LINCOM Studies in Semiotics

LINCOM.eu

Semiotics
The Science of Signs

Marcel Danesi
& Donato Santeramo

2021
LINCOM GmbH

Published by LINCOM GmbH 2021.

LINCOM GmbH
Hansjakobstr.127a
D-81825 Muenchen

contact@lincom.eu
www.lincom.eu

webshop: www.lincom-shop.eu

Bibliographic information published by the Deutsche Nationalbibliothek

The Deutsche Nationalbibliothek lists this publication in the Deutsche Nationalbibliografie; detailed bibliographic data are available in the Internet at http://dnb.dnb.de

Printed in E.C.

Contents

Introduction

Semiotics is in principle the discipline studying everything which can be used in order to lie. If something cannot be used to tell a lie, conversely it cannot be used to tell the truth: it cannot in fact be used "to tell" at all.

Umberto Eco (1932-2016)

We are bombarded on a daily basis by a plethora of signs—slang words in social media, images, memes, emojis, and so on. But we rarely stop to consider reflectively how they trigger thoughts in our minds and even impel us to action, nor how they are designed to package information in culture-specific ways, influencing how we view world and even ourselves. The science that deals directly with this critical aspect of human intelligence is called *semiotics*, defined simply as the "science of signs."

This book is our introduction to this science. It is intended primarily as a textbook for courses that deal with semiotics, directly or indirectly. For this reason, we have written it in as non-technical as tyle as possible, taking nothing for granted on the part of the reader. This manual is designed not only to cover the main aspects of semiotic theory and its traditional applications, but also to project it into the contemporary world of computers, social media, and artificial intelligence. To keep it within a reasonable length, we have made specific selections of what to treat in detail, what to discuss only tangentially, and what to ignore. We have also kept references to the technical literature to a minimum. Nonetheless, we have attempted to cast as a wide a thematic net as possible within logical boundaries of length.

Our overriding aim is to show that semiotics is a powerful investigative tool for understanding the nature of human thought, expressivity, creativity, and overall behavior, from the messages humans make with language to the visual images that are designed to shape the images in our minds. The vast repertoire and complexity of human sign-making distinguishes the human species from all others. The twentieth century philosopher, Ernst Cassirer (1944), went so far as to characterize the human species as a "symbolic species,"—a characterization that guides the purview of semiotics broadly as it attempts to understand why signs and symbols are so critical to humans beyond the instinctual survival. This manual is written so that anyone can get an initial glimpse into what semiotics has to offer to them.

This is not a critical book about semiotics. There are many excellent works currently on the market that look critically and technically at the various models, theories, methods, etc. of sign-making that the reader can consult—some of which can be found in the reference section at the back. It is intended, fundamentally, to impress upon readers that they already know a lot intuitively about signs and how they are used in everyday life. Our treatment simply aims to make this intuitive knowledge conscious. Also included in out treatment are topics such as Artificial Intelligence, cybernetics, the mass media, and other topics of current importance. We include a Basic Glossary of Semiotics at the end for practical future reference—this is, it is intended to list the main terms and ideas that make-up semiotics and can thus be used as a basic dictionary.

We are both instructors of semiotic courses at our universities—Queen's University and the University of Toronto. This manual is the product of decades of teaching the subject. It is fashioned to explain and illustrate the technical and often abstruse subject matter of semiotics in practical ways, with applications to contemporary culture. Our students have been our staunchest supporters and our most constructive critics. The suggestions and commentaries that they have passed on to us have guided every stage in the preparation of this book. We sincerely hope that it will truly reflect both what they and my own students have told me would be even more useful to them.

Marcel Danesi, *University of Toronto*

Donato Santeramo, Queen's University

1
Basic Principles and Notions

A science that studies the life of signs within society is conceivable. It would be part of social psychology and consequently of general psychology; I shall call it semiology (from Greek semeion "sign"). Semiology would show what constitutes signs, what laws govern them.

Ferdinand de Saussure (1857-1913)

Prologue

Consider the sounds represented individually by the following three alphabet characters: *a, t, c*. Now, let's combine them in a specific way: *c* + *a* + *t* = *cat*. The combination is no longer perceived by speakers of English as random sounds aligned together, but as a meaning-bearing unit structure, called a word (of course), that brings to mind the image of a small common feline. This is a truly remarkable phenomenon whereby a specific combination of sounds has the capacity to evoke the image of a specific type of animal in our minds, even when no such animal is present in our immediate surroundings for our sensory system to detect it. Words are reality-displacing and reality-replacing structures called *signs*—structures (such as specific combinations of sounds) that stand for something other than themselves (the actual sound combinations).

The science that studies signs is called *semiotics*, although the term *semiology* is sometimes used as a synonym. It is an ancient science, originating in early medicine as the study of symptoms, which like words, stand for something other than themselves in a specific way—as indicators of some malady, ailment, etc. Today, it has evolved into a sophisticated discipline, allowing access to patterns of human meaning-making as it manifests itself in its diverse forms, from story-telling to artistic practices; it also provides a particular interpretive lens through which we can assess and understand the meaning of contemporary media, events, and systems, from the Internet to Artificial Intelligence. Semiotics has also developed branches, such as literary semiotics, some of which will be discussed in this book as well.

The purpose of this opening chapter is to provide an overview of what semiotics is, what it studies, how it originated, and what its main principles, methodological and theoretical, are. This will provide a backdrop that will guide the discussions in subsequent chapters.

Historical Sketch

The term *semeiotics* (written with an "e") is traced to ancient Greek medicine. It was the early physician, Hippocrates (c. 460-377 BCE), who characterized a symptom as a *sēmeion* (sign, mark) and the diagnosis of symptoms as *sēmeiotikē*. Determining what a symptom (bodily mark, pain, abnormal skin pattern, etc.) stands for in terms of its physical structure (color, qualities, location, etc.) encapsulates what semiotic analysis is fundamentally all about—figuring out what something, such as a symptomatic form, stands for, namely a disease, an ailment, etc. For example, a dark bruise, a rash, or a sore throat might stand respectively for a broken finger, a skin allergy, or a cold respectively—called the potential referents:

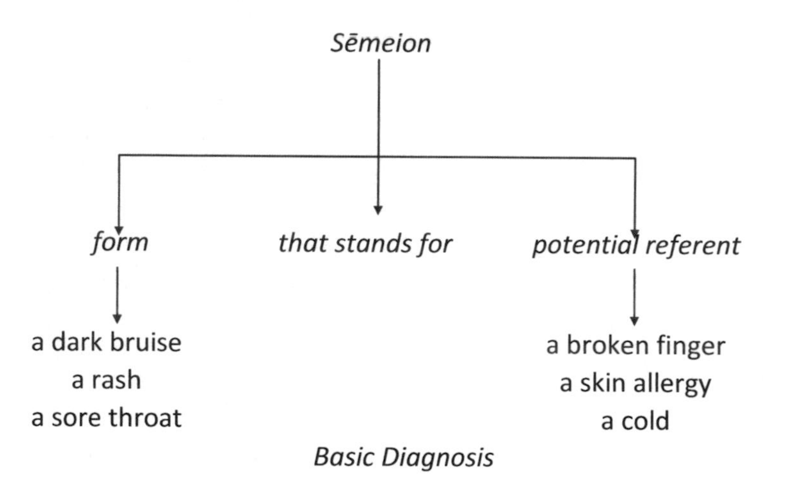

Basic Diagnosis

After Hippocrates, the question arose at some point in the ancient world as to whether or not there was any connection between natural (body) signs, such as symptoms, and a conventional (human-made) one, which was called a *symbol* (in Greek, *sumbolon*)—a possible connection first discussed by the so-called Stoic philosophers around 300 BCE, who argued that conventional signs (symbols) were analogous to natural ones (symptoms). It was the early Christian church father, St. Augustine of Hippo (354-430), who made a categorical distinction between the two, as well as putting forth an early theory of signs in his *De doctrina christiana* (Augustine 1887). He defined natural signs *(signa naturalia)* as signs that are produced by Nature, including bodily symptoms, the rustling of leaves, the colors of plants, the signals that animals emit, and so on. Natural signs are, in a word, *not* made by humans—they occur naturally, outside of human volition. However, humans have a desire to interpret them on their own terms. To do so, they invent and use conventional signs *(signa data)*, such as the names given to symptoms, to colors, etc. These are products of human intentions and needs, helping us understand Nature in our own way. St. Augustine also considered miracles to be signs, sent from God, and thus, as sacred forms. These can only be understood on faith, although such understanding is partly based on our specific interpretations—called *hermeneutic*. Augustine extended hermeneutic signs to such states as humility and love, as expressed in the Scriptures.

St. Augustine's views lay largely unknown until the eleventh century, when interest in the functions of signs was kindled by Persian scholars in Europe, who referred to the importance of ancient Greek thinkers in this domain of philosophy. This interest led eventually to the translation of ancient Greek works into European languages, which laid the foundation for the movement known as *Scholasticism*. The Scholastics were medieval theologians and philosophers who asserted that conventional signs, such as words, allowed humans to capture truths, and to reflect upon truth through them. But within this movement there were some—the so-called *nominalists*—who argued that "truth" was a matter of subjective opinion and that signs captured, at best, only illusory and highly variable human versions of it. The two best known nominalists were John Duns Scotus (c. 1265-1308) and William of Ockham (c. 1285-1349), who stressed that signs only referred to other signs, rather than to actual things. So, truth is human-made. The Scholastic theologian St. Thomas Aquinas (1225-1274) countered, however, that words referred to real things, even though they were subject to human interpretation and thus variation in sense-making. He saw sacred signs as especially crucial in understanding the world, even though they were beyond rational comprehension and had to be accepted on faith.

While discussions and debates about signs proliferated in the medieval and Renaissance eras, with some truly insightful attempts to classify them scientifically, as can be seen in the works of Roger Bacon (1214-1294), the autonomous study of signs had to await John Locke's (1632-1704) *Essay Concerning Humane Understanding* (Locke 1690), in which he revived the term *semeiotics* to a method of inquiry within philosophy. It is not clear where Locke got the idea to use this Hippocratic term. The same term was used two decades earlier in 1670 by the English physician Henry Stubbe (1632-1676) to designate the interpretation of signs within and outside of medicine. Locke may, however, be the source for fashioning an autonomous science of sign study, starting with the Swiss philologist Ferdinand de Saussure (1857-1913), the founder of modern-day linguistics as well. Saussure called the science *sémiologie* (semiology). As the following citation (Saussure 1916: 15-16) shows, he suggested that the main goal of semiology (should it ever come into being) was to understand the social function of signs:

> It is possible to conceive of a science which studies the role of signs as part of social life. It would form part of social psychology, and hence of general psychology. We shall call it *semiology* (from the Greek *sēmeĩon*, "sign"). It would investigate the nature of signs and the laws governing them. Since it does not yet exist, one cannot say for certain that it will exist. But it has a right to exist, a place ready for it in advance. Linguistics is only one branch of this general science. The laws which semiology will discover will be laws applicable in linguistics, and linguistics will thus be assigned to a clearly defined place in the field of human knowledge.

Saussure seems to have been unaware of the fact that the first appearance of the word *sémiologie* was in the *Dictionnaire de Trévoux* (1752) where it had, however, a medical meaning. The *Imperial Dictionary* of England (1883) also contained an entry for *semeiology* with the definition "doctrine of signs" that predated Saussure's use of *sémiologie*. At around the same time as Saussure's suggestion, American philosopher Charles S. Peirce (1839-1914), reintroduced Locke's term *semeiotics*. Given his enormous influence on modern-day sign study, starting at mid-twentieth century, Peirce's term, without the "e," is now the preferred one. It was adopted by the International Association of Semiotic Studies in 1969 as its official term. The term *significs*, coined by Victoria Lady Welby in 1896, is also used occasionally in the technical literature, but with a specific sense—the study of the relation among signs and the emotions.

In the twentieth century, a number of key scholars and scientists developed semiotics into the sophisticated discipline it has become today. Only a few will be mentioned here, as part of our schematic overview, focusing on their specific contributions to the development of semiotic theory. The American semiotician Charles Morris (1901-1979) divided semiotic method into: (1) the study of the relations between a sign and other signs, which he called *syntactics*; (2) the study of the relations between signs and their meanings, which he called *semantics*; and (3) the study of the relations between signs, their uses, and their users, which he called *pragmatics*—a term actually introduced by Peirce. This terminology has remained fundamental to this day. The Russian-born American semiotician Roman Jakobson (1896-1982) put forward the pivotal notion of "motivated signs," which he defined as the tendency to make signs represent the world through the simulation of sign referents—an idea that also originated with Peirce. The French semiotician Roland Barthes (1915-1980) illustrated the power of using semiotics to unravel the meaning structures hidden in everyday spectacles, performances, and common concepts; he also elaborated further the idea that signs exist on two levels or orders—the uncoded or literal level and the coded or connotative level (to be discussed in subsequently). French semiotician Algirdas J. Greimas (1917-1992) expanded the branch of semiotics known as *narratology*, which he defined as the study of how human beings in different cultures invent similar kinds of narratives (myths, tales, etc.) with virtually the same stock of characters, motifs, themes, and plots. Thomas A. Sebeok (1920-2001) was influential in expanding the semiotic paradigm to include the study of animal communication systems, which he termed *zoosemiotics*, and the comparative study of symptoms, signals, and signs in all living things, which he called *biosemiotics*. He also stressed that semiotic method should always unfold in an interdisciplinary fashion. The interweaving and blending of ideas, findings, and scientific discourses from different disciplinary domains was, Sebeok claimed, the distinguishing feature of the semiotic approach. Finally, the late Italian semiotician Umberto Eco (1932-2016) contributed significantly to our understanding of the relation between signs and reality. He also single-handedly put "semiotics" on the map of contemporary pop culture, so to speak, with his best-selling 1982 novel, *The Name of the Rose*, which became a major movie shortly thereafter.

In the twenty-first century, semiotics has been expanded to include the study of artificial minds, memetic culture, Internal discourse, and the like—which is attracting more and more semiotic scholars and researchers, and the founding of new branches, including a-signifying semiotics, the study of signs that have no meaning in themselves, such as the symbol systems used in computer programming, and media semiotics, which studies how signs are shaped by new media. Moreover, new disciplines, such as *visual rhetoric* (VR), have emerged from the platform of semiotic analysis. VR is now a field of inquiry aiming to analyze all kinds of visual images and texts as rhetorical structures—it is an offshoot of both visual semiotics, or the study of the meanings of visual signs in cultural contexts, and of the psychology of visual thinking, as opposed to verbal thinking—defined as the capacity to extract meaning from visual images. VR originated with semiotician Roland Barthes' pivotal 1964 article, *The Rhetoric of the Image*, in which he showed how to unravel the rhetorical meanings of visual images using simple semiotic analysis (Barthes 1964a). VR has spread as a technique to various disciplines, including psychology, anthropology, marketing, and graphic design, among many others. In a word, semiotics has spread its tentacles everywhere today, even though it might not be acknowledged or recognized as such.

Basic Principles

Semiotics has been defined in various ways throughout its history—as a doctrine (set of principles), as a technique or analytical tool for deciphering texts, from novels to programming languages, as an autonomous science, among others. The definition adopted in this book is that of the "science of signs" (Saussure 1916: 15). The late semiotician Umberto Eco (1976: 74) provided five reasons for defining semiotics in this way:

1. It is an autonomous discipline with its own lexicon of terms, methods of analysis, and scientific goals—for example, to understand the relation between signs and culture-specific meanings, signs and communication systems, signs and media, etc.
2. It has developed theories that allow semioticians to determine how signs and sign systems are constructed and how they function psychologically, historically, and socially.
3. It generates hypotheses about human behavior and cognition, and their reproduction artificially (in images, in computer models, etc.).
4. It makes predictions about how societies and cultures will evolve.
5. Its findings can have an impact on how people understand each other and thus can have an impact on changing the actual state of the world.

To this list, five general axioms can be added, which undergird how many semioticians view signs and sign systems (Danesi 2007):

1. Signs reveal similar structural properties and social functions the world over.
2. Differences in the manifestations of these properties are due to the histories and traditions of particular cultures and societies.
3. Signs and sign systems entail culture-specific classifications of the world.
4. These influence the way people think, behave, and act.

5. Perceptions of "naturalness" are thus tied to sign systems; that is, what is often considered to be "common sense" turns out often to be "communal sense."

A key notion, in addition to the principles and axioms, is that a sign is a *structure.* Recall the word *cat*, which is a combination of three sounds put together in a systematic way that stands, not for itself (the actual sounds in the word), but for a specific kind of animal. The reason why we perceive it as a word is because of the way in which the sounds have been combined is consistent with how English words are formed phonetically. They could have also been combined to form another legitimate word: *act.* Other combinations would be perceived as meaningless strings of sounds: *tca, atc, cta.* Structure, as used in semiotics, implies that the mind perceives physical forms, such as sound combinations, as meaningful (real or potentially) only if they reflect a recognizable shape (physical or mental). Structure is found throughout meaning-making systems. For instance, we recognize a triangle as a specific structure (as a particular kind of sign) because of the way in which three lines have been united—any other combination would not constitute a triangle.

Needless to say, the concept of structure involves more than combination; it can also involve contrastive selection. If we replace thc initial sound of *cat* with *r*, the result is *rat*, which is a legitimate new word. The contrast between *cat* and *rat* inheres in the change of one sound in the same phonetic position—a change that produces a new sign. This kind of structural relation, which is called *opposition*, occurs throughout sign systems, as will be discussed throughout this book. Suffice it to say here, that the notion of structure is a crucial one in semiotics.

Ferdinand de Saussure (mentioned above), put forward one of the first structural definitions of the sign, describing it as a binary structure composed of two interrelated components—a physical component (the sign itself) and a conceptual component (what it refers to and brings to mind). Saussure termed the former part, such as the sounds (known technically as phonemes) that make up the word *cat,* the *signifier*, and the concept or mental image that the sign elicits (the feline animal), the *signified* (literally meaning "that which is signified by the sign"). Saussure claimed, moreover, that there is no experiential connection between the signifier and the signified. So, the actual phonemic structure of the word *cat* is an arbitrary one, with no perceivable linkage between the sounds that make up the word and the animal itself—that is, the word *cat* is not constructed to simulate or imitate the sounds a cat makes, as in onomatopoeic constructions. Any other signifier would have sufficed—as long as it conformed to the laws of word formation in the language (that is, the rules for combining phonemes to form legitimate words). While this aspect of Saussurean sign theory is disputed by semioticians today, the main idea behind it is still a relevant one—namely that the parts of a sign imply each other conceptually. So, when we use or hear a word such as *tree* (the signifier), an image of the signified (a certain type of plant) crops up concomitantly in our minds—if we know English of course—even if a real tree is not present for us to observe. Now, if we do come across a tree in reality, then the word we use for it (*tree*) also comes to mind. In other words, when the word *tree* is used, an image of the arboreal plant occurs in the brain; vice versa when we see this arboreal plant the word *tree* is suggested concomitantly in the brain. This is why Saussure called word signifiers as sound images and their signifieds as mental images. The two are inextricably intertwined—one implying the other. Needless to say, wherever "trees" are not part of a culture's reality (such as, for example, in nomadic desert cultures), no signifier for them is required in the first place (since there is no signified to be encoded).

As the above discussion implies, and as stated in one of the axioms above, signs have a classificatory function. By naming a certain animal as a *cat* or a plant as a *tree* we have necessarily differentiated them conceptually from other animals and plants. At the initial point of naming a cat, we have divided the domain of animals conceptually into are *cats* and all the other animals, perceived provisionally as *non-cats*. Now, distinguishing *cats* from *non-cats* brings about cognitive consequences. By having the sign *cat* in our mental lexicon we are predisposed to attend to the presence of this creature in the world as real. Armed with that word, we now turn our attention to the world of *non-cats*. Within that larger domain, we start to perceive the existence of creatures that have physical affinities to *cats*. Features such as whiskers, tails, and retractile claws, for instance, seem to associate the cat conceptually to other animals. This suggests a larger category. In English, the name for that category is *feline*. The world of animals can now be divided into *felines* and *non-felines*. In the feline part, we can now devise further differentiations of cat-like creatures, naming them *lions, tigers, cougars, jaguars*, etc. We might then consider further distinctions as being useful. The words *Siamese* and *Persian* (indicating the origin of the cat) are two such distinctions. At that point, we stop classifying the feline world and consider the *non-feline* one. And the whole differentiation process starts over. Cultures stop their classificatory decision-making when they no longer see differentiations as useful or necessary.

In contrast to Saussure, Charles Peirce put forth a triadic model of the sign, consisting of the physical sign itself (which he called the *representamen*), the referent that it encodes (the *object*), and the interpretation that the sign elicits or reveals (the *interpretant*). In his writings, Peirce (1931-1958) called the dynamic interaction between the three parts as *semiosis*, which can be defined simply here as the making and interpreting of the meanings of signs. Consider again the word *cat*. It is not only a convenient well-formed structure (the *representamen*) standing for a specific kind of animal (the *object*), but also an acknowledgment that the object has special importance to those who coined the word (the *interpretant*). The *interpretant* is critical in guiding how signs are used and understood. In western culture, for instance, a cat is considered to be a domestic companion, among other cultural interpretants; in others, it is viewed instead as a sacred animal (akin to a sacred cow); and in others still it is considered to be a killer of rodents, as for example in the city of Venice, Italy. Thus, while different words for cat might *refer* to virtually the same physical mammal in different cultures (no matter what name is used), the *interpretant* of the words varies considerably, constituting the source of semiosis.

Unlike Saussure, Peirce viewed conventional signs (such as words) as originating, by and large, in an attempt to reproduce perceivable properties in their objects. Therefore, the Peircean model of the sign is defined as a *motivated* structure, whose construction is guided originally by an effort to imprint some aspect of the referent into the physical structure of the representamen. Peirce termed this a *firstness* dimension of semiosis, defined as the tendency to construct or understand signs as simulations of some perceived property of their objects. He called the sign-making process, *iconicity*. An obvious example of an *iconic* sign is the word *splash*, whose phonemic structure is clearly intended to echo the sound made by liquids when they are spilled to the ground. Saussure did admit that some signs were fashioned in this way—known as onomatopoeia or, more technically, sound modeling; but he maintained that this was the exception, not the rule. However, it is also true that many words possess a latent iconic quality, even though we are not aware of it consciously. Consider the word *duck*. It is one of an infinite number of phonemic assemblages that can be envisioned in English to refer to that animal. But the final *k* of that word hints at the kind of sound a "duck" is perceived to make, referenced much more directly in the word *quack*. This type of "latent sound modeling" is intrinsic to the creation of many kinds of words, even if it is not always obvious. Because phonemic iconicity is based on auditory perception, the meaning of sound-modeling words in different languages can be figured out even by those who do not speak them, if they are told what the sign stands for. Thus, if someone who does not speak English is told that the expression *cock-a-doodle-do* stands for the sound a rooster is perceived to make, then that person would have little difficulty imagining the resemblance between the word and its referent.

Peirce called the tendency of relating referents and sign-users in some way, *secondness*. This results in what he called *indexical* signs. The pointing finger is a perfect example of such a sign. When we point to something, we are in fact relating it to our location (or that of others) as a pointer. If it is close by, we can add words such as *near* or *here* to the pointing finger sign. If not, we can refer to it as *far* or *there*. These are indexes as well. Finally, Pierce claimed that there exists a *thirdness* dimension in sign construction, called *symbolism,* which consists in the signs developed in specific cultures and which have specific meaning to them. The cross figure used to stand for Christianity is understood as a symbol. Although it represents the figure of a cross on which Christ was crucified iconically, it is interpreted historically and conventionally as a sign standing for the religion that was founded after Christ's death.

Overall, the principles, axioms, and Saussurean and Peircean models of the sign discussed briefly above are adopted in part or in whole for diverse purposes by most semioticians. They also utilize ideas and findings from cognate disciplines—such as psychology, linguistics, anthropology, etc.—in order to carry out their analyses of sign systems and sign users. This *interdisciplinary* mode of inquiry is a two-way street, however, since ideas developed within semiotics are now found scattered across various disciplines. It was actually Saussure who originated the interdisciplinary orientation by claiming that semiology should be considered a branch of psychology and linguistics a branch of semiology, thus delineating an early interlacing pattern of connections among the human sciences.

Meaning

Semiotics is the science of signs and signs are structures that encode meanings. The question now becomes: What is the meaning of meaning? This was actually the topic of a classic 1923 book, titled appropriately *The Meaning of Meaning*, by Charles Ogden and I. A. Richards. The two scholars showed, first, that the English word *meaning* is problematic in any semiotic approach to signs. The reason is that it has itself many meanings, as the following common examples show:

1. She *means* to go and see that movie soon = "intends"
2. A red light *means* stop and wait = "indicates"
3. Our love *means* everything = "has great importance"
4. The look you gave him was full of *meaning* = "special import"
5. My life has no *meaning* = "purpose"
6. What does love *mean*? = "convey"

To circumvent the polyvalent semantics of the word *meaning*, Ogden and Richards proposed for the first time that the meaning of something is determined by the context in which it occurs—yet another principle of semiotics that will be discussed throughout this book. So, in place of the generic term *meaning*, semioticians prefer to use terms such as *reference, sense*, and *definition*. Using both Saussurean and Peircean models analogously, rather than equivalently, *reference* is the process of pointing out or identifying "something," whatever it may be (an object, a feeling, an idea, an imaginary construct, etc.) and encoding it in the form of a physical signifier or representamen; *sense* is what that "something" elicits cognitively, emotionally, historically, and socially (namely, the signified or interpretant); and *definition* is a statement about what that "something" implies or indicates.

Words may refer to the same (or similar) things, known as *referents,* but they have different *senses*. For example, the word *cat* refers to a specific type of mammal. But it bears different *senses*, from household companion to hunter of rodents, according to cultural context. This distinction was discussed at length by the German philosopher Gottlob Frege (1879). Frege used the following example that has since become a classic one—the "fourth smallest planet and the second planet from the Sun," which is named both *Venus* and the *Morning Star*. These two terms encode the same *referent*, but imply different *senses—Venus* designates the planet in a straightforward referential way (nevertheless with latent allusions to the goddess of love and beauty of Roman mythology), while *Morning Star* brings out the fact that the planet is visible in the east just before sunrise. The difference between *sense* and *reference* was explored further by philosopher Willard O. Quine (1953), who stressed, like Ogden and Richards, the importance of context in decoding the interpretation of a sign. As a simple example of how context shapes interpretation, consider the sentence, *The pig is ready to eat.* The word *pig* in the sentence will vary in meaning according to who, where, or why it is uttered: (1) It can refer to the actual animal called a *pig* if uttered, say, by a farmer at feeding time as he comments that a certain pig in a sty is hungry and is thus *ready to eat*. (2) It can refer to a cooked *pig* which is *ready to eat (to be eaten)*, if uttered by someone who has prepared a meal and is announcing it to guests. (3) It can refer to a *person* who appears gluttonous and overanxiously *ready to eat*, if uttered by an observer who interprets the person's behavior and facial actions in this way.

Definition is a statement about what something means by using other words or other signs (for example, pictures). As useful as it is, the act of defining something leads inevitably to circularity or looping structure. Take the dictionary definition of *cat* as "a small carnivorous mammal domesticated since early times as a catcher of rats and mice and as a pet and existing in several distinctive breeds and varieties." A problem that immediately surfaces from this definition is the use of *mammal* to define *cat*—one word has been used to define another. What is the meaning of *mammal*? A *mammal*, the dictionary states in another location, is "any of various warm-blooded vertebrate animals of the class Mammalia." But this too is hardly a viable way out of an emerging circle of references. What is an *animal*? The dictionary defines *animal* as an *organism*, which it defines, in turn, as an individual form of *life*, which it then defines as the property that distinguishes living *organisms*. Alas, at that point the dictionary has gone into a referential loop, since it has employed an already-used concept, *organism*, to define *life*. This looping pattern surfaces in all domains of human semiosis, not just in the area of definitions. It suggests that signs can never be understood in the absolute, only in relation to other signs. Suffice it to say here that it is within the looping structures themselves that meaning resides, even though it cannot be flushed out directly. It can only be inferred.

In semiotics proper, the terms *denotation* and *connotation* are preferred to *reference* and *sense*, thus permitting the use of meaning in specific ways. Consider the word *square*. The word elicits an image of a geometric figure made with "four equal straight lines meeting at right angles." It is irrelevant if the lines are thick, dotted, 2 meters long, or colored differently. If the figure has "four equal straight lines meeting at right angles," it qualifies as a square. This is its *denotative* meaning. More technically, it is called the sign's *denotatum*. All other meanings associated with the word *square* are *connotative*—meanings, called *connotate*, acquired through usage and projection onto other domains of understanding. Some *connotata* of *square* can be seen in expressions such as the following: *My friend is very square* ("old fashioned"); *My partner has a square disposition* ("forthright," "honorable"); *Put it squarely on the table* ("evenly," "precisely"). An old-fashioned person, an honorable individual, and the action of laying something down evenly imply the denotatum of a "square" in an allusive or suggestive way. Since the geometrical concept of square is an ancient one, probably known by everyone, the connotatum of "old-fashioned" fits in with this mental perception; it is also a figure in which every one of its parts is equal, hence the connotatum of "forthright;" and it is an even-sided figure, hence the connotatum of "evenly." Connotation encompasses all kinds of projections, analogies, allusions, etc. It produces an archive of culture-specific meanings that signs have accrued over time. It is the operative sense-making and sense-extracting mode in the production and decipherment of all kinds of texts, even technical ones. As current work on figurative language and the brain has shown, scientific theories and models involve connotative (metaphorical) reasoning, even though they end up being interpreted denotatively over time. Connotation is not a semantic option, as some traditional theories of meaning continue to sustain to this day; it is something we extract from a sign if we have access to its uses in cultural context.

Roland Barthes (1957, 1964b) saw these two levels of meaning as co-occurrent. The denotative level has pure informational value—it allows sign users to recognize some object such as a square. However, the sign also works at a different level connotative level, which constitutes a powerful unconscious system, called a *code* (to be discussed subsequently), which evokes all the additional meanings of the sign *square*. Barthes called the initial denotative reading of a sign as "non-coded" and the connotative one as "coded."

An example of how these two levels are immanent in sign usage, consider a word such as *red.* When asked what it means, the operation of the two levels come immediately into play. At a denotative level, it refers to a primary color located at the lower end of the visible spectrum; but this meaning is constrained by contextualized uses that are uncoded—What color is your new suit? That is a beautiful red color; etc. However, in virtually all other contexts, it has coded (connotative) meanings: Why is he wearing a red armband? What does it mean? Why is that sign painted in red? What does the color mean in this case?

The distinction between denotation and connotation is, of course, analogous to Frege's distinction between reference and sense, but it is much more useful in semiotics because it allows for a more focused understanding of the meaning of signs. It is also similar to philosopher Rudolf Carnap's (1942) distinction between *intension* and *extension*, with the former constituting the internal content of a concept (or sign), with the latter constituting the range of meaning encompassed by a concept (sign) beyond its internal content. So, while there are historical and notional differences among these terms, suffice it to say that in semiotic practice they are often interchangeable to varying degrees:

reference	=	denotation	=	intension
sense	=	connotation	=	extension

The distinction between denotation and connotation goes back considerably in time. However, as used today in semiotics and linguistics, it appears for the first time in American linguist Leonard Bloomfield's 1933 book *Language*, a distinction refined further by the Danish linguist and semiotician Louis Hjelmslev (1939, 1959) and Barthes (as discussed above).

Ultimately, signs allow people to recognize certain patterns in the world, encoding them as directive guides for taking action in the world. Signs are thus closely tied to social needs and aspirations—a fact emphasized by many semioticians, starting with the Russian theorist Mikhail Bakhtin (1981), who maintained that signs gain meaning only as they are exchanged by people in social dialogue, maintaining that human meaning is constructed socially. There is, however, a constant interaction between nature and culture, or between the *biosphere* and the *semiosphere*, as we saw with the ideas of St. Augustine. The latter term was coined by Estonian cultural semiotician Yuri Lotman

(1991) to imply that sign-formation and sign-interpretation are partly the result of adaptation to the biosphere and partly of exposure to the semiosphere—the universe of meanings in which humans are reared.

Semiosis

The term *semiosis*, as mentioned above, was introduced into semiotic theory by Peirce to designate the production and interpretation of signs and signals. Semiosis occurs across all species, hence, the fact that this very term has unified once and for all the study of potential connections between natural and conventional signs. It is the founding idea in biosemiotics—the branch dealing with semiosis and communication across species. As an organism (human or otherwise) lives and acts through its environment (called the *Umwelt*), its senses are activated and fine-tuned to its territory. To prevent sensory overload, each species selects or filters the information it needs for its life purposes. This implies that each organism has the capacity to eliminate irrelevant data. It is the relevant one that is encoded through semiosis via an activation of the autonomic or other biological systems that turn information into meaningful models of the world. As the late Thomas Sebeok (2001) suggested, semiosis may be the indication of whether something is alive.

It was the Estonian-born, German biologist Jakob von Uexküll (1864-1944) who saw differential forms of semiosis as the key factor that differentiated species (Uexküll 1909). The crux of his approach is the idea that animals with widely divergent anatomies do not process information in the same way. This means that a species interprets information, and reacts to it, in its own biologically-programmed way.

Semiosis manifests itself early on in childhood. When children come into contact with a new object, their instinctive reaction is to explore it with their senses—that is, to handle it, taste it, smell it, listen to any sounds it makes, and visually observe its features. This exploratory phase of recognizing or identifying the object constitutes a sensory stage. This produces an image of the object in the brain that allows infants to recognize the same object subsequently without having, each time, to examine it over again "from scratch" with their senses (although they might explore its physical qualities further for various other reasons). Now, as children grow, they start to engage more and more in semiotic behavior that displaces this sensory phase; that is, they start pointing to the object and imitating any sounds it makes, rather than just handling it, tasting it, etc. These imitations and indications are the child's first attempts at representing the object semiotically (Morris 1938, 1946). Thereafter, the repertoire of semiotic activities increases dramatically, as children learn how to refer to the world through the language (and other codes) to which they are exposed in cultural context, rather than through the senses or the instincts alone.

Semiosis is part of natural sign-making processes; the use of the products of semiosis (signs and models) in the human semiosphere is called, more precisely, *representation* is primarily a human capacity, although it is present different species in limited largely instinctual ways (Sebeok and Danesi 2000). It is defined as the use of signs and sign systems to create texts such as narratives, paintings, theories, musical compositions, and the like, for some psychological, philosophical, scientific, or social purpose. Representations influence how we come to view reality. Among the first to consider the connection between the two were the Plato and Aristotle. The latter saw our representations in art and poetry as the primary means through which we come to understand reality, identifying mimesis (imitation of life) as the main strategy for representing the world—so, a theatrical play is a mimetic representation of real-world or imaginary events and situations. Aristotle warned, however, that representations can easily lead people astray if they are believed literally. Plato went further than Aristotle, claiming that representations never tell the truth, but instead interfere with our perceptions of reality, creating illusions that lead us away from contemplating life as it really is. In contemporary semiotics, representation is defined simply as the use of signs to stand for something holistically—a novel might stand for some virtue or lack thereof, a scientific model might represent some physical process, such as light, etc.

Representation reveals how the human brain carries out its work of transforming sensory information into conceptual knowledge. The latter takes two main forms—concrete and abstract. A concrete concept is a referent encoded by a sign (such as a word) that is demonstrable and observable in a direct way, whereas the referent of an abstract concept cannot be demonstrated or observed directly. So, for example, the word *car* stands for a concrete concept because its referent—a self-propelled land vehicle powered by an internal-combustion engine—can be demonstrated or observed in the physical world. The word *love*, on the other hand, represents an abstract concept because, although "love" exists as an emotional phenomenon, it cannot be demonstrated or observed directly—that is, the emotion itself cannot be conceptualized apart from the behaviors, states of mind, etc. that it produces. This distinction between concrete and abstract concepts is, needless to say, a highly reductive one. In actual fact, there are many degrees of concreteness and abstraction in conceptualization that are influenced by various kinds of psychological and social factors. Suffice it to say here that most of the raw, unorganized information that is detected by the senses is transformed into concrete or abstract concepts as required. The type of conceptualization process enlisted also depends on the kind of meaning that the human mind seeks to extract from a specific situation.

The signs and conceptual structures that we acquire in childhood shape how we view the world—a basic principle of semiotics enunciated above. The linguists Edward Sapir (1921) and Benjamin Lee Whorf (1956) showed how this principle applies to the language we learn in childhood—a topic to be discussed subsequently. This does not mean that understanding between speakers of different languages is blocked. On the contrary, through translation and paraphrase people are always attempting to understand each other. Moreover, as Whorf claimed, the resources of any language allow its speakers to invent new categories any time they so desire. For example, if for some reason we decide that "strong blowing of the nose" is a discourteous action, not just a cold-related action , then by coining an appropriate word, such as *grooning,* we would in effect etch this concept into our minds. When we observe someone blowing their nose in this way, we would now be armed with a new concept, and thus be able to say "he is grooning," thinking of the action as exemplifying some aberrant behavior, rather than a simple nose-blowing action. When we name something, we are culling it into reality.

A classic example of how semiosis and representation put up filters to people's perception reality is in the domain of color perception. In English, as in other languages, some color names are considered to be basic—in English these would include words such as *red, blue, green, yellow, brown*, which are said to encode basic or *focal* colors. These are considered to represent "basic color" categories. Further distinctions are considered to be subcategories, that is, as shades or variants such as *crimson, navy blue,* and *pea green.* Now, the question becomes: What stretch of the light spectrum does a particular color term cover? Are there other ways to segment that same stretch? As it turns out, the ways in which we name the hues on a spectrum is a classificatory process—in effect, it is the strategy of organizing the hues into color categories, and these will vary from language to language and culture to culture. The stretch named *blue* in English is named in three ways in Italian—*azzurro, celeste,* and *blu*. These are not shades of *blue,* but distinct color categories.

Color has fascinated philosophers and scientists since antiquity. Sir Isaac Newton was among the first to make a distinction between focal colors (which he called primary) and subcategories of color. His color wheel may, in fact, be the first one to identify the English focal colors:

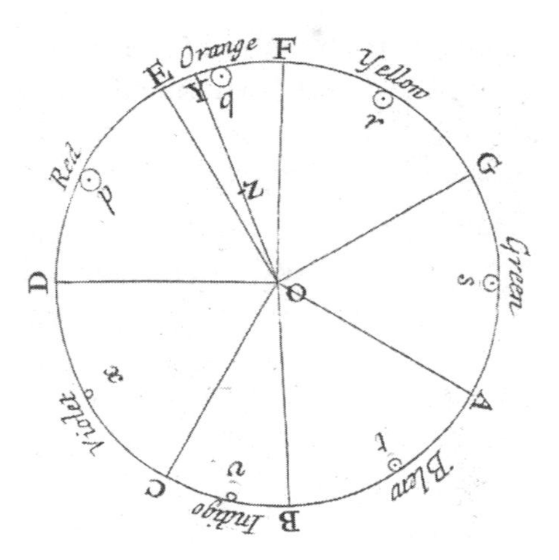

Newton's Color Wheel (Wikimedia Commons)

We use color terms not only to refer to gradations of hue on the light spectrum, but to select them and then encode them into the meanings of the words so selected. Consider what speakers of English would "see" if they were to put a finger at any point on the visible light spectrum. A speaker would likely perceive only a negligible difference in hue immediately adjacent to the finger at either side. Depending on where the finger is placed, however, the person might name the difference in a specific way. This is because the speaker has become accustomed to "seeing" the spectrum in terms of English color terms and thus, would organize it lexically and cognitively in specific ways.

In 1969, anthropologists Brent Berlin and Paul Kay argued that differences in color terms are only superficial matters that conceal universal principles of color perception which show up in a pattern of conceptual organization of color categories via specific linguistic principles. Using the judgments of the native speakers of widely-divergent languages, the two researchers collected naming data that led them to the conclusion that there were universal "focal points" in single-term color vocabularies which clustered in certain predictable ways. They identified eleven focal points, which corresponded to the English words *red, pink, orange, yellow, brown, green, blue, purple, black, white,* and *gray*. Not all the languages that they investigated had separate words for each of these colors, but they detected a pattern in the naming practices of the languages. If a language had two focal colors, then they were equivalents of English *black* and *white*. If it had three, then the third one corresponded to *red*. A four-term system had the equivalent of either *yellow* or *green*; while a five-term system had both of these. A six-term system included an equivalent term for *blue*; a seven-term one had *brown*. Finally, equivalent terms for *purple, pink, orange,* and *gray* were found to occur in any combination in languages that had the previous focal colors. Berlin and Kay thus had thus seemingly discovered a universal naming pattern based on principles of perception. So, languages with, say, a four-term system consisting of *black, white, red*, and *brown* did not exist, because they could not exist on the basis of human perception.

In 1975, Kay revised the sequence in order to account for the fact that certain languages—such as Japanese—encoded a color that can only be paraphrased in English as "green-blue." He gave it a name though, *grue*, and placed it both preceding or following *yellow* in the original sequence. Since then it has been found that further modifications are required because Russian does not have a single color for *blue*, but rather distinguishes "light blue" and "dark blue" as focal colors.

Debates on the Berlin-Kay study proliferated shortly after it was published. Its main findings and conclusions have not, however, been impugned. The main implication of the study is that color naming matches color perception, and this is why it follows a universal sequence across languages, even if some hues are perceived as more fundamental than others, and this is why additions to the sequence in a specific language also occurs in predictable way to else is expanded by other means—that is, a language with few focal terms might bolster its color terminology in creative ways, such as through metaphor. Swahili has three focal terms, but its color vocabulary is enlarged by figurative reference to objects (for example, yellow = *manjano* "turmeric") and through borrowing from another language (blue = *buluu*). The archeological record strongly suggests in fact that metaphor may be the source for the color terms themselves, which would go contrary to the Berlin-Kay study (Wescott 1980). In the ancient language Hittite, for instance, the words for colors initially designated plant and tree names corresponding to English *poplar*, *elm*, *cherry*, *oak*, and so on. But despite the fact that metaphor was not taken into account, the study by Berlin and Kay is remains a pertinent one. Above all else, it brought out how crucial semiosis is in how we filter reality. Much debate has emanated from the study, which need not concern us here. As David Ludden (2015) has aptly remarked, the it has made it obvious that:

> Although the colors of the visible light spectrum vary along a continuum, our visual system is maximally sensitive to four specific regions—red, green, yellow, and blue—which we then perceive as the four focal colors. Languages around the world tend to organize their color systems around these four focal colors. That is, languages will have names for these four colors before they'll have basic terms for colors like orange or purple. This four-color distinction is an important element of Westernized global color schemes, as for example in the four suits of an Uno deck or in the logos for Microsoft and Google.

The greatest weakness in the Berlin-Kay, from a semiotic perspective, remains the fact that it did not look at how the color terms in different languages matched each other in terms of the stretches they encoded on the spectrum. As it turns out, the fit is never perfect, and indeed many asymmetries and gaps can be seen in the comparison of different linguistic color terms. So, while the study showed how color naming may manifest itself broadly in synch with perception, it did not take into account how it is refined or elaborated in semiotic ways according to culture. We will return to this general topic in subsequent chapters.

Epilogue

To conclude this opening chapter, it is relevant to note that, indirectly, semiotics studies the strategies humans have developed ways to tame meaning, such as in constraining color terms to useful categories; without this function, it would be impracticable to refer to all the possible frequencies of color on the spectrum. Every branch of science employs such strategies so as to delimit its range of investigation. As such, every science can be seen as a semiotic enterprise. Astronomy uses a set of symbols to identify the sun, the moon, the planets, and the stars; Mathematicians use Greek letters and other symbols to make up their particular language; and so on and so forth. Conventionalized terms and symbols appear in such fields as commerce, engineering, medicine, packaging, transportation, music, etc. The reason in all cases is to fashion a common semiotic code that can be used to delimit the confines of each area—a notion introduced by Saussure (1916: 31).

A sign selects what is considered important to be known and recalled from the infinite variety of things that are in the world—it imprints important information into a structured form which filters out extraneous information, retaining within its content what is felt to be relevant. Although we create new signs to help us gain new knowledge and modify previous knowledge—that is what artists, scientists, writers, inventors, for instance, are always doing—by and large, we literally let our signs "do the understanding" for us, once we have acquired them in context. We are born into an already-fixed semiosphere that will largely determine how we view the world around us, allowing for culturally charged gradual change. Only if, hypothetically, all our knowledge (which is maintained in the form of semiotic codes) were somehow erased from the face of the earth would we need to rely once again on our instinctive meaning-making tendencies, that is, on semiosis, to represent the world all over again.

The Greek mathematician Eratosthenes (c. 276-195 BCE) developed an ingenious method for identifying prime numbers. These are numbers other than 1 that can be divided evenly by only 1 and themselves. Today, mathematicians use computers to identify prime numbers. But Eratosthenes's method, though much slower, always works. To find prime numbers with it, the series of integers starting with 2 is written out in a square arrangement. In it, every second number after 2 (the first prime number) is crossed out, thus eliminating all numbers that can be divided evenly by 2, except for 2 itself. Similarly, every third number after 3 (the next prime number) is crossed out, thus eliminating all the numbers that can be divided evenly by 3, except for 3 itself. This process is continued *ad infinitum*. Eratosthenes' method is called a "sieve" because the numbers that are not crossed out can be thought of as having passed through a sieve (strainer) that has caught all the rest. Any number that has not been crossed out is prime. It would take an infinite sieve, of course, to identify all prime numbers, making it an impracticable method. But what is of relevance here is the method itself. It provides not only a framework for investigating the nature of numbers in a concrete way, but. It becomes a "thought stimulus" for investigating previously unknown ideas in mathematics. Semiotics can analogously be thought of as a sieve—that is, as a method designed to sift sign-based phenomena from purely biological phenomena in human life, and thus to seek understanding of what may have been hidden beforehand. Like mathematics, semiotics builds its theoretical edifice from simple, yet ingenious, notions, which allow it to interconnect such apparently diverse phenomena, from color terms to how children acquire words, into an overall sieve of meaning-making that is unique among species.

2
The Sign

Words are but the signs of ideas.

Samuel Johnson (1709-1784)

Prologue

As mentioned in the previous chapter, the late semiotician Thomas Sebeok (2001) saw life as semiosis. Everyday life is, in fact, shaped by what he called a "perfusion of signs" (Sebeok 1977). Sign-based and sign-directed behavior manifests itself constantly—when we gesture, talk, write, read, listen to music, look at a painting, and so on. The primary task of semiotics is to identify and document this kind of behavior, assessing its functions in sustaining human life. Signs constitute mental filters that invariably condition how we think and act, largely replacing our instincts and our unconditioned responses to stimuli. As mentioned in the previous chapter, this does not mean however that there is a disconnection between natural and conventional semiosis in human beings—on the contrary, one of the main goals of contemporary semiotics is to discern what the connections between the two are. The study of signs is thus a study of human nature through a study of semiosis, which literally leaves its "signs" in biological, imaginative, expressive, and creative forms.

Recall that a sign is anything physical (that is perceptible by the senses)—a color, a gesture, a word, etc.—that stands for something other than itself because it possesses a specific kind of structure that allows us to identify it as a meaning-bearing form. The word *red* qualifies as a sign because it does not stand for the sounds *r-e-d* that comprise it, but rather for a certain kind of color in a linguistically-structured way—that is, according to the laws of English word-formation. Once acquired in a rearing or other learning context, this sign then guides our perception of a particular hue as it occurs in the world (or the imagination). So, when we see this hue manifest itself physically in, say, sunsets or traffic signals, the word *red* not only comes to mind, but may well be the reason why we detected the hue in these different contexts in the first place.

Semiotic inquiry is guided by three general questions: (1) What does something mean (such as the word *red*)? (2) How does it encode or portray this meaning (phonemically or in writing)? (3) Why does it mean what it means? Consider the following figure:

A "Bright Idea"

Question (1)—What does it mean?—is easily answered by those who are familiar with this figure as a sign standing for "a bright idea." How does it present this meaning? (question 2). It does so by showing a light bulb inside a bubble. Why is this configuration indicative of this meaning? (question 3). Answering this last question entails unraveling the cultural roots of the individual meanings of each component of the sign. The use of a light bulb is consistent with the general view of light as an analogue for intellect and intelligence in western culture. This can be seen, for instance, in such expressions as "to become *enlightened*," "to shed *light* on something," and so on. The use of a bubble to enclose the light bulb (the source of light) is derived from the comic book tradition of putting words and thoughts into bubbles. This simple example illustrates the sum and substance of semiotic method, albeit in a highly reductive manner. The point is that the same questions can be used to guide our understanding of everything from a simple visual figure (such as the one above) to a complex narrative or scientific theory.

As discussed in Chapter 1, a sign encodes two main kinds of referents: (1) a concrete referent, such as the color hue designated by the word *red*, and (2) an abstract referent, such as the "bright idea" concept designated by the light bulb figure above. The former is something that can be shown to exist in the real world—a red color can be indicated by simply pointing to something that is painted in this hue. The latter is imaginary and cannot be indicated by simply pointing to it. It can only be inferred through a historical understanding of symbols such as thought bubbles. In both cases, however, the sign itself allows us to refer to, or call to mind, referents—concrete or abstract—that might not be physically present for our senses to perceive. When we say or hear the word *red* a certain color hue comes instantly to mind, even if there is nothing around for us to perceive this color with our eyes. This feature of signs is called *displacement*, defined as the capacity of signs to refer to reality that is not present for the senses to process.

The referent that appears in the mind is called, more precisely, a *concept*. Consider the word *cat* (Chapter 1). If one were to ask us what kind of animal it is, we might answer that it is a type of *feline*, as is a *lion* or a *tiger*. If one were to ask us then to specify the type of cat that come into view, we might say that it was a *Siamese* or a *Persian* cat. The word *feline* encodes what is known as a *superordinate* concept. Such a concept has a general classificatory function. The word *cat* encodes instead a *basic* or *prototypical* concept. Cats, lions, and tigers are examples of basic (feline) concepts. Finally, the word *Siamese* encodes a *subordinate* concept. This is a word referring to a subtype of the cat category. In all cases, what crops up in the mind are referents that we may have seen or experienced in some way. Signs transform referents into concepts.

The distinction among levels of conceptualization above falls more directly under the rubric of psychology. The goal of semiotics is to examine how concepts are formed in the first place via sign structures. This chapter will thus look specifically at signs as conceptual structures and at the main kinds of structural relations they imply.

The Saussurean Model

As discussed in the previous chapter, a founder of contemporary semiotics was the Swiss philologist, Ferdinand de Saussure. As we also saw, Saussure envisioned the sign as a binary structure, that is, as a structure made up of two parts: (1) the sign's actual physical form (phonemic, visual, etc.), which he termed the *signifier*, and (2) a conceptual part, which he called the *signified*. In the case of a word such as *cat,* the signifier is more specifically a "sound-image," that is the image of sound in the mind that this specific combination of phonemes evokes in the mind. The conceptual part is the mental image of the particular kind of animal that the word refers to that comes to mind in tandem with the sound-image. The two parts are, therefore, inseparable cognitively. If we say or hear the word *cat*, then the sound-image (*c-a-t*) evokes simultaneously the conceptual image of a specific kind of animal which we have learned to connect to the sound-image; vice versa, if we were to come across this animal in the real world, the word *cat* would invariably come to mind concomitantly. Saussure showed this inherent binary relation with the diagram below:

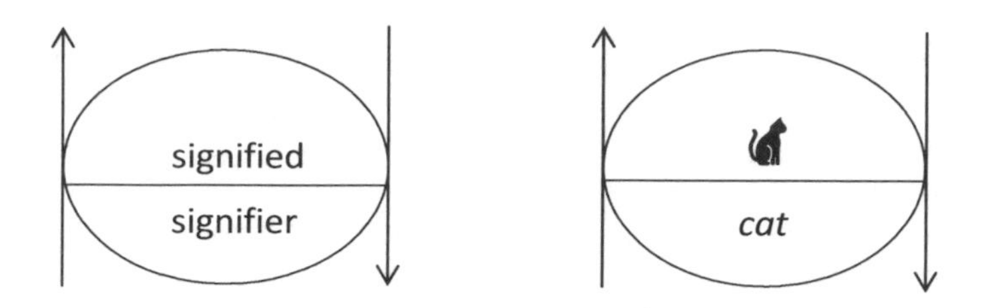

Saussurean Model of the Sign

The diagram shows the inherent connection between word and thought which, once established, is bidirectional or binary—that is, one implies the other. As also discussed in the previous chapter, Saussure considered this linkage to be an arbitrary one. To make his point, he noted that there was no evident reason for using, say, the word *arbre* in French or *tree* in English to designate "an arboreal plant." Indeed, any well-formed verbal signifier could have been used in either language. Saussure did admit, however, that there were some words that were fashioned intentionally to make the signifier resemble some sensory or perceivable property of the signified. Onomatopoeic words (*drip*, *plop*, *whack*, etc.), he granted, did indeed attempt to mirror real physical sounds in their phonemic structure. But, as discussed, Saussure maintained that this was not widespread. Moreover, the highly variable nature of onomatopoeia across languages showed that it was itself an arbitrary phenomenon. For instance, the word used to refer to the sounds made by a rooster is *cock-a-doodle-do* in English, but *chicchirichí* (pronounced "keekkeereekee") in Italian; the word employed to refer to the barking of a dog is *bow-wow* in English, but *ouaoua* (pronounced *wawa*) in French; and so on.

A counterargument to Saussure's arbitrariness argument is that many words are "latently onomatopoeic," that is, suggestive (implicitly) of the sensory properties of their referents. Consider the word *mash,* which refers denotatively to the concept of "crushing something to a pulp." The set of phonemes available in English to construct a word to refer to this concept, other than *mash*, is infinite. But the word *mash* seems intuitively more "natural" because its final sound, represented by *sh*, is suggestive of the sound made when something is crushed—indeed the word *crush* itself is indicative of the same sound. So, the question becomes: How extensive is this kind of "sound modeling?" This very question is actually studied under the rubric of *sound symbolism* theory in both linguistics and semiotics. The theory goes back considerably in time, but it was given a coherent formulation in the early twentieth century by Edward Sapir (1921) and a little later by Morris Swadesh (1951, 1959, 1971). Swadesh drew attention to the fact that most of the world's languages used front vowels (*i*-type and *e*-type vowels) to construct words in which "nearness" was implied, in contrast to back vowels (*a*-type, *o*-type, and *u*-type vowels) to construct words in which the opposite concept of "distance" was implied: in English common examples are *here*-versus-*there*, *near*-versus-*far*, *this*-versus-*that*, and so on. The same kind of pattern is found across languages, providing support to the possibility that it might be a universal tendency. Examples include the following:

Language	*"This"*	*"That/You"*
Chinook	-i-	-u-
Klamath	ke-	ho-, ha-
Tsimshian	gwii-	gwa-
Guaraní	tyé	tuvicha
Maya	li'	la', lo'
Binga	ti	ta
Fur	in	illa
Didinga	ici	ica
Tamil	idi	adi
Thai	nii	nan
Burmese	dii	thoo

Sound Symbolism in Various Languages

Since Swadesh, the research on sound symbolism has made it obvious that it might be an inherent tendency in word-formation, whether it is realized or not. For example, the *fl* cluster is found commonly in the make-up of English words that refer to things that move or run smoothly with unbroken continuity, in the manner that is characteristic of a fluid: *flow, flake, flee, float, fly*. On the other hand, the cluster *bl* is found in words that refer typically to actions that involve blocking, impeding, or some other form of occlusion: *block, blitz, blunt, blow* (Magnus 1999, 2013). The validity of this theory has actually been put to the test in various psycholinguistic studies (for example, Brown 1970: 258-273), which need not concern us here. The point is that Saussure's arbitrariness theory is not commonly accepted by semioticians today. However, his model of the sign still has value to this day. For example, it contains the seeds of so-called *opposition theory*, which will be discussed below.

The Peircean Model

Rather than a binary structure, Charles Peirce—the second major founder of contemporary semiotics (Chapter 1)—saw the sign as having a triadic structure. Moreover, he also saw a fundamental unconscious tendency in semiosis to make the sign resemble the referent in some way—he called this *motivation*, that is, the intent to make signs reproduce in their structure properties of their referents. So, sound symbolism in a Peircean model would be seen as an example of motivation in language.

To reiterate here for the sake of convenience (see Chapter 1), Peirce called the physical sign itself a *representamen*—that which represents something in some way—and the concept to which it refers the *object*. He termed the meaning (impression, cogitation, sense, etc.) that we get from a sign the *interpretant*. These three dimensions produce semiosis:

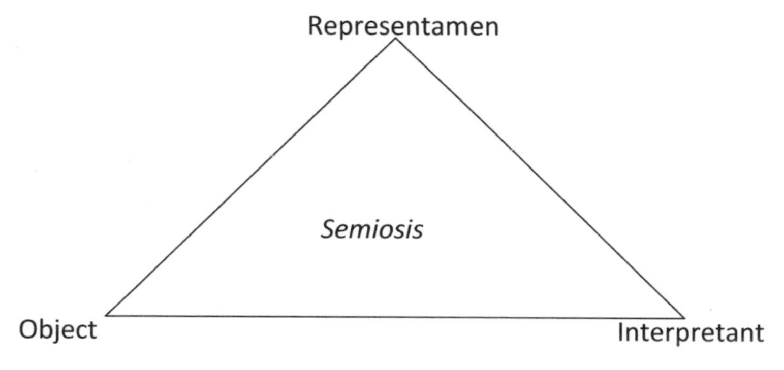

Peircean Model of the Sign

Peirce identified 66 different types of signs, of which three are used commonly in all kinds of semiotic work today. They are called *icons, indexes*, and *symbols*. These were discussed briefly as well in the previous chapter, and will be discussed in the next chapter in more detail. Suffice it to reiterate here that an icon is a sign that stands for a referent through some form of replication, simulation, imitation, or resemblance. Sound symbolism is an example of iconicity in language. But iconicity is found as well in the domain of nonverbal representation—a photo resembles its referent visually, as does a painting of a natural scene. An index is a sign that stands for a referent by pointing to it or by relating it (explicitly or implicitly) to other referents. Manifestations of indexicality include a pointing index finger, words such as *this* and *that*, *up* and *down,* and so on. A symbol is a sign that stands for its object by convention or agreement in specific contexts.

For example, a *rose* is a symbol of love in some cultures; the letter π stands, by agreement among mathematicians, for the number 3.14; and so on. Iconicity constitutes an attempt to simulate the sensory properties perceived in things. Indexicality is a strategy for referring to the existence and location of objects in time-space. And symbolism is the result of historical and social conventions, agreements, or pacts.

The typology of signs put forth by Peirce is a complex one, but once the terminology is deciphered, it is a truly useful, detailed way to describe semiosis. For the sake of convenience, a simplified illustration of how Peircean terminology works is in order. For example, Peirce suggested that a function of iconicity was the allusion of qualities of objects. He called the signs that involve this specific iconic function *qualisigns,* named in this way because they are intended to draw attention to the qualities of referents. In language, an adjective is a qualisign since it draws attention to the color, shape, size, etc. of noun referents. In other codes, qualisigns include the colors used by painters, the harmonies and tones used by composers, etc. A function of indexicality, on the other hand, is to single out the relative existence of certain referents in time-space. The signs that involve this function are called *sinsigns*—a pointing arrow, for example, is a visual sinsign, while a word such as *there* is a verbal sinsign. A function of symbolism is rule-governed semiosis. He called signs possessing this function *legisigns*. An example is a whistle that is blown by a referee during a hockey game. This means "stop play," as part of the rules of hockey. Each of these functions involves a specific type of interpretant: (1) a *rheme* is an interpretant of a qualisign; (2) a *dicisign* is an interpretant of a sinsign; and (3) an *argument* is an interpretant of a legisign. Although Peircean theory appears to be rather abstruse, once we grasp the logic of its particular terminology, it provides the most comprehensive theory of semiosis so far devised. In practice, though, the main notions used broadly by semioticians today are those of iconicity, indexicality, and symbolism, which will be discussed further in the next chapter.

Opposition Theory

Semiotics was born as a structuralist science, following Saussure's proposal for the establishment of *semiology* as a distinct discipline alongside linguistics and psychology, which were also emerging in the nineteenth century as distinct disciplines. Structuralism implies that signs are not understood in the absolute, but in minimal differential relation to each other. To give a simple example, we recognize the difference between an equilateral triangle and an isosceles triangle in terms of a minimal difference in their structure—namely, in the lengths of their sides, whereby in an equilateral triangle has all three sides equal to each other, while in an isosceles triangle, only two are equal. It is this minimal difference that defines the two as distinct structures. Saussure actually used the term *différence* in reference to such minimal contrasts. This relation occurs across sign systems. So, for example, we recognize the difference between *cat* and *rat* (as we saw in Chapter 1), via a single phonemic change at the beginning of each word. This *différence* is sufficient to distinguish them as separate meaning-bearing structures.

Saussure's notion was taken up and elaborated in the 1920s and 1930s by psychologists, linguists, and semioticians (Ogden 1932, Trubetzkoy 1936, 1939, Jakobson 1939), who refined it methodologically and elaborated its psychological implications in some detail. It was during this era that it came to be known as *opposition theory*—a theory that guided research in semiotics and linguistics, until the 1960s when it was assailed by several scholars, who initiated the movement of post-structuralism in (Derrida 1967)—to be discussed below. But the validity of the theory is evidenced by the fact that it was revived constructively and expanded in the 1990s (Andrews 1990, Andrews and Tobin 1996, Battistella 1990, 1996), and that it is used to this day in linguistics and semiotics for various analytical purposes.

Opposition theory is essentially a semiotic for determining meaning in signs. Verbal sounds in themselves (vowels, consonants, tones, etc.) have no meaning; they accrue it in differential relation to other sounds in the same system (consonants, vowels, etc.). For instance, in the minimal pair *pin*-versus-*bin* the sounds /p/ and /b/ form a phonemic opposition, since they constitute a minimal *différence,* allowing us to psychologically perceive the two words as distinct units of meaning. The theory has also been applied fruitfully to conceptual oppositions, to determine which concepts might be universal and might be culture-specific. For example, some oppositions seem to be cross-cultural (*right*-versus-*left, day*-versus-*night*), while others (*town*-versus-*country*) are culture-specific. One of the goals of early structuralism was, in effect, to establish which oppositions were universal and which were specific to particular societies.

Oppositional structure occurs at all levels of language and other codes, suggesting that the human mind is inclined by its nature to perceive the world in terms of complementary opposites and that these are the basis of a large portion of semiosis. This is probably due to the fact that much of human anatomy is structured in a symmetrical binary way—we have a left and right hand, eye, ear, foot, etc. The early founders of psychology, such as Wilhelm Wundt (1880) and Edward B. Titchener (1910), also envisioned an inherent oppositional structure in human thought. Their research agenda prefigured structuralism in psychology and its theoretical cross-fertilization in semiotics, linguistics, and anthropology. The first in-depth psychological study of opposition as a theory of mind was Charles Ogden's 1932 treatise, *Opposition: A Linguistic and Psychological Analysis*, which elaborated upon several key ideas he had discussed in 1923 with Richards in *The Meaning of Meaning.* Ogden claimed that a small set of conceptual oppositions, such as *right*-versus-*left* and *yes*-versus-*no*, appeared to be intrinsically binary in nature and that they were found across cultures. These were called *polar,* since they could be envisioned as two end-poles on a scale. Other types of concepts showed "gradience" between the two poles. For example, in a polar opposition such as *white*-versus-*black*, various color concepts such as *gray, red*, etc. could be located between the poles, a fact that clearly has both referential and conceptual resonance—gradient colors are distributed on the light spectrum, while *white* and *black* are not, forming instead conceptual endpoints on a color scale. Similarly, the polar opposition *day*-versus-*night* on a scale is filled-in with gradient concepts such as *twilight, dawn, noon,* and *afternoon*. In other words, polar concepts form a binary opposition and have, thus, paradigmatic structure, to use Saussure's insight, whereas gradient concepts do not—one cannot put *red* into a polar opposition with another color that would form a universal opposition (cross-cultural). Such concepts are "distributed concepts" on already-existing oppositional scales. They are culture-specific ones. As we saw in the previous chapter, all languages of the world (as far as can be told) have terms for the *white*-versus-*black* opposition; all the color terms are found distributed in specific ways between these. They are gradient concepts, rather than polar ones, and the research on color terms has essentially substantiated the underlying psychology of color perception as having this type of interconnected structure—polar and gradient. However, any concept on a scale can be extracted from it for specific purposes and put into an opposition. So, can put *red* in opposition to *green* if required to brings out a contrast, say, in fashion styles. Thus, what are gradient concepts can now be transformed into polar ones. This implies that there are levels of opposition. Universal polar oppositions are more properly called meta-oppositions, while polar oppositions that are specific to some culture or are relevant to a specific situation care called culture-specific oppositions.

Right after Ogden's work, opposition theory became *de facto* theory of semiotic structure, proclaiming that contrasts in form and meaning were the channels through which ideas and concepts gained physical form as signs and sign systems. It should be mentioned that although the theory derives from the Saussurean view of the sign, in no way has the Peircean approach ever been conceived to be antithetical to it, with various attempts having been put forward to reconcile opposition theory various aspects of Peircean sign theory (for example, Andersen 1989, 2001, 2008, Tomic 1989). Also, the so-called Tartu School of semiotics under the leadership of Yuri Lotman (1991)—a critical one today—never abandoned the basic idea that oppositional structure may be the conceptual glue that connected different codes meta-semiotically (so to speak), to produce culture as a sign-based system (see Andrews 2003 and Lepik 2008).

Semiotic research has identified different types and levels of opposition, by means of a simple commutative method. For example, by commuting a specific sound in a word such as *cat*, changing it to *rat* or some other minimally-different form *(bat, hat*, etc.), one could establish the phonemic status of its constituent sounds—in this case initial *c* (as we saw). A pair such as *cat*-versus-*rat* was called a "minimal pair" by Trubetzkoy (1939). Using this simple technique, linguists started discovering many aspects of phonological structure and its relation to the overall structure of a language. This technique remains central to linguistics to this day.

As work in structuralism gained momentum in the 1930s and 1940s, inevitably the question arose as to the psychological validity of opposition. It was Roman Jakobson (1942) who first tackled this question, by looking at childhood verbal development. He noted that phonemic oppositions that occur rarely in the system of the native language are among the last ones learned by children. Oppositions with nasal phonemes, such as *n* and *m* (*name*-versus-*game*, *more*-versus-*door*) exist in all languages and, Jakobson found, are among the earliest phonemes acquired by children. On the other hand, oppositions with laryngeals, such as the sound represented by *h* (*how*-versus-*wow*), are relatively rare. In this case, he found that they are among the last phonemes to be acquired. There may be other ways to explain this type of development, but subsequent research has not found evidence to negate Jakobson's conclusions. In effect, as Jakobson's work showed, the Prague School was starting to entertain broader implications of opposition theory before structuralism was marginalized by the various movements and trends mentioned above.

There are various types of oppositions. For example, phonemic oppositions (*cat*-versus-*rat*, which shows the opposition of *c*-versus-*r*) allow us to recognize physical cues in words that are distinctive. Conceptual oppositions, on the other hand, involve content (semantic) distinctions—*day*-versus-*night, right*-versus-*left*, and so on. The study of oppositions has also led to several insights into the actual relational structure of oppositions themselves. For instance, it has been found that the poles of an opposition tend to fall into the same typological category. For example, a left-pointing arrow is an indexical sign, and its polar opposite is a right-point one. This type of synchronization is not always present, but our tendency is to relate concepts that are based on similar semiotic properties. Now, the question becomes, what happens when a new concept, such as *Selfie*, comes into currency? Where is the opposition in this case? New concepts are never forged in isolation, but in relation to existing ones, which is a fundamental principle of structuralism. So, to grasp the meaning of this new concept, we instinctively relate it to photography. This, the opposition *Selfie*-versus-*photo* entails a whole array of connotations, which apply to new perceptions of photography and what it aims to do (which need not concern us here). The point is that we seem automatically to relate new concepts to previous ones.

Another key insight deriving from research on opposition theory is that not all oppositions show a binary structure. For example, the verb tense system of English has a ternary (not binary) oppositional structure—*present*-versus-*past*-versus-*future* ("I speak-versus-"I spoke"-versus-"I shall speak"). It has been found, in fact, that oppositions can be binary, ternary, four-part, graduated, or cohesive (set-based). The type of opposition that applies to some system depends on what system (language, kinship, etc.) or subsystem (phonemic, semantic, etc.) is involved. Anthropologist Claude Lévi-Strauss (1958), for example, showed that in some systems, such as the kinship one, pairs of oppositions often cohered into sets forming recognizable units. In analyzing kinship systems, Lévi-Strauss found that the elementary unit of kinship was made up of a set of four oppositions: *brother*-versus-*sister*, *husband*-versus-*wife*, *father*-versus-*son*, and *mother's brother*-versus-*sister's son*. A decade later, Algirdas J. Greimas (1966) elaborated the notion of the *semiotic square*—a model of opposition involving two sets of concepts forming a square arrangement. Given a sign s_1 (for example, *rich*), we determine its overall meaning by opposing it to its contradictory $-s_1$ (*not rich)*, its contrary s_2 (*poor*), and its contradictory $-s_2$ (*not poor*):

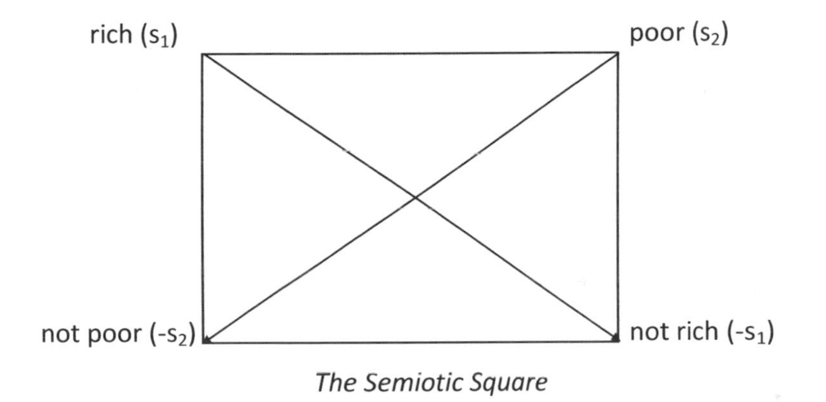

The Semiotic Square

For the sake of historical accuracy, it should be mentioned that the concept of semiotic square goes back at least to the fifteenth century, as the following diagram attests (attributed to a certain John Major, although this is not verifiable):

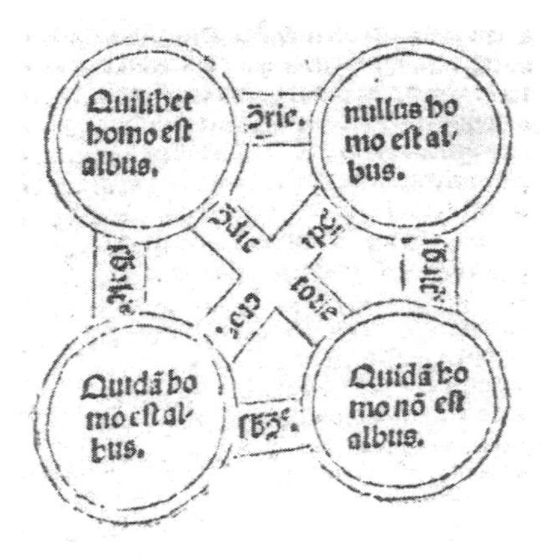

Fifteenth Century Semiotic Square

Roland Barthes (1967) argued that ternary and four-part oppositional structures surfaced frequently in specific codes. In the fashion code, for instance, he maintained that these included *tight fitting*-versus-*closely-fitting*-versus-*loosely fitting*-versus-*puffed-out* and *open*-versus-*side-by-side*-versus-*closed*-versus-*crossed*-versus-*rolled-up*. The gist of the theory is that signs do not bear meaning in isolation, but in relation to other signs.

The question of meaning comes up in oppositional analysis, which takes us back to the "meaning of meaning" problem discussed in the previous chapter. With the technique of opposition this question can be skirted, perhaps too conveniently, as Saussure (1916: 251-258) maintained by using the term *valeur* (*value*) as the minimal meaning we extract from oppositions—a minimal difference in sound, a minimal difference in tone, a minimal difference in orientation, and so on. Rather than bearing intrinsic meaning, Saussure argued that signs had *valeur* in differential relation to other signs or sign elements. To determine the value of an American quarter, for instance, one must know that the coin can be exchanged for a certain quantity (a *substance*) of something different and that its value can be compared with another value in the same system, for example, with two dimes and one nickel. While this skirts around the notion of meaning, it is certainly a useful notion for carrying out semiotic analysis without becoming enmeshed in the vagaries of the word *meaning*.

The Semantic Differential

As the foregoing discussion implies, connotative-cultural meaning is built into oppositions and their markedness structure. Among the first to examine how we extract connotations from oppositions in a systematic fashion were the psychologists Osgood, Suci, and Tannenbaum in 1957, who introduced the concept of *semantic differential* to do so. They suggested that connotative (culture-specific) meanings could actually be measured by asking subjects to rate a concept on seven-point scales, with polar concepts located at the end-points of those scales. The ratings are then collected and analyzed statistically. The number seven was chosen, incidentally, because the year before their study George Miller (1956) had shown that the ability to process meaningful cues in given information was limited to between 5 and 9 equally-weighted cues.

To grasp what the method entails, consider oppositions such as *fatherhood*-versus-*motherhood, femininity*-versus-*masculinity*, etc.—which in most semiospheres evoke specific social connotations (Bolinger 1968). Now, suppose hypothetically that subjects are asked to rate the concept *ideal father* in terms of seven-point oppositional scales such as *practical*-versus-*idealistic, flexible*-versus-*stern,* etc. The outcome of the survey would arguably yield a connotative profile of this concept. Results near the end of the scales (say, 1.4 or 6.4) would indicate high connotative content; results near the middle of the scales would indicate neutrality and, thus, equipollence in the oppositions. The ratings are collected and analyzed statistically in order to sift out any general pattern they might bear. The scales would look like this:

flexible	_	_	_	_	_	_	_	*stern*
	1	2	3	4	5	6	7	
practical	_	_	_	_	_	_	_	*idealistic*
	1	2	3	4	5	6	7	
modern	_	_	_	_	_	_	_	*traditional*
	1	2	3	4	5	6	7	
talkative	_	_	_	_	_	_	_	*quiet*
	1	2	3	4	5	6	7	
lenient	_	_	_	_	_	_	_	*strict*
	1	2	3	4	5	6	7	

Semantic Differential for the Ideal Father

A subject who feels that a father should be *flexible* would place a mark towards the *flexible* end of the top scale; one who feels that he should be *strict*, would place a mark towards the *strict* end; and so on. If we were to ask a large number of subjects to rate the father in this way, we would get a "connotative profile" of fatherhood in terms of the statistically significant variations in oppositional value that it evokes.

Research utilizing the semantic differential has shown, in fact, that the range of connotative variations is not a matter of pure subjectivity, but rather, forms a socially-based pattern. Younger people may tend to rate the ideal father as being flexible, older ones as stern, and so on. The connotative profile would also vary according to culture. Therefore, the method would shed light on how universal concepts are themselves subject to cultural shaping. In other words, the connotata of abstract concepts are constrained by psychological and cultural factors. A common critique of the technique, however, is that the poles used (*practical*-versus-*idealistic, flexible*-versus-*stern,* etc.) are themselves cultural concepts, utilized by the researchers to unconsciously guide subject choices along a certain path that is itself culturally-biased. In other words, they show what analysts want to show. But even if the scales are determined in advance, the results obtained may be unexpected ones and thus the whole technique would be legitimate as a form of randomized experimentation. In effect, the semantic differential remains a valid investigative tool into the nature of connotation, since it allows us to flesh out what something means in cultural terms (within limits).

Markedness

In any opposition, one of the poles is assumed to be the "default" or normal one and the other the "exceptional" one. So, in, say, the *health*-versus-*disease* opposition it is assumed that *health* is the normal state and that *disease* is the exceptional state. It is said that *disease* is "marked" psychologically, while *health* is "unmarked." This example illustrates, in microcosm, the essence of *markedness theory*, which is a derivative of opposition theory.

Work within structuralism revealed, from the outset, that polar concepts are processed cognitively in this way. So, for example, in *day*-versus-*night*, *night* is typically conceived by most people as being "absence of daylight," while *day* is rarely conceived analogously as being "absence of night." In other words, *night* is "marked" conceptually with respect to *day*, which is perceived to be the "unmarked" concept in the opposition. From such observations, the theory of markedness arose, allowing linguists and semoticians to examine sign systems in terms of the conceptually and socially marked implications. The question of which pole in an opposition was the marked one thus became a major line of inquiry, as well as what role culture or context played in markedness structure. For example, in the *give*-versus-*accept* opposition, either pole could be assigned unmarked status, depending on the situation or viewpoint of the people implicated in the opposition. In a situation where giving is the objective of some group, such as a charity agency, then *give* is the unmarked pole; vice versa, among people who survive through alms, then *accept* is the unmarked concept.

The foregoing discussion emphasizes that contextual criteria must always be enlisted to determine markedness relations, such as frequency, cultural events, situation, and so on. In phonological systems, the marked phoneme is generally more constrained than the unmarked one in the type and number of word-making combinations it may enter into, in the type and range of changes it may undergo, in the frequency with which it occurs, and so on. It was Trubetzkoy and Jakobson (mentioned above) who first identified and defined markedness as the asymmetrical relation whereby one pole is more constrained than the other pole on a particular level. As Battistella (1990: 2) observes, this principle comes from the fact that "the terms of polar oppositions at any level of language are not mere opposites, but rather that they show an evaluative nonequivalence that is imposed on all oppositions."

Markedness theory was applied from to both form-based (phonemic and grammatical) and conceptual oppositions. For example, in the indefinite article system of English grammar, *a* is the unmarked form, since it occurs before all consonants in the chain of speech (*a boy*), while *an* is the marked one, because it occurs more restrictively before vowels (*an apple*). The markedness criterion in this case is frequency, since there are more words beginning with consonants than vowels. However, internal grammatical rules do not always play a role in assigning markedness status. For example, in the *grape*-versus-*grapes* opposition, the singular form is the expected unmarked one grammatically, as it is for most nouns. However, on the semantic and discourse levels the singular form is marked, since the plural form, *grapes*, is referentially more common and is thus unmarked—"We love grapes;" "The grapes are ripe;" etc. As markedness was investigated across several disciplines, it became obvious that it provided insights into the interconnectedness of linguistic levels and their relation to the external world of reference, including social structure. In Italian, for example, the masculine plural form of nouns referring to people is the unmarked one, used to indicate any person, male or female, whereas the feminine plural form is marked, referring only to females. For instance, *i bambini* (which is masculine in form) can refer to all children, whereas *le bambine* refers specifically to female children. The fact that the unmarked form in Italian is the masculine gender is a clue to the historical roles played by the two genders in Italian society. Markedness theory can thus be seen to be a tool for unraveling social relations and codes of power. (This is not the case in many non-Western cultures as for example the unmarked forms in Mohawk are in the feminine, which underlines the prominent role women play in these societies). Terms like *chairman*, *spokesman*, etc. are examples of how the English language predisposed its users to view certain social roles in gender terms in the past. Their replacements (*chair, spokesperson,* etc.) show how the oppositional poles in the evaluative superstructure of language can be neutralized. Indeed, markedness theory suggests that we can potentially change social structure by changing linguistic structure. Consider job designations as a case-in-point. Over the past sixty years, as women increasingly entered into traditionally male-based occupations, their presence was perceived to be a deviation from tradition. Logically, their job titles were marked linguistically by adding suffixes such as *-ess* to words (*waitress*, *actress*, etc.). Use of this suffix today has lost its previous markedness structure. It is now used referentially simply to distinguish the sex of the server, carrying no social subtext with regard to gender as in the past. Moreover, the preference of many today is to not make any reference to gender (for example the common use of the word "actor" in English for both female and male actors).

Another insight that markedness theory has produced is the fact that the poles in an opposition generated related polar oppositions. As an example consider the *right*-versus-*left* opposition (Needham 1973). The *right* pole is perceived as the unmarked one at a denotative level because most people are right-handed. In this case markedness is a response to statistical factors. If the reverse were ever to happen, whereby left-handedness became the norm, then the markedness relation would be reversed. Now, once established, an array of derived oppositional relations based on connotative processes emerges across codes. So, *right* is associated with *good*, *light*, and *left* with *evil*, *dark*. This means that the *right*-versus-*left* opposition has become connotatively connected to derivative oppositions such as to *good*-versus-*evil,* to *light*-versus-*dark* and so on. The results on behavior are obvious—we shake hands with the right hand; we use the word *right* to suggest "correctness," but *sinister* (from Latin for "left") as something unwanted; and so on.

In sum, markedness theory has produced many insights into the connection between sign structures and social-cultural structures. It is applied to all sign systems to show how we evaluate and perceive signs in relation to each other.

Post-Structuralism

Despite its utility as a theoretical framework for discussing the relation between signs, concepts, and culture concretely, markedness theory became a target of criticism in the late 1950s and 1960s—a debate that spawned the movement known as *post-*

structuralism, spearheaded by two French scholars, Jacques Derrida (1967) and Michel Foucault (1972). Post-structuralism was, in hindsight, an ideological reaction against structuralism as ensconced in the theories of opposition and markedness theory. Derrida in particular pointed out that markedness was a logocentric concoction, and that it was ultimately perilous because of the inequalities it encoded. In a binary opposition such as *day*-versus-*night,* accepting *day* as the unmarked form and *night* as its marked counterpart entailed few, if any, social consequences. Problems arose, however, with oppositions such as *male*-versus-*female* and *self*-versus-*other*. Derrida (1976: 237) claimed that oppositions deconstruct themselves when analyzed reflectively, that is, they fall apart, revealing their biased origins:

> In idealization, to an origin or to a "priority" seen as simple, intact, normal, pure, standard, self-identical, in order *then* to conceive of derivation, complication, deterioration, accident, etc. All metaphysicians have proceeded thus: good before evil, the positive before the negative, the simple before the complex, the essential before the accidental, the imitated before the imitation, etc. This is not just *one* metaphysical gesture among others; it is *the* metaphysical exigency.

As discussed above, contrary to this view, markedness can actually be used to identify social stereotypes, not encode them. And this can, over time, actually lead to reversing markedness structure and the social inequalities it reflects. This has happened to the *male*-versus-*female* opposition in various modern societies, as discussed briefly above. Such reversals exist across oppositions.

Derrida also saw the Saussurean relation of the signifier and the signified as variable, not fixed, coining the term *différance (*spelled with an "a"), in contrast to Saussure's *différence*, to indicate an infinite deferral of meaning, and the absence of any true meaning to things outside of our signs and texts. As he put it (Derrida 1976: 12): "There is nothing outside the text." Derrida aimed to show that a structuralist science of signs cannot succeed since it must be carried out through language and thus will partake of the slippage (as he called it) it discovers. Sign systems are self-referential—signs refer to other signs, which refer to still other signs, and so on ad infinitum. Because written language is the basis of knowledge-producing enterprises, post-structuralists claimed that these end up reflecting nothing more than the writing practices used to articulate them. But in hindsight, there was nothing particularly radical in post-structuralism. Already in the 1920s, Jakobson and Trubetzkoy started probing the "relativity" of language oppositions in the light of their social and psychological functions. Basing their ideas in part on the work of German psychologist Karl Bühler (1908), they also posited that language categories mirrored social emphases, and thus did not really tell the truth in any objective sense. The goal of a true semiotic science, they claimed, was to investigate the isomorphism that manifested itself between signs and social systems.

Post-structuralism did, however, leave its imprint on important theories, including post-colonialism and critical race theory, which argue that certain binary oppositions have perpetuated and legitimized bias and stereotypes. The laudable goal on these theories has been to *deconstruct* the opposition, so as to make it obvious to everyone what its markedness structure entails. These have led to critical discourse theory, which has allowed us to deconstruct power structures in language as reflective of power structures in society.

Epilogue

As Saussure maintained, semiotics (semiology) is really part of psychology, because in documenting and investigating sign structures it is also investigating mental structures, and which ones are universal and which ones are shaped by culture. So, the theory of opposition to decipher which concepts are universal and which are culture-specific is essentially a theory of mind. Oppositions that seem to have universal status include *masculine*-versus-*feminine*, *light*-versus-*dark*, *good*-versus-*evil*, *self*-versus-*other*, *subject*-versus-*object*, *sacred*-versus-*profane*, *body*-versus-*mind*, *nature*-versus-*culture*, *beginning*-versus-*end*, *love*-versus-*hate*, *pleasure*-versus-*pain*, *existence*-versus-*nothingness*, *left*-versus-*right, something*-versus-*nothing,* among others. Most others are culture-specific, Consider bodies of water. In English, words such as *lakes, oceans, rivers, streams, seas, creeks,* and so on are used commonly. These are gradient concepts located on a *water*-versus-*land* oppositional scale. Now, people living in the desert have very few words for bodies of water, for obvious reasons. So, such concepts would no play as much of role in their culture as they do in others. In the latter, further oppositional refining, as it may be called, emerges. For example, size may enter the classificatory picture to produce lower-level conceptual oppositions—*ocean*-versus-*lake*—as does width and length—*river*-versus-*stream*—among other features.

The movement known as *cognitive linguistics*, which came to the forefront in the 1980s, after the publication of George Lakoff and Mark Johnson's groundbreaking book, *Metaphors We Live By* (1980), has lent more weight to the hypothesis that opposition theory is a theory of mind. Without going into details here, since it will be discussed subsequently, suffice it to say that cognitive linguistics has documented the fact that cultural meanings emerge from associations among concepts, called conceptual metaphors. The motivation behind this research enterprise is that the human mind seeks to understand reality by blending domains of meaning through bodily, historical, and affective processes. For example, by linking animals to human personality, we are seeking to understand the latter in terms of the former. This is why we interpret sentences such as *He's a fox*, *She's an eagle*, and so on, as personality constructs. It is not the denotative meaning of the animals that is built into the sentences, but rather their connotative (cultural) meanings. Upon closer reflection, this whole process can be seen to be the consequence of an ontological opposition: *humans*-versus-*animals*. This suggests that opposition is operative as well in figurative meaning. Gradience in this case is the actual allocation of specific animals (*gorilla, lion,* etc.) onto the oppositional scale—*John is a gorilla, She is a lion*, etc.

Lakoff and Johnson trace the psychological source of such polarity and gradience to mental image schemata that are produced by our sensory experiences of locations, movements, shapes, substances, etc. as well as our experiences of social events and of cultural life in general (Lakoff and Johnson 1980, 1999, Lakoff 1987, Johnson 1987). Upon closer scrutiny, these turn out to be oppositions: *up*-versus-*down*, *back*-versus-*front*, *near*-versus-*far*, *full*-versus-*empty*, *balance*-versus-*unbalance*, etc. Their manifestations occur in language (*I'm feeling up today, Inflation is going down at last, I'm full of memories, My sense of timing is out of synch*, etc.) and in other codes. For example, in music the *up*-versus-*down* opposition is expressed by the fact that the higher tones are perceived to express *happiness* and the lower ones *sadness*. The *up* pole is synchronized to *happiness* and *down* to *sadness* across the network of codes in a culture. Consider again the opposition *humans*-versus-*animals*. In American culture, it not only surfaces in discourse about human personality, but also in the naming of sports teams (*Denver Broncos*, *Chicago Bears, Detroit Tigers,* etc.), which imparts a certain character to the team in terms of perceived animal qualities, in fictional or cartoon characters *(Bugs Bunny, Daffy Duck,* etc.) to represent human personality types, in assigning surnames and nicknames *(John Fox, Mary Wolf*, etc.), and so on and so forth.

To conclude this chapter on a technical note, it should be mentioned polar concepts, which form a binary opposition and display what semioticians call *paradigmatic* structure, whereas gradient concepts do not—one cannot put *red* into a polar opposition with another color that would form a universal opposition (cross-cultural). Such concepts show, in other words, *syntagmatic* structure, since they are connected to the polar concepts in culture-specific ways. Consider one more time the words *cat* and *rat* once again. These are perceived as being structurally-appropriate English words, not only because they are recognizable as distinct through a simple binary opposition of initial phonemic cues, but also because the combination of sounds with which they are constructed is consistent with English word structure. On the other hand, *rtat* would not be recognizable as a legitimate word because it violates a specific aspect of such structure—namely, English words cannot start with the cluster *rt*. This is an example of violation of syntagmatic structure. The paradigmatic-syntagmatic pattern occurs across systems. In music, a melody is recognizable as appropriate only if the notes follow each other according to the rules of harmony. Paradigmatic structure is differentiation; syntagmatic structure is combination. When putting together a simple sentence, for example, we do not choose the words in a random fashion, but rather according to their paradigmatic and syntagmatic properties. The choice of the noun *brother* in the subject slot of a sentence such as *My brother loves school* is a paradigmatic one, because other nouns—*girl, man, woman,* etc.—could have been chosen instead. But the choice of any one of these for that sentence slot constrains the type—*love* vs. *drink*—and form—*loves* vs. *loving*— of the verb that can be chosen and combined with it. The co-occurrence of these two patterns is a structural feature of all meaning-bearing systems.

3
Sign Types

A sign is in a conjoint relation to the thing denoted and to the mind.

Charles S. Peirce (1839-1914)

Prologue

Semiosis mediates how we come to know the world beyond instinctual reactions to it. Because it is largely an information-filtering process—that is, a sign selects what is to be known and used by the mind from the infinite variety of things that exist in the world—it shapes worldview. The Prussian philologist Wilhelm von Humboldt (1767–1835) originated the idea that language, society, ethnic character, and worldview are intrinsically intertwined, and could not exist without one another (Humboldt 1836). Benjamin Lee Whorf (1956) also claimed that the lexicon and grammar of a language put up a mental filter for perceiving the "map of reality" (physical and non-physical). In effect, the map of the world coincides with the linguistic map of that world, as well as with musical, artistic, and other kinds of semiotic maps. The Polish-born scholar Alfred Korzybski, who founded the movement of *general semantics*, also argued that human knowledge is limited both by the human nervous system and the languages humans have developed, implying that we can never have direct access to reality. As he famously put it (Korzybski 1933: 58): "The map is not the territory."

Although we create new signs all the time to help us record new knowledge or modify previous knowledge, by and large, we let the signs we acquire in cultural context filter our understanding, as the above scholars maintained. We are born into an already-fixed system of signs that will largely shape how we will come to view the world around us. On the other hand, each time we come up with something new we encode it in new semiotic ways, and as these enter into groupthink they lead to changes in worldview. The paradox is that signs both record and ensconce previous knowledge, but semiosis is also the brain's strategy for changing knowledge. The implication is that, by studying signs and their various manifestations, we can gain insight into the connection between reality and our variable perception of it. The starting point in such study is classifying signs in order grasp how they encode reality in specific. ways. As discussed (Chapter 2), although there were classifications of signs before Charles Peirce, such as the typology by medieval philosopher and scientist Roger Bacon (c. 1214-1292), the Peircean system is the one that has become central to contemporary analysis. As discussed several times, three sign types within this system are now used diffusely—namely, icons, indexes, and symbols, also discussed briefly in the previous chapter. These can be summarized schematically in chart form as follows:

Type	*Relation to Referent*	*Examples*
Icon	encodes a referent by simulation or resemblance	onomatopoeic words *(splash*), photos, etc.
Index	puts referents in some relation	pointing finger, words such as *here, there, near, far,* etc.
Symbol	encodes a referent by convention	national symbols such as flags, advertising logos, etc.

Three Main Types of Signs

Three other kinds of signs also studied broadly across semiotic approaches are *names*, *symptoms*, and *signals*. This chapter will provide an overview of these six main sign types (Sebeok 2001).

Icons

An *icon* is a sign (a representamen)—a word, a figure, etc.—that is constructed and interpreted as resembling its referent in some way. Photographs, for instance, are icons of referents based on visuality; onomatopoeic words such as *splash, bang,* and *boom* have been made to resemble their referents in an acoustic way. Commercially-produced perfumes that are suggestive of certain natural scents are likewise iconic, because they simulate the scents in an artificial way. Iconicity crosses all levels and systems of semiosis and representation. It can be seen today in such new sign forms as emojis that stand artificially for facial expressions, from the smiley to the face with tears. It is found in music in the form of specific sounds—Beethoven's *Pastoral* symphony or Rossini's *William Tell Overture*, for example, contain musical sounds or leitmotifs that are evocative of the sounds found in nature (bird calls, thunder, wind, etc.).

Iconicity is not exclusive to the human species. Sebeok (1990, 2001a, 2001b) has documented its manifestations in different species, suggesting that the ability to manufacture concrete simulative models of the world, consciously or unconsciously, is a basic life scheme. For example, the walking-stick insect (*Phasmida*), which closely resembles the twigs of the plants on which it lives, has the ability to change minute details of its physical appearance that resemble other features in its environment. Similarly, the black chunky myna bird (*Sturnidae*) from Asia and the East Indies has a white spot on its wing and bright yellow wattles on the back of its head, which allow it to blend in with the visible features of its habitat. Sometimes, a creature even has the capacity to fabricate dummy copies of itself to misdirect predators. This iconic capacity is possessed, for instance, by different species of a spiders known as orb-weavers. These manifestations of iconicity are examples of natural iconicity. In humans, iconicity transcends biology, allowing humans to reproduce the world through representational practices. In effect, iconicity may be a law of nature, a modeling response to sensations, revealing instinctive efforts to know and understand the world through these responses.

The presence of iconicity in semiotic systems across cultures is strong evidence that human consciousness is, at its roots, attentive to the recurrent patterns of color, shape, dimension, movement, sound, taste, etc. that are monitor through human perceptual systems. The end-product of this attentiveness is iconic representation. Here are some examples of iconicity across sense modalities:

- Onomatopoeic words such as *drip, plop, bang, screech* are vocal-acoustic icons attempting to replicate the sounds that certain referents are perceived to make.
- Portraits of photos of people are visual icons intended to reproduce actual faces.
- Perfumes are olfactory icons attempting to simulate natural scents.
- Chemical food additives are gustatory icons designed to simulate the taste of natural foods.
- A block with a letter of the alphabet carved into it is a tactile icon because the letter's shape can be felt and figured out by touch.

Archeological evidence attests to the ancientness of visual iconicity. The first inscriptions, cave drawings, small sculptures, and relief carvings of animals and female figures found in caves throughout Europe, such as those at Lascaux in France and

Altamira in Spain, were created around 30,000 to 40,000 years ago. These are iconic representations that aim to represent objects in the world in terms of resemblance. As the hand movements used to make such works of art became more abbreviated, the figures became more condensed and abstract. This led, according to some theories, to the invention of writing. The earliest form of writing was, thus, vastly different from the alphabetic writing systems that we use today. The work of Schmandt-Besserat (1992) has shown, in fact, that the earliest precursors of modern writing systems were pattern-making forms, such as those found on clay tokens discovered in western Asia from the Neolithic era. The tokens were used as image-making objects.

The study of language origins presents a similar picture of iconicity at work in vocalization. Among the various theories, several stand out as being based in iconicity theory (Stam 1976):

- *Bow-Wow Theory*. This posits that speech originated as a result of attempts to imitate the sounds made by animals. This theory finds some validity in the fact that in the basic vocabularies of the world's languages onomatopoeic words are similar in their iconic properties (*bow-wow, meow)*.
- *Pooh-Pooh Theory*. This claims that speech originated out of the instinctive sounds and grunts our hominid ancestors made in response to pain, anger, love, and other affective states. The main evidence used in support of this theory is the universal presence of interjections—*Ah! Ouch! Yikes! Wow!* etc.—in the world's languages.
- *Ding-Dong Theory*. This postulates that speech resulted from vocal imitations of the sounds connected with objects or actions. For example, words such as *ding-dong, bing-bang, flip-flop,* suggest an iconic origin, revealing an attempt to reproduce sounds of various kinds through vocalization.
- *Yo-He-Ho Theory*. This posits that language crystallized from the chants made by early peoples as they worked and played together in vocal imitation of each other. The main evidence for this theory is the presence of prosodic features (tone, modulation, rhythm, etc.) in childhood, as children attempt to communicate early needs or to express early concepts. These features are said to be remnants of chanting.

- *La-La Theory.* This claims that language emerged as a consequence of the sounds our human ancestors made in response to lovemaking, play, and other social activities. Essentially, it claims that such imitative sounds were the basis of the first words.

These theories have been called *echoic*, originating in ancient Greece. The basic idea in echoism is that of iconicity as a primordial force in language creation. Stross (1976: 21) encapsulates the idea behind echoism in the following way:

> Humans and birds especially seem to have rather well developed abilities to imitate many environmental sounds, especially sounds made by other animals, and this ability could well have been very useful to protohominids for luring game. Could sounds used by protohominids to lure game or mimic sounds of nature come to represent the game or other objects in nature in the minds of these prelinguistic humans?

Iconicity is, in sum, a primary sign-making principle in the origin and evolution of language. As Derek Bickerton (2009: 218-222) has cogently argued, animal signal systems are largely made up of indexical signs (paw prints, pheromones, etc.), whereas human language originates through imitation. Our human ancestors used iconic signs to create new words and deploy old words in new way, further weakening the connection of words to situations, and thus allowing for the emergence of symbolic language.

It is relevant to note that, before Peirce's use of the term *icon* to refer to a specific type of sign, it was used in art to refer to the image of a religious figure. The word is still used with this meaning today. In this context, the icon is believed to be sacred in itself and, thus, to aid believers in contacting the represented figure through prayer or veneration. Beginning in the eighth century, *iconoclasm*, a movement that condemned the worship of icons as idolatrous, contributed to the destruction of much religious art throughout the Byzantine Christian world. It was not until the subsequent century that the sacred icons were restored to their former roles in religious observance.

Iconicity is also evident in childhood development, showing up in the tendency of children to make scribbles and elemental drawings at about the same time that they utter their first words. If given drawing materials around the age of two or three, young children instinctively start scribbling on the drawing surface. As time passes, their scrawls become more and more controlled; geometrical shapes such as crude circles, crosses, and rectangles, at first accidentally produced, are repeated and gradually perfected. Although children, with adult prompting, may learn to label circles as *suns* or *faces*, they do not seem inclined at first to draw anything in particular. The act of making shapes appears to be pleasurable and satisfying in itself. Of course, shapes eventually suggest "things" to the child as their ability to use language for naming purposes develops; but in the beginning, the child seems to engage in drawing solely for the pleasure of it, without attaching explicit associations of meaning to it. It is truly an example of "art for art's sake."

In the digital world, the term *icon* is used to designate a tiny picture on a computer screen. Each icon represents a command. The system of icons, pointer, and mouse is known as a graphical user interface, a system that provides a user-friendly way of interacting with a computer. Users can usually tell by the icons how to get the computer to do what they want. Without a GUI, the computer screen is black, and the only way to tell the computer what to do is to type in commands. There is little doubt that GUIs contributed to the rise of the personal computer in the mid-1980s, starting in 1984 when the Apple Computer company introduced the Macintosh, the first personal computer to include a GUI. Because they make computers easy to use, GUI's quickly became standard throughout the computer industry.

Iconicity is manifest throughout the digital world, from three-dimensional user interfaces to virtual reality (VR)—which is an iconic simulation, or more accurately, *simulacrum* of physical reality, to adopt the term used by Jean Baudrillard (1983), implying that simulated environments are perceived as real because of iconicity. VR technologies have been altering not only the way we interact with reality, but also the way we experience it and even interact with it. VR requires special interface devices that transmit the sights, sounds, and sensations of the simulated world to the user. These also record and send the speech and movements of the participants to the simulation program. In effect, the human subject is immersed in a world totally made-up, a kind of representational space where the user is interacting with the representation. To see in the virtual world, the user wears a head-mounted display (HMD) with screens directed at each eye. The HMD contains a position tracker to monitor the location of the user's head and the direction in which the user is looking. Using this information, a computer recalculates images of the virtual world to match the direction in which the user is looking and displays these images on the HMD. Users hear sounds in the virtual world through earphones in the HMD.

Clearly, the semiotic concept of iconicity is a powerful one for understanding the ways in which new media change people and societies. The iconicity on a screen literally comes to life in the imagination, and so we come to detach the image from the screen and generalize it to everyday life, whereby we start a process of inner perception that involves the image at its center.

Indexes

An *index* is a sign that refers to a referent in terms of its existence or location in time, space, or in relation to something or someone else. Smoke is an index of fire pointing out where the fire is; a cough is an index of a cold; and so on. These signs do not resemble their referents, like icons; they indicate or show where they are or how they are related to each other. The most typical manifestation of indexicality (as discussed several times) is the pointing *index* finger, which humans the world over use instinctively to point out and locate things, people, and events in the world. Many words, too, manifest an implicit form of indexicality: for example, *here*, *there*, *up*, *down* refer to the relative location of things when speaking about them.

Semioticians and linguists have identified several main types of indexicality:

- *Spatial Indexicality* is a form of reference by which the spatial locations of objects, beings, and events are either indicated or correlated by a manual sign like the pointing index finger, a pointing arrow, a demonstrative word like *this* or *that*, an adverb like *here* or *there*, etc.
- *Temporal Indexicality* is a form of reference by which the temporal relations among things and events are either indicated or to each, as for example, an adverb like *before, after, now*, or *then*, a timeline graph representing points in time as located to the left and right, or on top and below, of each other, etc.
- *Personal Indexicality* is a form of reference by which the relations among participants taking part in a situation are either indicated or correlated with forms such as a personal pronoun like *I, you, he, she,* an indefinite pronoun like *the one, the other*, etc.
- *Classificatory Indexicality* is a form of classificatory reference, such as an *index* at the end of a book is an alphabetized list of names, places, and subjects treated in a printed work, giving the page or pages on which each item is mentioned.
- *Mathematical Indexicality*: in mathematics an index is a number or symbol, often written as a subscript or superscript to a mathematical expression, that indicates an operation to be performed, an ordering relation, or the use of an associated expression.

- *Computer-search Indexicality*: a computer help users find the appropriate information on a computer via search engines have been designed so that indexes can be accessed to summarize the contents of the Internet. The user begins by entering a series of words, called a string, to tell the search engine what to look for. The search engine then tries to match the string to the available indexes.

The presence of indexicality in representational systems across the world is evidence that human consciousness is not only attentive to patterns of color, shape, etc., resulting in iconic representational activities, but also to the recurrent cause and effect patterns that are contingent on time and space constraints. The end-product of this form of attentiveness is indexical representation—that is, the activity of referring to objects, beings, and events in one's immediate line of sight by pointing, gesturing, etc.

Indexicality, like iconicity, can also involve metaphorical concepts. Consider the English expressions *think up*, *think over*, and *think out:* "When did you *think up* that preposterous idea?" "You should *think over* carefully what you just said"; "They must *think out* the entire problem together." Even though these refer to abstract ideas, they do so in ways that suggest imaginary physical location and movement: *think up* elicits a mental image of upward movement, portraying thinking as an object being extracted physically from an imaginary mental terrain; *think over* evokes the image of an internal eye scanning the mind; *think out* suggests the action of taking a deeply buried thought out of the mind so that it can be held up, presumably, for examination.

The presence of such expressions in languages across the world suggests something rather intriguing about the origins of language. The verbal simulation of the laws of physical perception suggests an evolutionary link between language and the senses. In Sanskrit, the word *maya* ("perceiving form in thought") contains the particle *ma* ("to measure or lay out"); in Italian, the verb *pensarci* ("to think about something, to think over") is constructed with the indexical particle *ci* ("here, there"); in English, *perceive* derives from Latin *cipio* ("to seize") and *per* ("through"), *examine* from *agmen* ("to pull out from a row") and *ex* ("from"), and *prospect* from Latin *spectus* ("looking") and *pro* ("forward, ahead").

Michael Silverstein (1976) has used indexicality as an analytical tool for studying the relationship between language and culture. This involves, concretely, the study of cross-references in actual speech, rather than on individual units as separate from speech texts. This idea was followed on by British-Australian linguist Michael Halliday (1985) who saw parts of speech that make up sentences, such as pronouns, as "text-governed" indexical structures, rather than items in a system of grammatical rules. Consider the following hypothetical conversation, which does not have pronouns in it. Although it is completely understandable grammatically, we nevertheless perceive it as awkward:

Speaker A:	Do you know Rina?
Speaker B:	Yes, I know Rina.
Speaker A:	Rina always likes to talk about Rina.
Speaker B:	Yes, Rina always talks about Rina.

The more appropriate version of the conversation is the one in which pronouns are used instead:

Speaker A:	Do you know Rina?
Speaker B:	Yes, I know *her*.
Speaker A:	*She* always likes to talk about *herself*.
Speaker B:	Yes, *she* always does.

The use of the pronouns (and the verb form *does*) are part of a "textual-indexical grammar" that allows speakers to connect the content part such as nouns in order to maintain the flow of conversation, like trace devices, by avoiding repetition.

Natural indexes are found in many species. For example, in *E.coli*—a bacterium normally found in the human gastrointestinal tract which is responsible for some diarrheal diseases—has multiple flagellae that it can rotate either clockwise or counterclockwise. In the former, they fly apart, causing the bacterium to tumble; in the latter they are drawn together into a bundle that acts as a propeller to produce smooth, directed swimming. In the intestinal tract, the bacterium explores a chemical field for nutrients by alternating—its context serving as operator—between tumbling and directed swimming until it finds an optimally appropriate concentration of sugar or an amino acid, for its replication. In doing so, it relies on a memory trace lasting approximately four seconds, allowing it to compare, over short periods of time and distances, where it was with where it is. On that basis, it "decides," whether to tumble, stay in place, or swim and search for another indexical match somewhere else. Another striking example of natural indexicality is evident in the behavior of a small family of picarian birds (*Indicator indicator*), which has developed a remarkable symbiotic relationship with certain ratels, baboons, and humans by employing an indexical strategy that is used to guide the latter to a source, such as a bees' nest. A bird will come to, say, a baboon, and emit chirps repetitively until followed, keeping out of sight of the pursue, leading the baboon to the honey.

Symbols

A *symbol* is a sign that stands for its referent in an arbitrary, conventional way. Most semioticians agree that symbolicity is what sets human semiosis apart from that of all other species, allowing the human species to reflect upon the world separately from stimulus-response situations. Words in general are symbolic signs. But any signifier—object, sound, figure, etc.—can be symbolic. A cross figure can stand for the concept "Christianity," as discussed previously; a V-sign made with the index and middle fingers can stand symbolically for the concept "peace;" *white* is a color that can be symbolic of "cleanliness," "purity," "innocence," whereas *dark* of "uncleanness," "impurity," "corruption;" and the list could go on and on. These are all established by social convention. The term *symbolicity* is used here specifically to allude to a sign type; *symbolism* is often employed as a synonym, but this can be confusing since the same term is used as referring to any artistic or literary movement or style using symbolic images and indirect suggestion to express mystical or metaphysical ideas. Symbolicity refers more specifically to signs that acquire their meanings through conventional-historical processes.

The presence of *symbolicity* in representational systems across the world is evidence that human consciousness is not only attentive to physical patterns (color, shape, etc.), resulting in iconic representational activities, and cause and effect patterns (contingent on time and space constraints), resulting in indexical representational activities, but also to pattern in itself. The end-product of this form of attentiveness is symbolic representation—that is, the activity of referring to objects, beings, and events in themselves with no apparent connection to physical or cause and effect phenomena.

In most models of the sign, symbolicity is seen as a derivative of the more fundamental iconic and indexical modes of representation. Symbols are thus seen "residues" of icons and indexes. The anecdotal evidence to support this view is substantial: for example, the child first learns to represent something by pointing to it (indexicality) and then naming it (symbolicity) later; people instinctively resort to iconicity (gesturing, making imitative sounds, etc.) and indexicality (pointing) when communicating with someone who does not speak the same language; iconic, indexical, and symbolic modes of representation often converge in the creation of a single sign; and so on. As discussed briefly, the Christian cross has all three modes. It is a symbol standing for Christianity, but the cross figure itself is an iconic evocation of the Crucifixion. Finally, the sign is also an index because when it is placed on a building, it indicates that the building is a church.

The foregoing discussion brings out the crucial role of context—the physical, psychological, and social environments in which a sign or text occurs—in the determination of meaning, as emphasized as well in previous chapters. Consider a beer can found thrown away on a city street. If we were to come across this item, we would no doubt view it as a piece of garbage or rubbish. But if we saw the very same object on a pedestal, displayed in an art gallery, "signed" by some artist, and given a title such as "Waste," then you would interpret its meaning in a vastly different way. We would, in fact, be inclined to interpret it as an artistic text, descrying a throw-away or materialistic society. Clearly, the package's physical context of occurrence and social frame of reference—its location on a sidewalk vs. its display in an art gallery—will determine how we will interpret it.

Symbolism (symbolicity) is everywhere. And it is the basis for forging international agreements on how to represent certain referents, constituting a shorthand system for recording and recalling information. Every branch of science has such a system—astronomy uses a set of ancient symbols to identify the sun, the moon, the planets, and the stars; in mathematics, Greek letters and other symbols make up an abbreviated language; and so on and so forth. Specific kinds of symbols appear in such fields as commerce, engineering, medicine, packaging, and transportation. All countries have official or unofficial national symbols. A flag or an anthem may symbolize a nation. Familiar symbols of the United States include Uncle Sam and the Statue of Liberty. Symbols for other countries include the maple leaf for Canada, John Bull for England, and the *fleur-de-lis* for France. Political parties also use symbols for identification. In the United States, a donkey symbolizes the Democratic Party, and an elephant represents the Republican Party.

Names

Names are signs that are normally formed as a blend of indexicality and symbolicity: they are indexical in that they are words identifying a person in some relational way (in relation to a kinship group, to a particular social context, etc.), and they are symbolic in that they are based on specific cultural traditions (Nuessel 1992). The study of *names* falls under the branch of both semiotics and linguistics called *onomastics* (from Greek *onoma* "name").

In Anglo-American culture, given (or first) names can stand for such things as a month or object (*May, June, Ruby, Daisy*), a religious figure *(John, Mary)*, popular personalities (*Elvis*, *Marilyn*), or classical mythic personages (*Diana*, *Jason*), among others. Until the late Middle Ages, one name was sufficient as an identification index. Duplications, however, began to occur so often that additional differentiations became necessary. Hence, surnames were assigned to individuals (literally "names on top of names"). These were at first either indexical, in that they identified the individual in terms of place of origin or genealogy, or descriptive, in that they identified the individual in terms of some personal or social feature (for example, occupation). For instance, in England a person living near or at a place where apple trees grew might have been called "Mary who lives nearby where the apples grow," hence, *Mary Appleby*. Surnames such as *Woods*, *Moore*, *Church*, or *Hill* have been coined in a similar way. Descriptive surnames such as *Black, Short, Long,* etc. were coined instead to highlight various characteristics of individuals. Descendant surnames were often constructed by prefixation—for example *Mac-*, *Mc-* in Scottish or Irish names or *Ap-* in Welsh names—or by suffixation—for example *-son* in English surnames and *-sen* in Scandinavian surnames (*Johnson* or *Jensen*, "son of John," *Maryson* "son of Mary," *Jakobsdottir*, "daughter of Jacob"). Surnames describing a person's occupation—*Smith, Farmer, Carpenter, Tailor, Weaver,* etc.—also assumed identifier function in the medieval period.

The Romans developed a system of three names: (1) the *praenomen* which was the person's given name; (2) the *nomen*, which indicated the *gens*, or clan to which the person belonged; and (3) the last name, or *cognomen*, which designated the family to which the person belonged. A person sometimes was assigned a fourth name, the *agnomen*, to commemorate an illustrious action or remarkable event in their life. Family names gained widespread use in Europe in the late tenth century. Nobles were the first to adopt them, in order to set themselves apart from common people, passing them on to their children. A family name thus became the mark of a well-bred person, and so all classes of people aspiring to ascend the social ladder began adopting this practice too.

Names are perceived throughout the world to be much more than indexes. They are laden with all kinds of symbolic meanings. Across cultures, a neonate is not considered a person until given a name. The act of naming is a semiotic rite of admission into personhood. The ancient Egyptians believed that a name was a living part of an individual, charting the person's destiny throughout life and even beyond. They also believed that if an individual's name was forgotten on earth, the deceased would have to undergo a second death. To avoid this danger, names were written multiple times on walls, tombs, and papyri. Political rulers would sometimes erase the names of previous monarchs as a means of rewriting history in their favor, since removal of a person's name meant the extinction of the person from memory. In Hebrew culture, the ancient art of *gematria* was based on the belief that the letters of a name could be translated as digits and rearranged to form a number that contained secret messages encoded in it. The Romans, too, thought names were prophetic, believing that *nomen est omen*—a "name is an omen."

Naming trends are remarkably stable in most societies. This is because names link people to the history and culture of the society into which they are born. However, in some contemporary societies, fashion trends often play a role in name-giving. The late rock musician and composer Frank Zappa (1940-1993), for instance, named his daughter *Moon Unit* and his son *Dweezil*. Actor Gwyneth Paltrow called her child *Apple*. Although this is somewhat consistent with tradition of naming children after flowers *(Daisy, Lily, Rose*, etc.) and occasionally after some fruits (*Peach*), it is rare (to the best of our knowledge) that a child would be named in this way. Perhaps Paltrow's intention was to connect her child to the many connotations built into the apple

In various parts of the ancient world, names were believed to be coded messages from divinities. Not only, but by invoking a god by name, it was thought that the god's power could be summoned for magical or spiritual purposes. In the Bible, characters are given names at birth that reflect something spiritually important or which are omens for the course that their lives would take: for instance, Solomon meant peace, perhaps impelling him psychologically to reign without war. In ancient cultures, it was believed that even knowing the name of a deity would give the knower great power—for example, in Egyptian mythology, the sorceress Isis created a serpent to poison the sun god, the supreme Egyptian deity. She would give him the antidote only if he revealed his true name, which was Ra. Upon knowing the name, she passed it on to Horus, bolstering his authority.

In many cultures, the name given to children is meant to continue the lineage of ancestors and is thus perceived to weave a sort of magical protective aura on the individual named after them. The Inuit, for instance, believe that a newborn baby cries because it wants its name, and will not be complete until it gets it. In some traditional indigenous cultures, individuals will not utter their names, fearing that this senseless act could break the magical spell of protection that it brings with it. As Epes Brown (1992: 13) puts it: "the fact that when we create words we use our breath, and for these people and these traditions breath is associated with the principle of life; breath is life itself. And so if a word is born from this sacred principle of breath, this lends an added sacred dimension to the spoken word."

Nicknames also reach back considerably in time. They are more likely to stand out than real names because they are designed to be character profiles. This is why they are common among organized criminal gangs (Nicaso and Danesi 2013). Mafioso Lucky Luciano, born Salvatore Lucania, was called "Lucky" because of the noticeable large scars around his neck that permanently recorded his fortuitous escape from death after being slashed and left dead by criminal rivals. The nickname of "Scarface" was given to Al Capone because he was involved in an altercation that left him with three noticeable scars on his face. These nicknames emphasize the fearlessness of each individual. Such names constitute a form of antonomasia, or the substitution of an epithet or title for a proper name. Because of its psychological connotative power, it is a marker of self-importance and an implicit form of braggadocio. Below are some nicknames of famous Mafiosi that show how they are intended to bring out some feature of the Mafioso's character, appearance, or personality (Danesi 2013):

- Vincent "Chin" Gigante (who had a prominent chin)
- Richard "Shellackhead" Cantarella (from his hair pomade)
- Vincent "Vinny Gorgeous" Basciano (who always dressed in dapper clothes and slicked his hair in style)
- Earl "Squint" Coralluzzo (because he squinted a lot)
- Thomas "Tough Tommy" Contaldo (because of his brutality)
- Salvatore "Sammy the Bull" Gravano (who had a neck like a bull and was a capable fighter)
- Ettore "Killer" Coco (for his ruthlessness)
- Thomas "Tommy Karate" Pitera (used martial arts in his vicious killing sprees)

Interestingly, many animals use signals that have comparable naming functions (at least as we humans interpret them). In birds, for example, it has been found that when partners are absent, the remaining bird will use the sounds normally reserved for the partner, with the result that the partner will return as quickly as possible. Whales apparently emit clicks that seem to have the same purpose of beckoning a partner to come back speedily. Dolphins have distinctive whistles, to which they will respond even when there is no other information to clarify which dolphin is being referred to.

Interestingly as we, we name animals, brand products, and even hurricanes. In the latter case, we are creating a *meteorological character* to represent a dangerous climactic event, recalling ancient mythic practices of naming meteorological phenomena as governed by deities. Although people do not think of a hurricane literally as a person, they nonetheless find it convenient to blame or thank "Him" or "Her" rather than some abstract process, for certain weather conditions. This mirrors, no doubt, how the original mythic characters were imagined—the difference being that the mythic characters of the past were likely believed to be real beings, not narrative models of physical events. So fundamental is our association between name-giving and life that this should come as no surprise. So, when brand products or tropical storms are given names they seem to take on a human personality.

Symptoms and Signals

Recall from Chapter 1 that semiotics emerges in the domain of medicine in antiquity as the study of symptoms, which are signs that provide vital clues to bodily functions or dysfunctions. The bodies of all animals produce symptoms as warning signs, but what they indicate will depend on the species. The biologist Jakob von Uexküll (1909) argued, the symptom is a reflex of anatomical structure. Animals with widely divergent anatomies will manifest virtually no symptomatology in common. It is interesting to note, by the way, that the term *symptom* is often extended metaphorically to refer to intellectual, emotional, and social phenomena that result from causes that are perceived to be analogous to physical processes: "Their behavior is a *symptom* of our times;" "Their dislike of each other is a *symptom* of circumstances;" etc.

A symptom can be subjective or objective. Tiredness is typically a subjective symptom whereas a cough or a fever are objective symptoms. In medical practice, a distinction between symptom and sign is often made (Danesi and Zukowski 2019). In contrast to a symptom, a sign is a clue to a disease or as determined by a medical practitioner. For example, paresthesia—the tingling sensation caused by pressure on peripheral nerves—is a symptom, since it is the person experiencing it who can describe it in this way; while erythema—a reddening of the skin—is a sign, since anyone can confirm that the skin is redder than usual and a practitioner will be the one to determine its connection to any disease. Clinical signs such as rash and muscle tremors are observable both by the patient and anyone else. Some signs can only be discovered through medical diagnosis—for instance, hypocalcemia or neutropenia require blood tests to be diagnosed.

All animals are endowed with the capacity to use and respond to species-specific signals for survival. Birds, for instance, are born prepared to produce a particular type of coo, and no amount of exposure to the songs of other species, or the absence of their own, has any effect on their cooing. A bird reared in isolation, in fact, will sing a very simple outline of the sort of song that would develop naturally in that bird born in the wild. This does not mean, however, that animal signaling is not subject to environmental or adaptational factors. Many bird species have also developed regional cooing "dialects" by apparently imitating each other. Vervet monkeys, too, have the usual set of signals to express emotional states and social needs, but they also have developed a particular predator signaling system—a specific call alerting the group to eagles, one to four-legged predators such as leopards, another to snakes, and one to other primates. The calls and general categories they represent seem innate, but in actual fact the young of the species learn them only by observing older monkeys and by trial and error. An infant vervet may at first deliver an aerial alarm to signal a vulture, a stork, or even a falling leaf, but eventually comes to ignore everything airborne except the eagle.

Most signals are emitted automatically in response to specific types of stimuli and affective states. The response patterns suggest strongly that animals have a species-specific form of reflective consciousness. A large portion of bodily communication among humans also unfolds largely in the form of unwitting signals. It has been shown, for example, that people are attracted to those with large pupils during courtship, which signal unconsciously a strong and sexually tinged interest, as well as making individuals look younger (Sebeok 1990). But humans are capable as well of deploying witting signals for some intentional purpose—for example, nodding, winking, glancing, looking, nudging, kicking, head tilting. As the linguist Karl Bühler (1934: 28) aptly observed, such signals act like regulators, eliciting or inhibiting some action or reaction. Signaling systems can also be created for conventional social purposes. The list of such systems is extensive, and includes: railway signals, smoke signals, semaphores, telegraph signals, Morse code signals, warning lights, flares, beacons, balefires, red flags, warning lights, traffic lights, alarms, distress signals, danger signals, whistles, sirens, beepers, buzzers, knocking, gongs, bells, drums.

The Morse Code requires some commentary, since it shows how signals and sign structures overlap. The first commercial telegraph system was developed in the 1830s. In 1844, the American inventor Samuel F. B. Morse (1791-1872), developed the binary code that bears his name (the Morse Code) for sending messages via telegraphy. The code utilized *on* and *off* signals to represent individual letters of the alphabet. The telegrapher at one end of the line would tap on an electrical key, and the telegrapher at the other end would decode the tapping signals as they came in, write down the message they contained, and send it to the recipient by messenger. Below is the set of signals of the Morse Code:

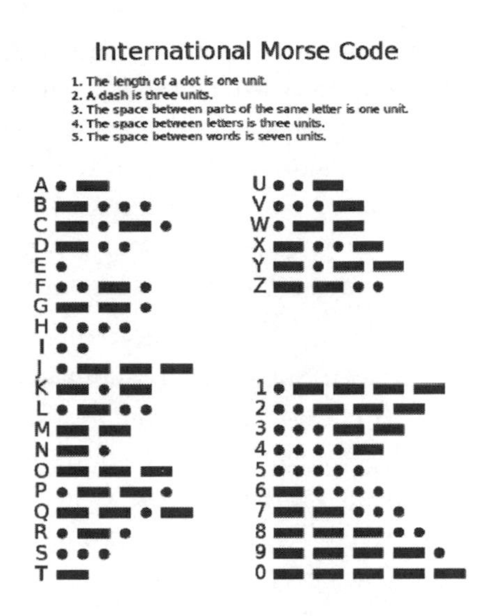

The Morse Code

This is a mini-model of (artificial) semiosis, since the binary signifiers form a paradigm in the set that gains meaning when they are combined in structured ways (syntagmatically). The dots and slashes stand for nothing until they are used in this semiotic way. Saussure introduced the concept of code into semiotics as a system of rules that convert one form of information into another. The Morse Code shows how signals based on a binary code can actually be used to encode all kinds of meanings. Most digital systems are based on a similar binary code to the Morse Code, although the use of binary numbers precedes the current computer age. In 1874, Émile Baudot, a French telegraph engineer, invented the first means of digital communication, consisting of a five-bit code used as a replacement of the Morse Code. The code had 32 five-digit words for representing every alphabet letter plus other symbols. Baudot's code was developed into a seven-bit code by the American Standard Code for Information Interchange (ASCII), called an octal code, that continues to be used by computers to this day.

Epilogue

As argued in this chapter, semiotic analysis begins by specifying what constitutes a sign and how many kinds of signs are possible. As mentioned at the start, only the main types are discussed here, although as Peirce showed there are at least 66 types (most of which are subtypes, however), some of which were described briefly in the previous chapter.

So, the solution to the meaning problem (Chapter 1) is not to examine meaning in itself, but how it is encoded in specific ways through structures that have specific representational functions—resemblance (iconicity), relation (indexicality), conventionality (symbolicity). As Ogden and Richards (1923) stressed in their study of the problem of meaning, meaning is to be understood not by analyzing isolated units, but by taking into account entire forms or events of mental processes. In this view, the real meaning unit is the form: a mental structure that takes its attributes from a corresponding structure of brain processes.

A general way to classify signs was suggested by the American philosopher, Susanne K. Langer (1895-1985), who wrote extensively on aesthetics and on analytic and linguistic philosophy (Langer1942). Langer makes an important distinction between the *presentational* symbols found in art, which allow a variety of interpretations, and *discursive, representational* symbols found in science and ordinary language, which have dictionary meanings. This scheme has been a useful one in distinguishing between signs according to their functions. Interestingly, she approached the problem of meaning in terms of *fantasy*, that is, as something that the imagination recognizes as something existential. She puts it as follows (1948: 129)

> Suppose a person sees, for the first time in his life, a train arriving at a station. He probably carries away what we should call a "general impression" of noise and mass. Very possibly he has not noticed the wheels going round, but only the rods moving like a runner's knees. He does not instantly distinguish smoke from steam, nor the hissing from the squeaking. Yet the next time he watches a train pull in the process is familiar. His mind retains a fantasy which "means" the general concept, "a train arriving at a station." Everything that happens the second time is, to him like or unlike the first time. The fantasy…was abstracted from the very first instance, and made the later ones "familiar."

It is useful to conclude this chapter recalling Thomas Sebeok's (1990) six cognitive features that characterize semiosis, which allow us to complete the picture of *how* signs work:

- *Inner/Outer:* All organisms possess *inner* modeling capacities that allow them to respond in kind to their *outer* experiences. In humans these become iconic, indexical, or symbolic responses based on the specific type of experience.

- *Vocal/Nonvocal:* Semiosis in humans can enlist either or both of these two channels—hence, verbal signs, gestures, writing signs, etc.. Vocalization is not restricted to humans. Birds, for instance, possess the capacity to change their songs subtly, in a "dialectal" fashion.
- *Verbal/Nonverbal:* This is a basic distinction between human and all other semiotic systems. Only humans are capable of verbal semiosis. Note that *language* is verbal, but not necessarily vocal; *speech* is both vocal and verbal.
- *Witting/Unwitting:* Certain signs or signals are unwitting or unconditioned (e.g. pupil responses), while others are constructed in a deliberate and witting manner.
- *Left/Right:* Semiosis involves the psychological functions associated with both the left and right hemispheres of the brain. It would seem that the left hemisphere's characteristics in verbal semiosis are peculiar to the human species.
- *Formation/Dissolution:* Communication and sign systems are *formed* within the organism, in part from genetic inheritance and in part from context. All such systems are subject to change and even *dissolution* over time.

In sum, semioticians try to answer the question "What is the meaning of *x*?" They do this by studying what signs are, as well as how signs possess "meaning"—that is, how they are intended by users, how they designate (make reference to things and ideas), and how they are interpreted by others. The goal of semiotics is to match the meanings of signs—what they stand for—with the process of assigning those meanings. It also asks a philosophical question (implicitly): "To what extent are we in the sign?" This implies that we are the makers of our own sign structures and even those that come from Nature are subjected to our interpretive capacities.

4
Texts

The frontiers of a book are never clear-cut: beyond the title, the first lines, and the last full stop, beyond its internal configuration and its autonomous form, it is caught up in a system of references to other books, other texts, other sentences: it is a node within a network.

Michel Foucault (1926-1984)

Prologue

Individual sign structures, such as single words, hand gestures, visual images (such as computer icons), etc. are like pieces of a jigsaw puzzle. In themselves, they show only fragments of the picture of reality that humans aim to encode—a word such as *cat* in isolation simply selects a part of that reality that is seen as relevant by the coiners of that word. The word might imply various connotations, but by and large it is essentially a means of cutting out a specific slice of reality to give it cognitive-cultural salience. Now, putting signs together cohesively allows us to encode a larger picture of reality. A simple utterance such as *Cats are really friendly companions* expands the range of reference that involves the word *cat*, connecting it to other referents in such a way that a broader representation of reality emerges. That representation is called a *text* in semiotics. Stories, utterances, drawings, myths, paintings, films, websites, scientific theories, mathematical proofs, etc. are all texts of one kind or other. While an individual sign stands for some referent, a text stands for some message or connected information.

We are constantly making messages and informational structures by constructing texts—conversations, emails, speeches, musical compositions, science textbooks, etc. A text can be characterized as a "weaving together" of signs, sign elements (signifiers), and other meaning-making cues in order to express something that encapsulates a complex notion, such as the fact that cats are companions. Texts manifest paradigmatic and syntagmatic structure in their composition. In the utterance above, the words—*cats, are, really, friendly, companions*—have been selected paradigmatically from subsystems of words organized according to their grammatical and semantic function, and they have been put together, not randomly, but according to the rules of English grammar.

Analogously, a novel has been constructed with words, selected from a specific language, and they are according to the rules of the language's orthographical and grammatical systems. But the intent of the organization is to portray events in time and space as perceived by the human mind as interconnected to each other. So, a novel is not interpreted in terms of its individual constituent parts (words, sentences, etc.), but holistically as if it were a single sign structure. This is why when we ask someone what a novel means, the person will typically couch the answer in this way: "The novel *Crime and Punishment* paints a grim portrait of the human psyche."

A text involves a specific kind of interpretation—we understand a work of literature, a building, a style of clothing, etc. not in terms of the constituent parts of which they are composed considered individually but in how these are interconnected structurally to produce a meaning or message. As an example, consider how we read *clothes* as messages standing for personality, social status, character etc. Take, for instance, the traditional masculine business suit, such as one worn by a CEO of a major company (to this day). How do we read this? Certainly not in terms of the individual clothing items (signifiers) that distinguish it. These have been selected from a *code* (to be discussed in the next chapter) and put together in a certain way that conforms to what we recognize broadly as a *business suit.* Here are the kinds of selections (clothing signifiers) that constitute the (traditional) code:

Code	*Selections and Options*
Shirt	white or some other conservative color, long sleeves, no designs, preferably buttoned at the collar
Tie	conservative color that should match the suit, tied neatly around the neck with a standard knot
Jacket	gray or blue, or some other color that does not stand out
Pants	matching color
Shoes	black (preferably with shoelaces)

There is, needless to say, some latitude to the selections that can be made to create the appropriate male business suit. But we know for certain that we cannot put on sneakers or wear a red shirt and yellow jacket, because these combinations would not make up the clothing text that is anticipated according to the code—a text that is consistent with its business meaning. In effect, as this simple example shows, clothing styles are derived from codes that allow us to make clothing texts for a specific occasion. When worn they send out messages about social status, our beliefs, etc. This is why uniforms are required by special groups like sports teams, military organizations, religious institutions, and the like. In each case, the dress is a standardized text.

The purpose of this chapter is to describe the semiotic approach to texts, in a generic way. The overriding goal is to argue that everything we do, such as writing novel, constructing a website, or engaging in a fashion style, is subject to the same laws of textuality A text can thus be seen as a "complex sign structure" made up of individual signs that are connected in such a way as to portray an aspect of reality that is felt to have connected elements in it. The text can have denotative, connotative, allegorical, metaphorical, etc. meanings, A denotative text is, for example, a specific GPS map that shows how to go from one place to another via the parts on the map that represent locations and their relative distances; an example of a connotative text is a poem that uses all kinds of figurative strategies to create meaning. To limit the discussion in this chapter to a manageable range, three specific kinds of texts will be used as illustrative—narrative, digital, and visual.

Textuality

Textuality can be defined simply as semiosis at a textual level—that is, as meaning-making through the use of signs and sign structures in combinatory ways, as discussed above. Everyday conversations are perfect examples of how textuality unfolds unconsciously in a routine way. First, we do not understand speech as the semantic sum of individual words, but as holistic texts in themselves. Second, each part of a dialogical back-and-forth is shaped by unconscious discourse codes, which contain values, worldviews, beliefs, interests, and biases that interlocutors tend to share. Without these two features, conversations would be meaningless. This view of *discourse* was put forward formally in the 1920s by Russian literary critic Mikhail Bakhtin (1981), who anticipated many key notions of current textual theory. The fact that conversations are based on specific discourse codes is evident in common terms such as "political discourse" or "sports discourse." Each one is based on a code (signs and their structural relations) that allows speakers to select appropriate words, create phrases and sentences, etc. that bear specific meanings and messages to them as they converse. Conversations are thus characterized by recurring discourse-based sign structures that not only appear frequently in conversations among members of a group, but also assign meaning to them.

Discourse codes are subdivided generally into *specialized*, *common*, *ritualistic*, and *critical*. The former is the type of discourse code that is characteristic of the speech of specialized groups as they converse in their normal settings—doctors, lawyers, mechanics, professors, etc. It involves the use of specialized vocabularies, a particular style, and a shared understanding of subject matter. Common discourse codes are characteristic of every day common speech habits, used by those sharing or cohabiting a common social setting or else interacting routinely. Media discourse, sports discourse, office discourse, school discourse, etc. are examples of common discourse types. Ritualistic discourse codes are used in rituals and rites of various kinds—religious ceremonies, rallies, debates, etc. Critical discourse refers to the type of speech that reflects power relations and ideologies—for example, "conservative discourse," "Marxist discourse," and so on.

A structural feature of all discourse is the presence of established textual practices and previous textual influences that come out constantly, albeit unconsciously, in conversations and in writing practices generally. The term used to indicate how specific texts are shaped by previous texts is *intertextuality*, a feature that provides the conceptual glue that makes specific conversations within social settings relevant and meaningful to the members of a community. This notion can be traced to semioticians Roland Barthes and Julia Kristeva, among a few others. Barthes (1981) saw any text as constituted by bits of codes, various conventional formulas, specific kinds of discourse codes, previous textual allusions, etc. all of which pass into the text and are reconfigured within it. For Barthes the text is, thus, a blend of unconscious quotations, without quotation marks. For Kristeva (1980), a text is the result of other texts converging on it through the author's own memory. Any text is, thus, the result of an author absorbing and transforming other texts. Intertextuality can also be conscious. It occurs when we cite someone or something during a conversation, when we use references in written texts, and so on. In effect, a text in itself is constructed through an interweaving of other texts, either implicitly or explicitly.

Intertextuality varies according to discourse code. For instance, the citations from, or allusions to, Biblical figures, events, and sayings figure prominently in religious discourse; on the other hand, allusions to Shakespeare, Dante, or other authors are part of a generic literary discourse. Some texts are especially critical. These are called *canonical*. For instance, Martin Luther King's speeches are alluded to often in activist political discourse, while citations from Karl Marx are intrinsic to some types of political discourse. Intertexuality also involves certain conventions and related textualities, such as the following:

1. A *paratext* refers to the physical and conventional characteristics associated with certain kinds of texts. In speech, paratexts include such strategies as contact protocols, which vary according to situation and

medium—oral speech versus writing. Paratextual features in writing practices include such things as titles, headings, prefaces, epigraphs, dedications, acknowledgements, footnotes, illustrations, and so on.

2. An *architext* is the prototype from which similar texts are derived—for example, a classical symphony with four movements (fast-slow-medium fast-fast) is the architext on which most symphonies are based as replicas, modifications, elaborations, etc.
3. A *metatext* is a text that makes an explicit or implicit critical commentary on another text. For example, an essay on, say, narrative, is a metatext—it is about another type of text.
4. A *hypotext* is a text based on another text which, however, it alters, elaborates or extends. Parodies, spoofs, sequels, and translations are all examples of hypotexts.
5. A *hypertext* is a text within a digital text that is designed to explain it or to provide further information about some of its components. The term was coined in 1965 to describe computer textuality as opposed to the linear textuality of traditional print texts. Hypertexttuality permits the user to browse through related topics, regardless of the presented order of the topics. These links are often established both by the author of a hypertext document and by the user, depending on the intent of the hypertext document. Hypertext has changed the way we read and consume texts. Reading a printed page is a one-dimensional process. If something in the text is unclear then we need to consult other physical print texts (such as reference texts) or else seek information from someone else. In the case of a hypertext, the linking functions give access to the Web, allowing us to remain in the same location (physically and psychologically) to complete the reading of the text. This is sometimes called "clicking literacy," given that a click (or touch) on a screen permits navigation through the text's sources or allusions with great facility.
6. The term *subtext* is also used commonly in semiotic textual analysis—it designates any message or meaning in a text that is not immediately accessible to interpretation, but is implied. A subtext is, to put it differently, a text implied or embedded within the main text. For

example, when we say that someone *has fallen from grace*, the subtext is the Garden of Eden scene.

As the last point implies, many subtexts are based in significant historical texts. In effect, a simple conversational text is hardly an isolated semiotic structure—it is part of a web of textualities that we acquire unconsciously as we learn to speak. Speech and writing practices are thus textual phenomena, allowing us to connect their individual meanings to the culture's repertoire of textualities and set of institutionalized meanings. Paradoxically, as in all semiotic phenomena, breaking away from this web of textualities involves constructing new texts—new narratives, new scientific theories, etc. Paradox is, seemingly, a hidden principle of human semiotic life.

Narrative Texts

One of the first areas to which text theory has been applied is in the study of mythic texts, because they provide the subtextual and intertextual structures for many subsequent texts, thus unconsciously shaping all kinds of discourse codes, conversations, and writing practices. A *myth* is a narrative text that seeks to give order and coherence to experiences and perceived events by relating them to some existential purpose in terms of time, space, and cause. Indeed, the appearance of narrative in human life can be traced to the early myths. Narratives are texts that related events in some sequence that is felt to be meaningful or purposeful. In the early stages of human culture, myths functioned as genuine "theories" of the world. Mythical narratives continue to form the basis for imparting knowledge of the world to children. There is no culture without its mythic stories, fables, and legends to explain the origins of things, people, morals, values, etc. to children. Myth-creation and story-telling in general reveal something rather unique about humans. Unlike other species, humans possess the demonstrable capacity to invent narrative texts of all kinds, true or not, to explain themselves and the world they inhabit. Narrative textuality is a fundamental sense-making operation of the human mind; indeed, we remember stories more easily and vividly than we do isolated concepts and words.

The themes of the first myths have not disappeared; they continue to reverberate in intertexts and subtexts in everyday narratives and discourse practices—a discovery of semiotician Roland Barthes (1957). In For instance, the mythic *good*-versus-*evil* opposition of ancient myths theme is found throughout films, novels, adventure stories, etc. It also manifests itself subconsciously in sports events, which are portrayed and experienced as dramatic mythic battles between good armies (the home team) and evil armies (the visiting team). The whole fanfare associated with preparing for the World

Series of baseball or the Superbowl of American football, has a ceremonial quality to it that invokes the same kind of pomp and circumstance that ancient armies engaged in before going out to battle and war. The symbolism of the home team's (= army) uniform, the valor and strength of star players (= the heroic warriors), and the strategic and tactical capacities of the coach (= the army general) stir the emotions of the fans (= the warring nation). The game (= the battle) is thus perceived to unfold in moral terms: i.e. as a struggle of good against the forces of evil.

The *narrative* text is a central target of a branch of semiotics called *narratology*, a term proposed originally by semiotician Tzvetan Todorov (see 1982). Narratology is based on the idea that narrative texts are implanted on a universal mythic code that generates stories that vary only in detail, not in substance. Semiotician Vladimir Propp (1928) was among the first semioticians to put forward this view with his analysis of Russian folktales. Propp showed that there are a small number of narrative units, which he called *narremes*, which are essentially mythic oppositions (*good*-versus-*evil*, *natural*-versus-*supernatural*, etc.) that allow us to recognize a text as narrative. These oppositions manifest themselves in stories where imaginary creatures intermingle in the lives of human beings, where good characters fight evil doers, where a hero must overcome challenges, etc. Propp identified 31 narremes that, he assumed, would, in effect, explain why narrative is the medium through which our values, ethics, morals, etc. are established and transmitted to subsequent generations.

Propp's basic model of narrative was pursued by the late Algirdas J. Greimas (1966, 1970). According to Greimas, the narremes (mythic oppositional structures) are connected in terms of a trajectory of what he called *actants* (characters, situations, etc.). Each part of the narrative sequence therefore manifests an actantial structure. So, for instance, in a modern-day story, such as a *Star Wars* episode, a *James Bond* movie, or a *Harry Potter* novel, a sequence such as the following one occurs typically both inside certain particular parts of the plot and, in some cases, as an overall structure in the narrative:

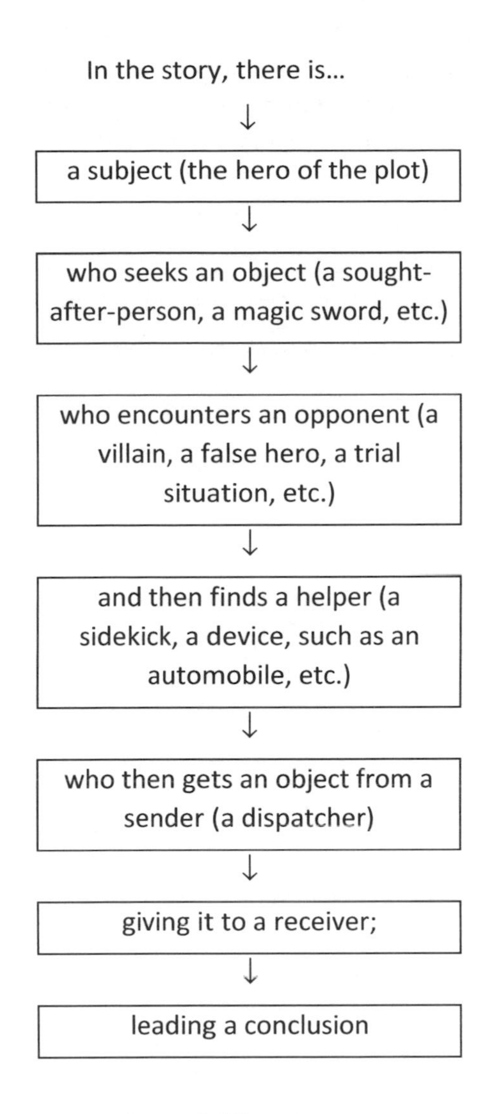

Actantial Structure

An actant can be converted into specific roles or subplots along a certain number of specified positions in the trajectory. In a mystery novel, for instance, the subject, or hero, may have several enemies, all of whom function actantially as a single opponent. In a love story, a male lover may function as both object and sender. The actants and oppositions that they entail are, upon close analysis, the same ones found in the ancient myths. To reiterate here, as the foundational narrative texts of humanity, therefore, the myths continue to provide the subtexts and intertexts that constitute narrativity.

Each character in ancient myth is a sign standing for some human quality, idea, emotion, need, or intrinsic reality. Take for, example, the Greek and Roman gods. As the list below shows, each one represented something in nature or human society:

- Poseidon (Neptune) = god of the sea and of earthquakes
- Zeus (Jupiter) = sky god, wielder of thunderbolts and thunder
- Hades (Pluto) = god of the underworld and dispenser of earthly riches; associated with death
- Demeter (Ceres) = goddess of grain and of fertility
- Hera (Juno) = goddess of marriage and childbirth, consort of Zeus
- Ares (Mars) = god of war
- Apollo (Apollo) = god of archery, prophecy, music, healing, and youth
- Hermes (Mercury) = herald and messenger of the gods; god of business, god of thieves; guide of the dead to the underworld
- Athena (Minerva) = virgin goddess of wisdom and the practical arts
- Hephaestus (Vulcan) = god of fire and metalworking
- Dionysus (Bacchus) = god of wine and fertility
- Aphrodite (Venus) = goddess of love, sexual desire, and beauty

A similar list, with the exact same kinds of signifieds, could be drawn up for any mythical tradition in any language—indeed, some philologists would claim that the origin of language myth are coincident. Anthropologist Claude Lévi-Strauss (1962, 1971) saw mythic oppositions as the original source for discourse, culture, and other semiotic codes. The oppositional clusters in myth are thus built into all kinds of meaning systems and institutions. These include: *good*-versus-*evil*, *right*-versus-*wrong*, *male*-versus-*female*, etc. which, as discussed previously, form universal oppositions. Crucial to Lévi-Strauss' conception of myth is the Saussurean notion of *value* (*valeur*) (Chapter 2). Rather than carrying intrinsic meaning, these oppositions produce *valeur*, which itself then becomes "values" in ethical and moral systems.

Opposed to the view of (mythic) narrative as a mirror of life was Jacques Derrida, who, as discussed (Chapter 2) saw oppositional structure as meaningless beyond the intent of an author who employs it, and even that is subject to variable interpretation. Thus, Derrida claimed that, because there are an infinite number of legitimate interpretations of a narrative text, it is useless to try to figure out what an author wanted to say or what it aims to say itself in terms of human values. But, as Umberto Eco (1990) responded, common sense tells us that the meaning of a text is not infinitely variable, nor without some central purpose. Concretely speaking, it is unlikely that anyone today would interpret John Bunyan's (1628-1688) novel, the *Pilgrim's Progress,* as an erotic tale. While someone reading it with "modern eyes" would not see in it the same kinds of Christian meanings that seventeenth century readers saw in it, one would still not interpret it in vastly different terms.

It was Mikhail Bakhtin (1984) who was among the first semioticians to argue that the novel, as a popular narrative text, changed society drastically when it was introduced broadly in the fifteenth-sixteen centuries. It was not only an early form of reading entertainment, but a socially-subversive tool, because a novel depicts social conditions and personages as fictitious, using verisimilitude, so that author cannot be directly held responsible for libel or political treason. The novel, unlike sermons, for example, made it possible for readers to enter into a silent dialogue with authors, coming out of it transformed; it also gives voice to different characters (in the novel itself). Bakhtin called this type of dialogue "polyphonic" defined as "plurality of independent and unmerged voices and consciousnesses, a genuine polyphony of fully valid voices" (Bakhtin 1984: 6). We can literally hear the different voices in Fyodor Dostoyevsky's novels, such as *Crime and Punishment* (1866), in contrast to the monologue—speeches, laws, lectures, and so on. The power of this new kind of "voicing" is particularly evident in the works of French satirist François Rabelais (Bakhtin 1983), in which boisterous and libidinous language ushered forth the modern world, marking the collapse of rigid moralism. Rabelais' novel *Gargantua and Pantagruel* (1534) portrayed the everyday culture and language of common folk that "was to a great extent a culture of the loud word spoken in the open, in the street and marketplace" (Bakhtin 1984: 182). Rabelais' work was thus as much a socio-political statement as it was satire; it attacked the pompous attitudes of the self- appointed moral guardians of order and respectability, thereby undermining the already-moribund medieval system.

The Book

The novel was one of the first narrative texts produced massively through print technologies in the latter part of the fifteenth century. It became influential because of this fact. As the Canadian communications theorist Marshall McLuhan (1911-1980)—to be discussed further in a subsequent chapter—the novel led to the book becoming itself a powerful new form of textuality. At one level, the book extends human memory across time and space, since it allows us to preserve ideas in a more permanent way than through oral transmission. At another level, a book is a code, a structured set of signs that allows for the expression of broader messages than is possible with single words. So, it also extends human language. The forerunners of books were the clay tablets, impressed with a stylus, found in the societies of ancient Mesopotamia and other places. These were followed by scrolls, which consisted of sheets of papyrus formed into a continuous strip and rolled around a stick. The strip, with the text inscribed with a reed pen in narrow, closely spaced columns on one side, was unrolled as it was read. During the fourth to first centuries BCE, a long roll was subdivided into shorter rolls, stored together in one container. In the first century CE, the container came to be called a *codex*, the direct ancestor of the modern book.

Used at first by the Greeks and Romans for recording and preserving business accounts and for schooling purposes, the codex was a small, rectangular container consisting of two or more wooden tablets covered with wax, which could be marked with a stylus, smoothed over, and reused many times. Readers could refer ahead or back to parts in the codex. In the Middle Ages, codices were used primarily to preserve sacred writings in the observance of the liturgy. Indeed, the word *codex* is part of the title of many ancient handwritten books on topics related to the Bible. Parenthetically, it should be mentioned that a parallel history of the book and its functions can be written for civilizations across the globe, from China and Japan to Africa and elsewhere. It is fascinating to note that the same kinds of inventions occur in different parts of the ancient world, virtually synchronically, where little or no contact among the societies would have been possible. This suggests an intrinsic "tool-making instinct" in the human species that manifests itself throughout the world in different ways, but retaining a common and deeper essence.

The advent of books as texts for encoding knowledge, for reading pleasure and other intellectual-expressive-aesthetic activities constituted a paradigm shift in human civilization and consciousness. In the first centuries of the Common Era the chief ones were papyrus and parchment. Parchment (made from the skin of a sheep or goat) was not as light as papyrus (made from the pith or the stems of sedge); but it was more durable. Paper was invented in the second century CE by the Chinese, who developed it from silk fibers. Persian scholars took the Chinese technology to Europe in the eleventh century. Paper was lighter than all other materials used for writing up to that time, and thus more portable. It was also relatively inexpensive and thus spread throughout Europe widely. Copyists called scribes, many of whom were monks, made duplicates of paper manuscripts. But they were very expensive, because the scribes decorated them with pictures and designs, and so were bought and read by aristocrats and clergymen.

Although a Chinese printer named Bi Sheng invented movable type in the 1000s, it was not until 1447 that a German printer named Johannes Gutenberg (c. 1400-1468) perfected movable metal type technology, developing the first mechanical printing press capable of producing numerous copies of paper documents quickly and cheaply. The event was monumental in the history of communications. Printing shops sprung up all over Europe, publishing books, newspapers, pamphlets, and many other kinds of paper documents inexpensively. As a result, more books became available and more people desired to gain literacy because it became an increasingly useful and necessary skill. With more and more people able to read, ideas could be spread more broadly than ever before. This situation is cited by historians as the basis for the revolutions of an educational, religious, political, social, and scientific nature that led eventually to the Renaissance, the period marking the transition from medieval to modern times. Standardized ways of doing things in the scientific, education, and business worlds emerged, bringing people of different countries more and more into contact with each other, consequently leading to the spread of foreign language instruction. In a phrase, the invention of the printing press was the technological event that paved the way to the establishment of a global civilization. McLuhan called this new world order the "Gutenberg Galaxy" (McLuhan 1962).

In the 1600s, printed newssheets called *corantos* appeared in the Netherlands, England, and other European nations. The coranto differed from previous pamphlets in format—it included a title on the upper first page and adopted a two-column format, unlike previous single-column formats. Corantos reported mostly business news, and introduced a new feature in print communications—advertising, with brief announcements of goods and services, prefiguring the classified ad style. After the Industrial Revolution in the 1700s, print literacy became increasingly a widespread social value, as books, magazines, and newspapers, made information available to more and more readers. As a result, a new type of communications problem surfaced—plagiarism and illegal copying. In 1709, the British Parliament passed the first copyright law, as literary property became commercially valuable. Publishing surged during the late 1700s.

It is mind-boggling to think that the emergence of a textual form—the book—has the capacity to change human life permanently. The spread of books in the 1500s made the attainment of literacy—reading for knowledge and for imaginative purposes—a possibility for one and all, thus changing the evolutionary course of humanity radically. Literacy introduces a level of abstraction in human thought that forces people to separate the maker of knowledge from the knowledge made, leading to the sense that knowledge can exist on its own, spanning time and distance. This is, arguably, what is meant by the term *objectivity*: knowledge (the object) unconnected to a knower (the subject or maker). Before literacy became widespread, humans lived primarily in oral cultures, based on the spoken word. The human voice conveys emotion. The orator and his or her message were perceived as inseparable. On the other hand, in book-based cultures, the written page, with its edges, margins, and sharply defined characters laid out in neatly layered rows or columns, induces a linear-rational way of thinking in people. And because the maker of the written text is rarely present during its reading, the reader is thus free to extract from it whatever he or she wants. It is the object, in the Peircean sense (Peirce 1931-1958), that comes out of the reading process—the meaning extracted from the reading itself. The spread of book-based literacy has, *ipso facto*, been the unconscious force in the "objectification" of knowledge.

The book also made individualism an ever-spreading reality. As McLuhan himself put it: "The portability of the book, like that of the easel-painting, added much to the new culture of individualism" (McLuhan 1962: 233). But, at the same time that the book fostered a sense of individualism, a latent form of communal consciousness was retrieved through the profession of the printing press: "The book is a private confessional form that provides a point of view," but "the press is a group confessional form that provides communal participation" (McLuhan 1962: 204).

Digital Texts

As computers became household items in the 1980s, the medium for textuality started gradually becoming the digital-electronic one, with the screen complementing and even replacing the printed page. Computers have amplified the functions of book-based textuality considerably—including human memory and text-making versatility: "People never remember but the computer never forgets" (McLuhan 1969: 69). The spread of computers and the Artificial Intelligence (AI) field has retrieved a form of magic that induces us to believe that our machines are able not only to replace us but also to become more intelligent than us. McLuhan warned against this deceptive belief, since the computer, like the book, is a human invention, and thus cannot replace the mind that made it, as various artificial intelligence researchers claim. As he put it: "Computers can do better than ever what needn't be done at all. Making sense is still a human monopoly" (McLuhan and Barrington 1972: 109).

The computer is a great technological achievement, constituting a paradigm shift that parallels the advent of print technology. It has had a definitive impact on human life, again parallel to, and even surpassing, the one that the printing press had five centuries ago. The PC, which can be traced to the Apple II in 1977 created by American computer designers Steven Jobs and Steven Wozniak, has rendered many other information-based technologies of the past obsolete. Jobs and Wozniak later founded Apple Computer Corporation. Their initial plan was to manufacture PCs to provide sophisticated gaming software for people to pit their logical skills against those of the software programmers. In 1984 the first Apple Macintosh was manufactured. It featured a graphical user interface, combining icons with windows (boxes that contain an open file or program). The interface function made computers easy to use, eliminating the need to type in complex commands. computers have since become as intrinsic to the system of modern living as automobiles and TV sets. They enable artists to create all kinds of texts—images, musicians to record music, businesses to keep track of their finances and forecast performance, journalists, students, instructors, and many more professionals to compose their verbal texts and communicate them to others from remote locations. In effect, computers have allowed us to interface with worldwide communication networks in order to find information on any subject and to interact with others on a global scale. In a phrase, the computer has extended the capacities and the reach of books infinitely. It is a meta-extension that has enhanced ways of writing and of encoding information that would be literally unimaginable to people in any previous era of history, including the Print Age.

The institutionalization of computer technology has subsequently brought about so many shifts in meaning-making textuality, as discussed above. The interconnection of computers via the Internet has allowed hypertextuality to become a central mode of text-making, virtually replacing previous modes which have become much more specialized in function—for example, university essays are still written in print-age style and textuality, bit text messages are multimodal and hypertextual. We no longer live in the Gutenberg Galaxy. Rather, because of the computer and the Internet, we now live in a new Galaxy that seems to know no bounds. But this hardly means that there has been a radical break with the previous functions and modes of communication. On the contrary, as electronic devices, satellite systems, and other sophisticated digital technologies allow people to break down barriers of communication and interaction of the past, there is a renewed strong desire in people to live in the "real" world, as can be seen by phenomena such as mass tourism—indicating arguably that people now want to meet each other in the flesh rather than on screens. This may be an over-simplification, but it is certainly a plausible hypothesis. The desire to connect with others is, perhaps, a stronger motivation for rampant tourism than higher levels of affluence among people. Indeed, the more the computer is used to conduct everyday affairs, the more people seem to resort to, or at least desire, more basic communal and real-world forms of interaction. The paradox of everyday life in the "global village" is, as McLuhan often pointed out, that it engenders both "individualism" and "tribalism" at once. As he so aptly put it, in his own inimitable way: "The tribalizing power of the new electronic media, the way in which they return us to the unified fields of the old oral cultures, to tribal cohesion and pre-individualist patterns of thought, is little understood. Tribalism is the sense of the deep bond of family, the closed society as the norm of community" (McLuhan and Betterman1985: 60).

The notion of hypertext has had some interesting implications for the semiotics of text-interpretation. At one level, successful interpretation entails knowing the codes with which the text has been assembled. For instance, if a verbal text is written in Finnish, in order to derive any meaning from it, the decoder must know the Finnish language, the conceptual metaphors that characterize Finnish modes of speaking, and so on and so forth. This can be called the level of the "textual signifier." At a different (conceptual) level, successful interpretation involves knowledge of how signification unfolds in the specific text, that is, of how the text generates its meanings through a series of internal and external signifying processes. This requires knowledge of cultural codes other than the strictly verbal or nonverbal ones used to physically create the text. It constitutes the level of the "textual signified." It is the level at which we ask ourselves the question: What does it mean? Finally, various contextual factors enter into the entire process to constrain the interpretation, such as what the individual reader will get from it, what the intent of the author was, etc. The interaction of these dimensions guides the extraction of meaning from the text. A little reflection will reveal that this whole process is hypertextual in nature because the reader of the text must possess not only the ability to understand its "surface textual signifiers," but also to navigate through the various codes that it harbors within it. This type of "mental clicking," as it can be called, is analogous to what is done on a computer screen by clicking keywords and icons physically. In effect, the structure of hypertextuality on the computer screen may well constitute a kind of "mirror model" of how people interpret texts psychologically.

The advent of digital textuality has, brought about a new form of literacy—digital literacy—without which people's ability to function in modern society would diminish considerably. This has expanded the traditional definition of literacy considerably. Today, it is used as a synonym for competencies in various domains of knowledge—hence, media literacy, technological literacy, computer literacy, and so on. In schools, traditional literacy practices still prevail. However, it is not uncommon for educators and students to be given the choice to move back and forth between online and offline literacies.

Visual Texts

The study of *visual texts*—texts produced in terms of visual sign structures—became central to semiotic theory after the publication of three influential studies: Rudolf

Arnheim's *Visual Thinking* (1969), Jonathan Berger's *Ways of Seeing* (1972), and Roland Barthes' *Image-Music-Text* (1977). These brought to the attention of all semioticians the crucial role visual textuality plays in people's attempts to understand the world. Visual semiotics is now a flourishing branch of semiotic theory (see, for example, Bogdan 2002, Tomaselli 2009, Crow 2010, Jappy 2013, Zantides 2014).

Drawing pictures, making charts, sketching diagrams, and the like are such common everyday activities that we hardly ever realize what they imply. Consider, for instance, what can be accomplished with three straight lines of equal length: Can they be combined in some way to create recognizable referents? They can be joined in specific configurations to represent by resemblance (iconicity) a triangle, the letter H, or a picnic table (among other things):

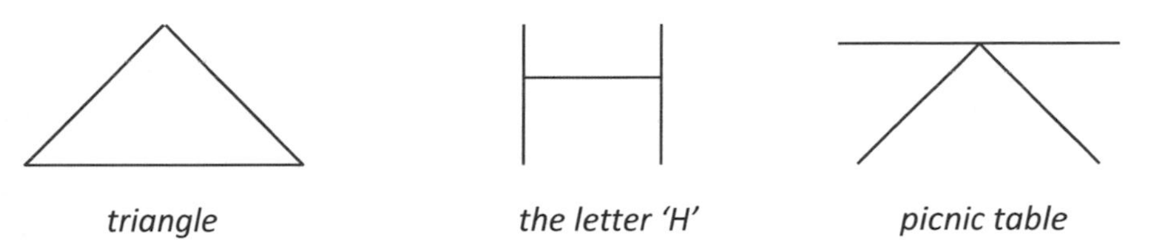

Three Visual Texts

We perceive these figures as textual wholes rather than as amalgams of three lines—Visual textuality works broadly in this way, with lines, points, shapes, colors, etc. constituting the basic visual signifiers that go into the make-up of visual texts—we shall discuss paintings subsequently as special types of visual texts. Consider three kinds of visual signifiers—hue, color, and texture. Hue refers to the darkness or lightness of a line or shape. It plays an important role in the portrayal of contrasts, such as *dark*-versus-*light*. Hue conveys mood, feeling, and atmosphere in a visual text such as a painting. This is why we speak of "warm," "soft," "cold," or "harsh" colors, as part of a system of culture-specific connotations: for example, in American culture *yellow* connotes cowardice, in China it connotes royalty. Texture is the use of visual forms to evoke certain sensations. Wavy lines, for example, tend to produce a pleasant sensation in a viewer than do angular ones. By increasing the number of edges on angular lines, the unpleasant sensation tends to increase proportionately:

pleasant sensation

unpleasant sensation

Visual Texture

This is evidence that visual representation is often intermodal, eliciting different sensory modalities in tandem. The term that is used to characterize this phenomenon is *synesthesia*, defined specifically in visual semiotics as the evocation of one sensation by another, as when a loud noise produces the image of a blinding light, or vice versa. Lines and shapes can also be combined to create three-dimensional figures, which are visual texts that are constructed in such a way as to create an illusion of depth in the viewer—a technique developed by Renaissance artists such as Filippo Brunelleschi (1377-1446) and Albrecht Dürer (1471-1528). Many optical illusions are probably caused by this technique. In the following plane figure there are 12 flat lines. The way they are put together, however, induces us to interpret it as a three-dimensional box:

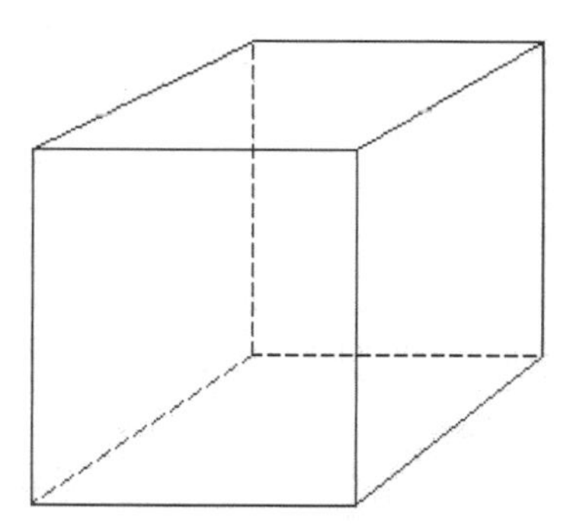

Perspective Drawing of a Box

The reason for this is that perspective drawing dupes us into viewing objects as the human eye perceives them in three dimensions. The flat surface is known as the picture plane; the horizon line is called the horizontal eye-level line that divides a scene in the distance; and the vanishing point is located on the horizon line where parallel lines in the scene appear to converge. This makes certain parts of the figure appear to be closer than others, as the following sketch shows:

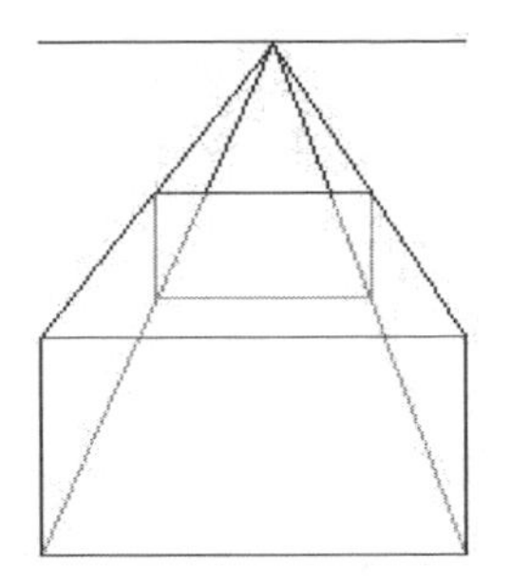

Vanishing Point

To reiterate, the vanishing point technique reflects our visual sense of space. When we look down a long, straight road, it seems to grow narrower in the distance. Trees and poles along the road appear to become smaller and smaller as they stretch away toward the horizon.

Two types of visual texts that have been targets of great interest within semiotics are *diagrams*. A diagram is a schematic drawing using basic visual elements (points, lines, shapes) to "explain" visually how something works or to clarify the relationship between the parts of some whole. A chart is a type of diagram containing or displaying information of various kinds. Diagrams are cognitively-powerful texts that are indispensable in science and, typically, are the sum and substance of theory-making. The original diagram of the atom as a miniature solar system with a nucleus and orbiting particles is, *ipso facto*, a theory of the atom, allowing us to envision it in a particular way. Diagrams allow for the organization and display of information in a compact yet insightful way. Scientists thus use diagrams and models to gain further insight into physical processes—literally to get views that are not possible in any other way. A chemist might devise a diagrammatic form that reveals the energy levels at which molecules react with one another to produce a given substance, perhaps revealing how the substance could be produced with less energy. Engineers and architects draw up diagrams to help them see how one part fits together with other parts. They might first enter into the computer a set of mathematical equations describing how each part of a machine would react to forces. The computer would apply the numbers to the equations and display the resulting pictures.

The importance of diagrammatic representation to knowledge-making was brought out by Charles Peirce with his Existential Graph Theory (see Stjernfelt 2007). An Existential Graph is a diagram that maps of one group of relations onto another, revealing the essential nature of those relations. These do not simply portray information, but also mirror how thinking about the relevant information occurs in the mind. Peirce called them "moving pictures of thought" (because in their form we can literally "see" a given argument or thought process). In effect, Existential Graphs are icons of how we perceive quantity, space, and their interrelations in a schematic way, making the mental images observable in the form of diagrams.

A graph is, in effect, a picture of cognitive processes in action. And it thus doubles back on itself to suggest further information or ideas. As Peirce called it, it is an "abductive" (inferential) process that leads to discovery. The following citation encapsulates Pierce's notion of graph. In it, we see him discussing with a general why a map is used to conduct a campaign (Peirce 1931-1958, volume 4: 530):

> But why do that [use maps] when the thought itself is present to us? Such, substantially, has been the interrogative objection raised by an eminent and glorious General. Recluse that I am, I was not ready with the counter-question, which should have run, "General, you make use of maps during a campaign, I believe. But why should you do so, when the country they represent is right there?" Thereupon, had he replied that he found details in the maps that were so far from being "right there," that they were within the enemy's lines, I ought to have pressed the question, "Am I right, then, in understanding that, if you were thoroughly and perfectly familiar with the country, no map of it would then be of the smallest use to you in laying out your detailed plans?" No, I do not say that, since I might probably desire the maps to stick pins into, so as to mark each anticipated day's change in the situations of the two armies." "Well, General, that precisely corresponds to the advantages of a diagram of the course of a discussion. Namely, if I may try to state the matter after you, one can make exact experiments upon uniform diagrams; and when one does so, one must keep a bright lookout for unintended and unexpected changes thereby brought about in the relations of different significant parts of the diagram to one another. Such operations upon diagrams, whether external or imaginary, take the place of the experiments upon real things that one performs in chemical and physical research.

A simple illustration of the underlying principles of Existential Graph theory (EG) is the graph below, which Peirce used in place of A > B, which shows the relation much more iconically than this previous symbological form:

A is greater than

is greater than B

A Peircean Existential Graph

The line is called a line of identity by Peirce. In any EG any line of identity whose outermost part is evenly enclosed refers to something, and any one whose outermost part is oddly enclosed refers to anything there may be. (Peirce 1931-1958, volume 4: 458). The following graph shows, essentially, how any EG can be used to represent logical statements (from Roberts 2009):

Existential Graph of a Logical Statement

The first graph (where the outermost part of the line is evenly, zero, enclosed) says that something good is ugly, and the second graph (where the outermost part is enclosed once) says that everything good is ugly.

Peirce extended the notion of Existential Graph to numerals, equations and other mathematical sign structures. An equation is, thus, a graph consisting of signs (letters, numbers, symbols) organized to reflect the relation of the signs to each other in terms of the information they encode. It may show that some parts are tied to a strict sequence, whereas others may be connected through associative relations of sorts. As an example, consider the Pythagorean equation: $c^2 = a^2 + b^2$. As an Existential Graph, it is a visual portrait of the indexical relations among the variables (originally standing for the sides of a right-angles triangle). But, being a graph, it also tells us that the parts may entail other meanings beyond the initial triangle referent, such as the fact that there infinitely many Pythagorean triples, or sets of three integers that satisfy the equation. Expressed in language ("the square on the hypotenuse is equal to the sum of the squares on the other two sides"), we would literally not be able to *see* this hidden implication. Now, once we have this equational EG, it becomes the source for more inferences and abductions, such as the previously-hidden concept of Pythagorean number triples. Eventually, it gave rise to a new theorem, namely that only when n = 2 does the general formula hold ($c^n = a^n + b^n$)—called Fermat's Last Theorem. This, in turn, led to many other discoveries (Danesi 2020).

Today, visual semiotics has become an important analytical tool in the study of online representational practices, which are increasingly multimodal (involving visual, audio, and verbal expressive modalities). Digital signs such as emojis have captured the attention of semiotic analysis because of the suggestive ways in which they relay specific types of emotional information visually. In a phrase, the study of multimodality in online contexts and in all forms of digital communication is becoming a major area of semiotic investigation.

In his 2001 book, *Media Unlimited: How the Torrent of Images and Sounds Overwhelms Our Lives*, Todd Gitlin characterizes modern media pas having made the visual sign dominant. "Images," he states, "depict or re-present realities but are not themselves realities" (Gitlin 2001: 22). We know the difference, but we prefer the virtual to the real—a point made effectively before the Internet age by Jean Baudrillard (1983), who referred to this blurring of the line as the simulacrum effect (discussed briefly in Chapter 3). This means, essentially, that the power of visual images is such that we can no longer distinguish, or want to distinguish, between the real and the hyperreal (the world created by images). One of the themes within visual semiotics today is the study of media images and simulacra. The term *simulacrum* comes from Latin where it meant "likeness" or "similarity," and was used in the nineteenth century by painters to describe drawings that were seen merely to be copies of other paintings, rather than emulations of them. Aware of this designation of the term, Baudrillard insisted that a simulacrum is not the result of a simple copying or imitation, but a form of false consciousness that emerges on its own after long exposure to images through four stages: (1) a basic reflection of reality (the normal state of consciousness); (2) a perversion of reality; (3) a pretense of reality; and (4) the simulacrum, which bears no relation whatsoever to reality. Eventually, as people engage constantly with the hyperreal everything—from politics to art—becomes governed by simulacra.

The 1999 movie *The Matrix* understood Baudrillard's warning perfectly, (so much that the French philosopher's book *Simulacra And Simulation* shows up in the film on Neo's bookshelf as a hollowed out volume in which he keeps his stash), portraying a world in which life is shaped by the computer screen. Like the main protagonist, Neo, we now experience reality "on" and "through" the computer screen, and our consciousness is largely shaped by that screen, whose technical name is the *matrix*, as the network of circuits that defines computer technology is called. The same word also meant "womb," in Latin. The movie's transparent subtext is that people are now born through two kinds of wombs—the biological and the technological ones.

Humans have, of course, always created and experienced visual forms throughout their history. The difference is one of degree—today visual images seem to be more dominant in social communication than they have ever been in the past. Semiotics has emerged as a critical discipline for examining the power of these images with the tools of semiotic analysis.

Epilogue

As something standing for something else, a sign can take any form, or "size," as long as it does not violate the structure of the code to which it belongs and as long as it conveys meaning in some recognizable way. A sign can thus be something "small," physically speaking, such as a word or two fingers raised vertically (for example, the V-sign); or it can be something much "larger," such as an equation or a narrative. If we show the equation $c^2 = a^2 + b^2$ (above) to mathematicians, they would instantly recognize it as a specific form standing for the Pythagorean theorem, not as a combination of unrelated variables (letter signs). If we ask someone who has just read a novel what that person got out of it, we would receive an evaluation of its overall message, not an interpretation or analysis of its separate words and parts.

As discussed throughout this chapter, in semiotic theory, "larger signs," such as equations and novels, are called texts; and their meanings, or "larger signifieds," that they encode messages or information structures. Texts include conversations, poems, myths, novels, television programs, paintings, scientific theories, musical compositions, and the like. Consider again the novel (discussed above). It is a verbal text constructed with "smaller" language signs (which are, more accurately, the "signifiers" of the text) in order to communicate some overarching message (the "larger signified"). Its organization is sequential, mirroring the sequence of events. In western languages this means writing it from left-to-right, in others, such as Semitic ones, from right-to-left. In both cases, however, the sequence itself is integral to the narrative representations. Specific codes (next chapter) provide the signs for constructing and interpreting texts (as discussed in the previous chapter). Using Saussurean theory, it can be said that the code constitutes a form of *langue* (the abstract knowledge of how certain signs and their relations can be used and interpreted), and the text created on the basis of the code a form of *parole* (the concrete utilization of the code to represent something).

As discussed as well, we extract meaning from some texts, such as narrative ones, not directly, but through processes inference, implication, or suggestion—processes termed intertextual and subtextual. For example, extracting a meaning from John Bunyan's (1628-1688) novel *Pilgrim's Progress* (1678) is contingent upon knowing the

Bible narrative, since it constitutes an allegorical tale of a Christian's journey from the City of Destruction to the Celestial City. Analogously, James Joyce's (1882-1941) novel *Ulysses* (1922) takes its title from parallels Joyce established between the adventures of his main character, Leopold Bloom, and those of Homer's Ulysses (Odysseus in Greek), who was the hero of the *Odyssey*. Because of its dense intertextuality, *Ulysses* is one of the most challenging novels ever written. It is filled with allusions to many areas of knowledge, including theology, mythology, astronomy, Irish legends, history, and such languages as Hebrew, Latin, and Gaelic.

5
Codes

The photographic image is a message without a code.

Roland Barthes (1915-1980)

Prologue

Recall two codes discussed briefly in previous chapters—the Morse Code and the male business suit code. In the case of the former, the code consisted in a set of symbols for changing one sign system, the alphabet, into another, a binary system of dots and dashes (delivered as short and long sounds). In the case of the business suit, the code consisted in assigning specific connotations to clothing items, such as shirts, ties, pants, etc. All codes work in this way—they are systems within which specific signs or signifiers are assigned meanings, either by translating one system into another (Morse Code) or else assigning specific types of meanings to the signs within the system. So, in a general way, a semiotic *code* can be defined simply as the meaning-assigning pattern that inheres between signs organized in a certain way, with a certain function, or bearing specific information, and their referents. Recall the definition of the sign as something that stands for something else in a certain way. A code is the term for the "stands for" relation, which is completed with "in a certain way."

There are many uses of the term code within and outside of semiotics. But in all cases, the notion of collection of forms that assign meaning, function is implicit. The genetic code, for example, consists of DNA and RNA molecules that carry genetic information in living cells; a computer code is a set of instructions forming a computer program which, like the Morse Code, can be translated into other codes, such as language.

In semiotics, a code can be defined more specifically as the meanings assigned to signs that are organized according to their functions or to the type of meaning-bearing information they entail. Language, dress, music, and gesture are examples of codes—that is, of systems of signs that are organized and used in specific ways, allowing for the creation of specific texts—conversations, clothing styles, etc. Recall again the male business suit. Its items are interpreted in terms of a code that specifies what it means to dress in this way, with each part of the suit bearing specific connotations that are relevant to the business world, as we saw. In this case, it is a subcode of dress as an overall code—it specifies what items to select (paradigmatic process), how to combine them (syntagmatic process), and what kinds of messages they convey, from the overall dress code.

Codes can vary in "size, as can texts. The business suit code (or subcode) exemplifies a code with limited range. A language, on the other hand, is a code with infinite range of functions and meaning-bearing structures. As discussed, words are signs. But words in isolation are virtually meaningless outside of pure referential function (naming things as in a dictionary) unless they can be combined to form texts. But to produce meaning-bearing texts they cannot be stringed together haphazardly. So, the forms of language, from its sounds (phonemes) to its uses (conversations) are coded in specific ways, as will be discussed, in terms of subcodes—phonological, grammatical, semantic, pragmatic, etc. Similarly, single musical notes are practically meaningless in themselves (although they might evoke some emotional response); they become part of some musically-based text or message when they are combined according to specific codes, such as the harmonic subcode, the rhythmic subcode, etc. Note that each code (or subcode) is an organizing grid of specific types of signs or signifiers—sounds, words, etc.

This chapter will discuss the semiotic concept of code, illustrating it with language, nonverbal codes, material culture codes, and architectural. Artistic codes will be discussed in chapter 7.

Code Theory

Codes in themselves have no meaning, nor do the individual signs or signifiers that constitute them. It is when they are used to make messages that they gain meaning. Codes can also contain elements of signs that provide the means for creating them. An example is the alphabet code. It contains specific signifiers, called letters, that stand for sounds, and which can be selected to write words in lieu of uttering them. To write the words knowledge of the letter-to-sound code is required.

The term *code* derives from the Latin word *codex* ("wooden book"), revealing that a book is itself a type of a code that has structure, coherence, predictability, and meaning-making potential. The term has been used in cryptography from ancient times to mean a system of making messages in secretive ways. In order for someone to read the original text, which is *encoded,* the person must know the code and use it to *decode* it. The term *code*, as mentioned, was introduced by Saussure in his *Cours de linguistique générale*

(Saussure 1916: 31). For Saussure the code was a generic form of *langue* (the abstract knowledge of how signs such as words, grammatical structures, and their relations can be used and interpreted). The texts, forms, and messages that it allows people to encode (construct) and decode (understand) was a form of *parole* (the concrete utilization of the code to represent something).

Codes are found in all domains of human aesthetic, intellectual, and social life, from the juridical (for example, the *legal code*) to the aesthetic sphere (for example, *musical codes*). They provide the specific kind of signs (words, musical sounds, etc.) for constructing specific kinds of messages, carrying out actions, enacting rituals, and so on. Stories, fashion styles, musical trends, and so on are all code-based phenomena. The code provides the key to extracting meaning from some message text, etc. To understand certain kinds of dress, for example, one needs to know the social code behind them, which in consists of clothing items (signifiers) and style details. Consider blue jeans. In the 1930s and 1940s, these were cheap, strong, and mass-produced blue-collar working clothes. High fashion articles, on the other hand, were manufactured with expensive materials and fabrics. As early as the mid-1950s, the youth culture of the era adopted blue jeans as part of its dress code. By the 1960s and 1970s, blue jeans were worn by the new generation of young people to proclaim equality between the sexes and among social classes. The dress code thus became a political code. By the 1980s, this subversive meaning was forgotten, and the same clothing item became fashion statement. Blue jeans became much more expensive, much more exclusive, often personalized, and available at chic boutiques. In that era the blue jean became part of a fashion code. Today, jeans are just jeans—comfortable clothing worn by people of all ages in informal settings. In effect, the story of blue jeans brings out a basic principle of code theory—signs can crisscross codes and engender meanings that are shaped by historical trends and other accrued meanings. The code is what changes—namely, the inherent meanings that the dress items convey.

It would be a futile task to classify codes according to how they allow for meaning-making to be institutionalized or carried out. This would be tantamount to documenting the entire meaning-making resources of a culture. So a more generic approach must be used. A basic way to classify codes is to say that they can be *natural* or *conventional*, recalling St. Augustine's typology of signs (Chapter 1). The former are those that are produced by nature (for example, the *genetic code*). Natural codes are decoded by humans in various ways, leading to human-knowledge conventional codes (science, for example). These change over time as they become falsified by ongoing exploration and research. Conventional codes are those that are produced by people to represent, organize, explore, and record meaningful culture-specific events, practices, and traditions. These govern all aspects of human life. In order to make contact with someone successfully we must know the appropriate body and verbal language codes. These provide the meaningful forms and actions (words, expressions, how the hands are to be used in the contact ritual, the length of the contact, and so on) and rules for combining them that make contact rituals successful or meaning-bearing. Similarly, writing, music, painting, and other kinds of codes provide and specify the ways in which tones, harmonies, colors, figures, and so on can be selected and combined to produce symphonies, portraits, and so forth. These ways are not invented on the spot. They are shaped by historical processes and, thus, are subject to change, although they retain an intrinsic essence across time. Modern music is based on the same harmonic code that was established over 250 years ago in Europe. The musicians of that era, in turn, came to fashion their own harmonic practices on the basis of previous codes used in the music of earlier centuries.

The Language Code

Some codes are codes within codes (or subcodes); others are meta-codes, that is "larger codes" that encompass these subcodes—although this distinction is rarely made in semiotics for practical purposes—it is a theoretical distinction. So, the term *code* used here can refer to a meta-code or a subcode, with each term used distinctively if necessary. An example of a larger all-encompassing code is language. Each level within it has coded structure. For example, knowledge of words entails knowledge of (1) how they cluster into phrases and sentences; (2) how they are inflected; and (3) which words (known as *function words*) can be used to relate the other words in a sentence to each other; and other structural features.

As discussed, Saussure called the language code itself, *langue*, and the ways in which it is used or expressed, *parole*—rendered generically in English as *language* and *speech* respectively. Language is a mental code. Speech is how language is delivered, involving the intentional use of the organs of the vocal apparatus—the tongue, the teeth, the epiglottis, etc.—to articulate sounds and words. Language can also be delivered or expressed through other physical modes—writing, gesture, and so on. One can have language without speech (as do individuals with impaired vocal organs), because it exists in the mind. But one cannot have speech without language, because speech depends on the language code.

Language literally comes naturally to us. We acquire it as speech without effort or training during our infancy. And we learn how its signs allow us to cut up the world around and within us. Then words acquired in context, for example, become filters for perceiving the world (Whorf 1956). Consider a practical example. In Italian, the word *orologio* is used to refer to any "time-keeping device," no matter what its shape, form, or function might be. In English, on the other hand, two words are used, *watch* and *clock*—the former refers to a time device that is carried, worn, or put on bodies (on wrists, around the neck, in pockets, etc.), while the latter refers to a time device that is placed in specific locations (on a table, on a wall, etc.) and not carried around. This does not mean Italians are incapable of making this very same distinction. They can do so by using the construction: *da + place*, with *da* meaning approximately "for:" *orologio da polso* = wristwatch ("watch for wrist"), *orologio da tavolo* = table clock ("clock for table"), and so on. Unlike speakers of English, speakers of Italian are not accustomed to differentiating conceptually between carryable and non-carryable time-keeping devices. Their language has predisposed them to see this small part of the world differently. In effect, like our color terms (discussed previously), our verbal signs become lenses through which we perceive the things of the world. This is one aspect of codes that cannot be over-emphasized. Codes are organizing grids of signs and of the mental processes they activate in tandem.

As a semiotic code, language is subject to the laws and structural features of semiosis, including laws of iconicity, indexicality, and symbolicity. Consider the phonemic construction of words—that is, how words are created with specific sounds and combinations of sounds. As discussed, this process is often an iconic one; that is, a process whereby the word is made to resemble, simulate, or reproduce some property of its referent, to add sonority to an expression, to convey emotional states, etc. Some common iconic patterns are discernible:

- in alliteration, or in the repetition of specific phonemes to represent certain perceived sonorities or for intentional phonic effects: *sing-song, ping-pong, no-no, tick-tock, choo-choo*, etc.;
- in the lengthening of phonemes for emphasis or for some emotional response: *Yesssss!, Noooooo!*, etc.;
- in patterns of intonation to express emotional states: *Are you absolutely sure? Don't you dare say that again!* etc.;
- in sound symbolism (discussed previously), which can be seen, for instance, in the speech representations of cartoons and comic books: *Zap!, Boom!, Pow!*, etc.;
- in onomatopoeic descriptions of people and things: *splash, bang, crack*, etc.;

- in the use of tone and volume—loudness conveys anger, an increased rate of speech urgency, etc.

Iconicity manifests itself as well in other areas of language. The American linguist Ronald Langacker (1987, 1990, 1999), for example, has shown how grammar is an unconscious iconic code. Nouns, for instance, are designed to elicit images of referents that appear to trace a "region" in mind-space—for example a count noun is imagined as referring to something that encircles a bounded region, whereas a mass noun is visualized as designating a non-bounded region. The noun *water* elicits an image of a non-bounded region, whereas the noun *leaf* evokes an image of bounded region. This conceptual iconicity produces grammatical effects—*leaves* can be counted, *water* cannot; *leaf* has a plural form (*leaves*), *water* does not (unless the referential domain is metaphorical); *leaf* can be preceded by an indefinite article *(a leaf)*, *water* cannot; and so on.

Indexicality and symbolicity are also involved in various linguistic subcodes. For example, languages across the world have indexical words: (1)for referring to the relative location of things—*this*, *that*, *here*, *there*, *up, down,* etc.; (2) for referring to events that are in temporal relation to each other—*before*, *after*, *now*, *then, yesterday, tomorrow,* etc.; and (3) for referring to the participants taking part in a situation—*I, you, he, she, the one, the other*, etc. Symbolicity is diffuse, of course, in encoding concepts that involve s social convention, agreement, or common practices. It can be seen, for example, in the creation of words made with the prefix *cyber-* such as *cyberspace, cybercafé,* etc., which pertain to the Internet era.

As discussed in this book, one of the fundamental methods of semiotic analysis is opposition theory. This can be applied effectively to the semantic subcode, making it possible to establish the following basic semantic-conceptual relations among words:

- *Synonymy.* This is the relation whereby the meanings of words overlap, as can be seen by oppositions such as *hide*-versus-*conceal, near*-versus-*close,* etc. The overlap is partial, and rarely completely coincidental. It is more a feature of gradience than polarity.
- *Homonymy*. This is the relation whereby two or more meanings are associated with the same word or phrase, as can be seen by oppositions such as *Shakespeare's play*-versus-*He likes to play* in *play* is a homonym.
- *Antonymy.* This is the relation by which different words stand in a discernible semantic contrast, as can be seem in oppositions such as

love-versus-*hate, hot*-versus-*cold,* etc. reveal. Again antonymy is a matter of degree or gradience, rather than of categorical or polar difference.

- *Hyponymy:* This is the relation by which the meaning of one word is included in that of another: as can be seen in oppositions such as the meaning of *scarlet*-versus-*flower* and *water*-versus-*liquid,* in which the second pole is the generic category and the first one an exemplar of that category.
- *Proportionality:* This is the relation by which distinctions among certain words are maintained through oppositional *proportions* that can be set up among signs: (1) *man*-versus-*woman*-versus-*child,* (2) *bull*-versus-*cow*-versus-*calf).* The proportionality between set (1) and (2) is based on the triadic opposition: *adult male*-versus-*adult female*-versus-*non-adult person*

Needless to say, there are myriad other relations in the subcodes of language. These need not concern us here, since our goal is simply illustrative, selecting a few aspects of language to exemplify its semiotic codability features.

Now, as mentioned above, language is delivered as speech, which is also subject to the laws of codability. Among the descriptions of the speech code, the one by the late Roman Jakobson (1960), is the one most used within semiotics. Jakobson posited six "constituents" that characterize the speech code:

- an *addresser* who initiates a communication;
- a *message* that the addresser wishes or aims to convey, recognizing that it must refer to something other than the single meanings of the words used;
- an *addressee* who is the intended receiver of the message;
- a *context* that provides the framework (psychological, physical, social, etc.) for encoding and decoding the message—the phrase *Help me* would have a different meaning depending on whether it was uttered by someone lying motionless on the ground or by someone in a classroom who was working on a math problem.

- a mode of *contact* by which the message is delivered between an addresser and an addressee
- a *code* providing the signs for encoding and decoding messages.

Jakobson then pointed out that each of these constituents determined a different communicative function, which he named as follows:

- *Emotive function.* This refers to the intent of the addresser in constructing a message—it is described as emotive in the sense that, no matter how literal the message might be, its mode of delivery invariably involves the latent presence of the addresser's emotions, attitudes, social status, etc.
- *Conative function.* The message invariably has an effect on its receiver, known as "conative," no matter what the message contents might be, because the way it is delivered by the addresser involves such subjective features as tone of voice, individual selection of words, and so on.
- *Referential function.* This refers to any message that is constructed to convey information ("Main Street is two blocks north of here"). The message is tied indexically to a context, referring to something in some way.
- *Poetic Function.* This refers to any message that is constructed to deliver meanings effectively, like poetry ("Roses are red, violets are blue, and you know I love you"). It is a form of contact that is based on some iconic or metaphorical strategy, rather than a literal exchange of information.
- *Phatic function.* This refers to any message that is designed to establish, acknowledge, or reinforce social relations ("Hi, how's it going?").
- *Metalingual function.* This refers to any message that is designed to indicate the code used ("The word noun is a *noun*."). It is also the awareness that language and other codes are involved in the delivery of messages. The term *metacommunication* was used to indicate this

idea first by anthropologist Gregory Bateson (Ruesch and Bateson 1951), which seems to have inspired Jakobson.

Jakobson's analysis suggests that verbal discourse goes well beyond the function of simple information transfer. It is a coded phenomenon that involves *who* says *what* to *whom*; *where* and *when* it is said; and *how* and *why* it is said; that is, it is motivated and shaped by the setting, the message contents, the participants, and the goals of each interlocutor. Discourse makes an emotional claim on everyone in the social situation.

The phatic function, requires some further commentary. It is not just a way of indicating how greetings are coded, but more broadly of how speech functions ritualistically. It was first described by anthropologist Bronislaw Malinowski (1923), who saw it as a critical speech function. It is manifest in all kinds of rituals and religious practices—in sermons, political rallies, ceremonial gatherings, etc. are all phatic events are anchored in speeches, either traditionally worded or specifically composed for the occasion. The use of language in ritual is not to create new meanings, but to reinforce traditional ones and, thus, to ensure cultural cohesion. Societies are held together as a result of such phatic verbal rituals.

Language is a truly distinctive achievement of the human species. With it, we can organize the world in our minds. Without it, we would have to rely on other codes, such as nonverbal ones (see below). But these can hardly do the same kind of powerful cognitive work that the language code does. We would not have been able to organize and classify knowledge without it.

Nonverbal Codes

Codes that do not involve language are called, simply, *nonverbal.* Consider, as a practical example, the zones that people maintain between each other during contact and greeting rituals. The closer people stand to each other, the more they are on familiar or intimate terms. In other words, the zones between people are used coded for social meaning. The anthropologist Edward T. Hall started measuring these zones starting in the late 1950s (Hall 1959, 1966). Hall discovered that in American culture a distance of under 6 inches was experienced as an intimate zone reserved for lovemaking, comforting, and protecting; a 6–18 in. zone was experienced instead as a zone where family members and close friends should interact; a 1.5–4 ft. zone is felt to be the minimum comfortable zone that non-touching individuals tend to maintain; a 4–12 ft. zone is perceived as non-involving and non-threatening by most individuals; and a 12 ft. and beyond zone constitutes a formalized zone used for public communication (lectures, speeches, and so on). The zone dimensions vary, as might be expected, from culture to culture. So, while the basic code, which he called *proxemic,* is universal, the various zone-based oppositions it encompasses will vary. In effect, the proxemic code is a perfect example of what a nonverbal code implies.

Across cultures, the body signs and the codes that regulate nonverbal behaviors are the result of a perception of the body as something more than physical substance. Winks, hand gestures, facial expressions, postures, and other bodily actions all communicate something culturally relevant in particular social situations. Nonverbal behaviors seem "natural" because they are acquired osmotically (unreflectively) in a cultural context. In reality, they are largely a matter of historically-based codes, not of naturalness or lack thereof. Consider the behaviors that we associate with *gender* as a case-in-point. Most humans, like other animals, sense and respond instinctively to the sex (male or female) of another human being. But the human story of sex does not end there. Throughout the world, certain behaviors are perceived as constituting appropriate manifestations of male and female sexuality. These are the result of *gender codes* that define "masculinity" and "femininity" within a tribe or society. This is why sexual behaviors and practices vary considerably. These codes can be expanded, to include other sexual possibilities (as in LGBTQ+ and fluid sexuality), and as result guide how we change our behaviors and our perceptions.

One area of nonverbal semiosis that has become of great interest to semiotics is the area of facial expressions in human beings, which are partially a result of our common evolution with other animals and partly a result of social codability. The former are, in effect, signals, which psychologist Paul Ekman has called *microexpressions* (Ekman 1982, 1985, 2003). These are the characteristic components—eyebrow position, eye shape, mouth shape, nostril size, etc.—which in various combinations determine the facial expression. Ekman found very little variation across cultures in the microexpressions of the basic emotions—fear, anger, happiness, sadness, surprise, disgust, contempt. Indeed, he has shown that it is possible to write a "grammar" of the face that shows less cross-cultural variation than do language grammars. However, many other expressions are coded socially. So, expressions that involve irony, gazing for courtship purposes, etc. are all socially coded.

The semiotic story of the human face does not stop at a study of such expressions. The face is perceived the world over as a sign of Selfhood. This is why we tend to evaluate a stranger's personality on the basis of facial appearance. And, we are inclined to judge the "beauty," or lack thereof, of a person on the basis of how that person "looks," in relation to the standards of what is "beautiful" in our semiosphere. This is why facial decorations and alterations constitute critical Self-representational props and activities that reach back into the origins of culture. From the beginning of time, human beings have made up their faces to convey identity and attractiveness. As the anthropologist Helen Fisher (1992: 272-273) has aptly remarked, the available archeological evidence suggests, in fact, that the sexually-constructed face is a characteristic Self-representational phenomenon that goes right back to our Cro-Magnon ancestors, who spent hours decorating themselves, plaiting their hair, and donning garlands of flowers to show off for one another around the fire's glow. In effect, the face is itself a code—a code of identity and of Self-presentation. This coded perception underlies the practice of portraiture. A portrait is a visual representation of a subject whose facial appearance, as depicted by the artist, is typically interpreted by viewers as a signifier of the Self, that is, as betraying the subject's character, social position, profession, etc. A portrait is a probe of human character.

Eye contact is another area of nonverbal semiosis. It is not unique to the human species. A dog uses a direct stare as a threat or challenge. The dog will break eye contact as a sign of surrender to a more dominant (powerful) dog or person. But it is also a socially-coded phenomenon, reflecting cultural meanings and fitting in with social interaction patterns. Aspects of the variable coding involve, the length of time in eye contact, which conveys what kinds of relationships people have with each other, how gazing patterns are tied to speech, etc. Making eye contact early or late during a verbal exchange will indicate the kind of relationship one wishes to have with the interlocutor. People in some cultures will tend to look more into each other's eyes during conversation than do North Americans; in other cultures males do not look into female eyes unless they are married or members of the same family. The eye-gazing code is of special interest because of its cultural variability. For example, in western culture, gazing in certain contexts might be interpreted as indicative of sexual wonder, fascination, awe, or admiration; staring as sexual curiosity, boldness, or insolence; ogling as staring in an amorous, usually impertinent manner; and the list could go on and on. The point here is that such codes are directive of behavior since they imply specific meanings, especially socially connotative ones.

The overall study of nonverbal semiosis and communication comes under the rubric of *kinesics*, developed by the American anthropologist Ray L. Birdwhistell, who used slow-motion films of conversations to analyze speakers' behaviors. He borrowed many terms and techniques from linguistics to characterize the basic motions that made up meaningful body language. He reported the results of his findings in two well-known books, titled *Introduction to Kinesics* (1952) and *Kinesics and Context* (1970). Kinesic signs cohere into *kinesic subcodes* that regulate how people behave in certain social situations. These include the facial expressions, gazing, eye contact, and other codes (some of which were described briefly above), which can now be defined as subcodes within an overall kinesic code. In most cultures, a basic form of greeting involves handshaking, which is a kinesic *tactile code*, that is, by a code that governs the patterns of touch in interpersonal situations. The study of touch goes under the rubric of *haptics*. The anthropologist Desmond Morris (1969) claims that the western form of handshaking may have started as a way to show that neither person was holding a weapon. It thus became a "tie sign," because of the bond it was designed to create. Throughout the centuries, the sign became a symbol of equality among individuals, being used to seal agreements of all kinds. Indeed, refusing to shake someone's outstretched hand continues, to this day, to be interpreted as a "counter-sign" of aggressiveness or as a challenge. Predictably, this form of greeting reveals a high degree of cross-cultural variation. People can squeeze the hand (as Europeans and North Americans do), shake the other's hand with both hands, shake the hand and then pat the other's back or hug him or her, lean forward or stand straight while shaking, and so on. Haptic communication is not limited, of course, just to handshake greetings. Other forms include patting someone on the arm, shoulder, or back to indicate agreement or to compliment; linking arms to indicate companionship; putting one's arm around the shoulder to indicate friendship or intimacy; holding hands with family members or a lover to express intimacy; hugging to convey happiness at seeing a friend or a family member; and so on. During the COVID-19 pandemic in 2020, such kinesic codes were changes to take the coronavirus spread into account. So, handshaking was replaced by other means of contract, such as elbow touching or head nodding, which has actually been a form of greeting in many cultures before the pandemic.

One other area of special interest to nonverbal semiotics is the domain of gesture codes. Gesture can be defined simply as the use of the hands, the arms, and to a lesser extent, the head to make physical signs (Kendon 2004). Although there are cross-cultural similarities in gesture, substantial differences also exist both in the extent to which gesture is used and in the interpretations given to its particular uses. For example, the head gestures for "yes" and "no" used in the Balkans seem inverted to other Europeans (Morris et al. 1970). Gesture is also found in primates. Chimpanzees raise their arms in the air as a signal that they want to be groomed; they stretch out their arms to beg or invite; and they have the ability to point to things. These gestures are purposeful and regulatory of the actions of other chimps. But the number of gestural forms of which chimpanzees are capable is limited. Human gesturing, on the other hand, is productive and varied. It encompasses, for instance, the many sign languages used in communities of the hearing-impaired, the alternative sign languages used by religious groups during periods of imposed silence, the hand signals used by traffic personnel, and the hand and arm movements used to conduct an orchestra. Some gestures can have quite specific meanings, such as those for saying good-bye; for asking someone to approach, the clenched fist of anger, the raised palm of peace, the "V" for victory or for peace, the "thumbs down" for disapproval, and the gesture for hitchhiking.

Gesture spans the entire range of semiosis. Using the index finger is the most common manifestation of indexical pointing, although any body part that can be moved directionally (lips, nose, tongue, etc.) can also be used to point out referents in the immediate environment, to indicate directions, etc. Iconic gestures are employed commonly to represent the shape of objects: for example, to refer to a round object people the world over tend to use both hands together moving in opposite—clockwise (the right hand) and counter-clockwise (the left hand)—directions. Such a gesture is characterizable as a kind of spatial drawing technique. Symbolic gestures are those used to stand conventionally for social functions or for carrying out interactional protocols such as greeting, affirmation, negation, etc.

The linguist David McNeill (1992) has shown that gesture is often a complement of vocal language, forming a co-speech code. He videotaped a large number of people as they spoke, gathering a substantial amount of data on how gesture complements vocal language. The gestures that accompany speech are known more specifically as *gesticulants*. McNeill's findings suggest that gesticulants are complementary components of vocal communication—exhibiting images that cannot be shown overtly in speech, as well as images of what the speaker is thinking about. Speech and gesticulation constitute a single integrated communication system in which both cooperate to express the person's meanings. McNeill classified gesticulants into five main categories. First, there are *iconic* gesticulants which, as their name suggests, bear a close resemblance to the referent or referential domain of an utterance: for example, when describing a scene from a story in which a character bends a tree back to the ground, a speaker observed by McNeill appeared to grip something and pull it back. His gesture was, in effect, a visual icon of the action talked about, revealing both his memory image and his point of view (he could have taken the part of the character or the tree instead). Second, there are *metaphoric* gesticulants. These are also pictorial, but their content is abstract, rather than strictly iconic of a referent. For example, McNeill observed a male speaker announcing that what he had just seen was a cartoon, simultaneously raising up his hands as if offering his listener a kind of object. He was obviously not referring to the cartoon itself, but to the "genre" of the cartoon. His gesture created and displayed this genre as if it were an object, placing it into an act of offering to the listener. This type of gesticulant typically accompanies utterances that contain expressions such as *presenting an idea, putting forth an idea, offering advice*, and so on. Third, there are *beat* gesticulants. These resemble the beating of musical tempo. The speaker's hand moves along with the rhythmic pulsation of speech, in the form of a simple flick of the hand or fingers up and down, or back and forth. Beats are indexes, marking the introduction of new characters, summarizing the action, introducing new themes, etc. during the utterance. Fourth, there are *cohesive* gesticulants. These serve to show how separate parts of an utterance are supposed to hold together. Beats emphasize sequentiality, cohesives globality. Cohesives can take iconic, metaphoric, or beat form. They unfold through a repetition of the same gesticulant form, movement, or location in the gesture space. It is the repetition that is meant to convey cohesiveness. Fifth, there are *deictic* gesticulants—deixis is the term used to designate all kinds of pointing or indicating signs. Deictic gesticulants are aimed not at an existing physical place, but at an abstract concept that had occurred earlier in the conversation. These reveal that we perceive concepts as having a physical location in space.

McNeill's gesticulant categories are actually subtypes of the more generic category of gesture known as an *illustrator*. Other categories are *emblems, affect displays, regulators,* and *adaptors:*

- *Emblems:* These directly translate words or phrases. Examples are the *Okay* sign, the *Come here* sign, the hitchhiking sign, waving, and obscene gestures.
- *Affect Displays:* These communicate emotional meaning. Examples are the typical hand movements that accompany states and expressions of happiness, surprise, fear, anger, sadness, contempt, disgust, etc.
- *Regulators:* These monitor, maintain, or control the speech of someone else. Examples include the hand movements for *Keep going, Slow down, What else happened?*
- *Adaptors:* These are used to satisfy some need. Examples include scratching one's head when puzzled, rubbing one's forehead when worried, and so on.

Many societies have developed "gesture languages" for the use of hearing or speech-impaired individuals. These are known generally as *sign languages*. These share many structural and semantic features with vocal languages. The spatial and orientational use of hand movements, as well as facial expressions and body movements, make up the grammar and lexicon of sign languages. In American Sign Language (ASL), for instance, the sign for "catch" is formed with one hand (in the role of agent) moving across the body (an action) to grasp the forefinger of the other hand (the patient). ASL signifiers are made by one or both hands, which assume distinctive shapes and movements. A number of manual communication systems use the sign vocabulary of ASL in combination with other hand movements to approximate the syntax of English. Sign languages are also used by hearing peoples for various purposes. One of the best-known examples is the sign language developed by the Plains people of North America as a means of communication between tribes with different vocal languages. The manual signs represent things in nature, ideas, emotions, and sensations. For example, the sign for a white person is made by drawing the fingers across the forehead, indicating a hat. Special signs exist also for each tribe and for particular rivers, mountains, and other natural features. The sensation of cold is indicated by a shivering motion of the hands in front of the body; and the same sign is used for "winter" and for "year," because the Plains peoples count years in terms of winters. Slowly turning the hand, relaxed at the wrist, means vacillation, doubt, or possibility; a modification of this sign, with a quicker movement, is the question sign. The sign language is so elaborate that a detailed conversation is possible using the gestures alone.

Gestures may also be used for sacred symbolic purposes, revealing the ancientness and thus "mythic symbolism" of the hands. For example, in Christianity the "sign of the cross" is a gesture that aims to recreate the central event of Christianity—the Crucifixion. In Buddhism, the gestures known as *Mudras* are used during ceremonies to represent meditation, reasoning, doctrine, protection and request, enlightenment, unification of matter, and spirit. The "devil's hand," with the index and little finger raised, on the other hand, belongs to the domain of superstition, symbolizing, in some cultures, a horned figure intended to ward off the evil eye and in others a sign of "cuckoldry."

Material Culture Codes

The clothes people wear, the food they eat, the objects they value as important, the buildings they construct, etc. all form an overall cultural code that anthropologists call material culture. Of the subcodes that make it up, dress and food codes will be discussed in this section, while architectural codes will be discussed in the subsequent section.

At a biological level, clothes enhance survivability. They are, at this denotative level, human-made extensions of the body's protective resources; they are additions to our protective bodily hair and skin thickness. As Werner Enninger (1992: 215) aptly points out, this is why clothing styles vary according to where a group or society is located geographically: "The distribution of types of clothing in relation to different climatic zones and the variation in clothes worn with changes in weather conditions show their practical, protective function." But as is the case in all human systems, clothes invariably take on a whole range of connotations in social settings, as discussed vis-à-vis the business suit. These are shaped by the various *dress codes* that inform people how to clothe themselves in social situations, how to present oneself to others, and even to change one's image through the clothes (Hollander 1988). And they overlap with other cultural codes, such as gender, professional, and other codes. In Amish culture, a blue

Mutze is a jacket which indicates that the wearer is between 16 and 35 years of age, a charcoal one indicates that he is over 35. The Russian *kalbak* is brimless red hat worn in rural areas, but traditionally it was an index of profession, indicating that the wearer is a medical doctor.

Clothing can also be used to lie, like language: con artists and criminals can dress in three-piece suits to look trustworthy; a crook can dress like a police officer to gain a victim's confidence, and so on. To discourage people from deceiving others through clothing, some societies have enacted laws that prohibit misleading dressing, defining who can dress in certain ways. In ancient Rome, for instance, only aristocrats were allowed to wear purple-colored clothes; and in many religiously oriented cultures differentiated dress codes for males and females are regularly enforced.

For some semioticians, such as Roland Barthes (1967), the history of fashion is the history of culture. Up until the nineteenth century, fashion was mainly the privilege of the rich and wealthy. The Industrial Revolution, however, made fashion for the masses an economic reality. Since then, fashion for almost everyone has become an intrinsic feature of modern lifestyles. Outside the western world, however, clothing styles in many nations continue to be anchored in traditions, retaining their coded values. Fashion can be defined as the prevailing style or custom of dress wither for a particular group or class of people, or generally for the entire society. It is a kind of macro dress code that sets style standards according to age, gender, class, etc. To understand how fashion codes emerge, let us return briefly to the code of the business suit, and specifically the male business suit. The subtextual message underlying the apparel text is, *dress for success.* It is a contemporary version of Puritan dress. The toned down colors (blues, browns, grays) that the business world demands are the contemporary reflexes of the Puritan's fear and dislike of color and ornament. During the "hippie" 1960s and early 1970s, the office scene came briefly under the influence of a new form of fashion. "Cavalierism," with its emphasis in the wearing of colorful suits, of turtle neck sweaters rather than of white shirts, of longer hair, of sideburns, of Nehru jackets, of medallions, and of beards made its pitch to take over the world of corporate capitalism. But this fashion experiment was bound to fail, as the Cavalier 1960s were overtaken by conservative neo-puritanical forces in the late 1970s and 1980s. The "business suit" model became once again the dress code for all of the corporate world, with only minor variations in detail, until the advent of the Web society and the emergence of geek entrepreneurs, who founded such mega-companies like Google and Facebook. Their dress is a counter-statement to the traditional business suit—T-shirt, sweater, jeans, etc. The dress code's subtext is: *we do not need to dress for success, we have succeeded with our brains.* As this implies, fashion codes can also constitute ideological statement. This new "geek ideology," as it can be called, may be the reason for the decline of importance of the traditional fashion shows and fashion modeling. This ideology stands in contrast with the ideology of other parts of the business world, where the suit continues to bear its long-established connotations. Finally, since the early 2000s gender-neutral dress codes have been in practice.

Like clothing, food is much more than survival substance. Survival without food is, of course, impossible. So, denotatively food can be defined as survival substance. But, in the cultural settings, food and eating styles invariably take on a whole range of connotations. Thus, food and eating codes inform people about what to eat, how to make food, and what certain foods imply socially. The earliest people ate whatever plant food they could find, including wild fruits, mushrooms, nuts, roots, and seeds. They caught fish and small land animals as food sources. Food supply was also connected to cultural location—if the food supply in an area ran out, they apparently moved on. Over time, people roasted some of their food over burning wood from fires that started naturally. After they discovered how to make fire, they could roast food more often. After they learned how to make pots, they also started to boil and stew food. By about 8,000 BCE, people had begun to raise plants and animals for food—hence the rise of farming as a communal activity, assuring people of a steadier food supply. It also meant settling in one area instead of traveling about in search of food.

As the anthropologist Claude Lévi-Strauss (1964) has emphasized, the origin of human culture can be traced to the advent of "cooking technology." He claimed that this transformation was accomplished by two processes—roasting and boiling—both of which were among the first significant technological advances made by humanity. Roasting is more primitive than boiling because it implies a direct contact between the food and a fire. But boiling reveals an advanced form of technology, since the process in this case is mediated by a pot. Boiling, Lévi-Strauss, was a major event that led to the institution of true culture—which implies the sharing of food in the community of others. At that point food takes on symbolic meanings—that is, these early hunting-gathering societies soon developed complex belief systems with regard to the world, and food became a symbolic part of ritual that enacted these systems. To this day, food invariably is a primary constituent of all kinds of ceremonies and rituals, from feasts (weddings, Bar Mitzvahs, etc.) to simple social gatherings, such as parties or get-togethers. We plan our days around meals. Even going out on a common date would be anomalous without some eating component associated with this ritual,

To illustrate how symbolism is embedded in food, consider the apple as a case-in-point. Many of its symbolic meanings derive from numerous accounts of human origins. The discovery and cultivation of the apple dates back considerably. Ramses II of Egypt cultivated apples in orchards along the Nile in the thirteenth century BCE. The ancient Greeks also cultivated apple trees from the seventh century BCE onwards. They designated the apple "the golden fruit," in Greek mythology after the hero Heracles, as a part of his Twelve Labors, had to travel to the Garden of the Hesperides and pick the golden apples off the Tree of Life growing at its center. This symbolism has also been ascribed to the apple in Christian tradition, even though the "forbidden fruit" is not identified as such in the Book of Genesis. The forbidden fruit became an apple probably influenced by the story of the Garden of Hesperides. As a result, the apple became a symbol for knowledge and human weakness at once.

As another example, consider lamb meat, which is a particularly important. As another example, consider lamb meat, which is a particularly important food in most Jewish and Christian traditions. In most Christian traditions it is eaten at Easter which is the time period of the liturgical year because it represents Jesus and relates His death to that of the lamb sacrificed on the first Passover. This is why Christians traditionally refer to Jesus as "the Lamb of God." In many homes, a lamb-shaped cake also decorates the table at Easter. Many Eastern Orthodox Christians even hang pictures of the Easter lamb in their homes.

Similar historical accounts can be sketched for virtually any of traditional foods we continue to eat today. Symbolism is also the reason why the meat of certain animals is not eaten by the people of certain cultures. And it is also the reason for fasting. Fasting is one of a number of rites in which physical activities are reduced or suspended, resulting in a state of quiescence symbolically comparable to death, or to the state preceding birth. The Assyrians and the Babylonians observed fasts as a form of penance. In Hebrew tradition, fasting is a symbolic form of purification, observed on the Day of Atonement, Yom Kippur. In many indigenous communities young people hold fasts to seek direction in life. Political fasting, known as "hunger striking" has also been employed as a political weapon ever since Mohandas Gandhi, leader of the struggle for India's freedom, used it effectively in the early and mid-1900s. The counterpart to fasting is indulging in food. One tradition based on indulging is *carnival*, which in Christian traditions consists of feasting and merrymaking just before Lent, such as the Mardi Gras in New Orleans, which takes place just before Ash Wednesday, the beginning of forty days of penance, including some form of fasting.

Eating codes, like all other kinds of social codes, are regulatory systems—they regulate what kinds of food are eaten, when they are eaten, who is allowed to eat them, and so on and so forth. Predictably, these vary considerably from culture to culture (Goode 1992: 236-245), guiding how eating events are organized, including:

- the order in which dishes are presented
- what combinations can be served in tandem
- how the dishes or food items are to be placed on the table

- who has preference in being served
- who must show deference
- who does the speaking and who the listening
- who sits where
- what topics of conversation are appropriate

All cultures, moreover, have a discrete set of table rituals and manners that are inculcated into the members of the culture from birth. If one does not know the *table-manner code* of a certain culture, then that person will have to learn it in order to continue living in that culture without censure or disapprobation. Such codes also involve the use of flatware. In Egypt, Greece, and Rome this use was the privilege of the aristocracy; made of precious materials, including silver and gold, and sometimes decorated. The Romans also possessed skewers that were forerunners of the fork. From the Middle Ages until the Renaissance, the knife remained the principal table utensil. Forks came into common table use in Italy in the 1500s. At the same time spoons made the transition from kitchen utensils to table items. From that time onward, flatware came to be used by all peoples of all classes. During the nineteenth century numerous other items of flatware were created, such as teaspoons, butter knives, and salad forks. These have become signs in their own right—knives, for example, connote much more than eating utensils. They are also perceived as weapons or symbols of power.

Objects are signs that evoke a broad range of meanings across the world's cultures. This is why archeologists reconstruct ancient societies on the basis of the artifacts they discover at a site. The jewelry, clothes, furniture, ornaments, tools, toys, etc. that they find there are signs that allow them to reconstruct the society's traditions, values, rituals, etc. to varying degrees of completeness. Artifacts provide clues as to what an extinct culture was probably like. The symbolism of objects, in fact, was the basis for the emergence of the craft of alchemy, defined as the art of transmuting materials, such as iron into gold. The principal activity of the alchemists was the search for the "philosopher's stone"—popularized as a unique object by the highly popular *Harry Potter* movies of the early 2000s—and the production of gold by artificial means.

Architectural Codes

One final area of commentary with regards to codes involves meanings of buildings, cities, and other architectural constructions. These codes are themselves subject to the meanings of *spatial codes*, divided into three main categories—*public*, *private*, and *sacred*. Public spatial codes are those that regulate to how people interact at public sites; the proxemic codes discussed previously would fall under this category. Private spatial codes are those that regulate how we perceive private spaces, as extensions of ourselves, while sacred spatial codes regulate interaction at sites that are purported to have spiritual qualities. Public spaces are felt to be extensions of a "communal body." This is why societies are often described by people as being "healthy," "beautiful," "organized," etc. And this is why a public place is defaced, it is felt as having violated the entire community. Conflicts between societies, groups, or nations are often ignited by such acts against the communal body.

In the same way that public spaces are perceived to be parts of a semiotic communal body, so too private spaces are felt typically to be extensions of Self-space. A home, whether a crude hut or an elaborate mansion, is a shelter providing protection from weather and intruders. It is felt, therefore, to be an extension of the body's protective armor. Indeed, when one steps inside, one feels as if one has entered into one's own body. Thus, when people build and decorate their homes, they are primarily engaged in making images of themselves to suit their own eyes. The identification of Self with the home is characteristic of all cultures.

Homes are subject to various meanings, which fall under the rubric of architectural codes. In some societies the house tends to be a single volume, a room for all activities, reflecting an uncomplicated experience of Self. It is usually built directly against neighboring structures and often close to the tribal meeting-house or religious site as well. In city cultures, the experience of home is much more diversified. In China, for instance, the walled-in form of the courtyard house, which has persisted for centuries, reflects the need for privacy that is inherent in Chinese social traditions. But rows of single-volume dwellings, each with a small court or garden, are also found in China, reflecting a different type of perception. At the other end of the scale are the imperial palace compounds, of which the Forbidden City in Beijing is the perfect example. The various buildings of these compounds, laid out to form a vast, symmetrical complex, constitute an architectural text symbolizing the divine claims of the emperors and the society they governed.

Within the home, the rooms are themselves meaningful "sign spaces" eliciting a specific constellation of emotive connotations. Concealing bedrooms seems to have a biological basis. Humans are extremely vulnerable when sleeping, and so it is certainly judicious, if not essential, to keep sleeping areas hidden from view. This is perhaps why people are especially protective of their bedrooms. In a bedroom, an individual unwinds, relaxes, and expresses his or her inner Self through decoration and personal objects. The bedroom is a refuge and asylum from the outside world. Only intimates are allowed to share that space physically and symbolically. This is why when someone steals something from a bedroom, or defiles it in some way, it is felt to be a personal violation. When people cannot procure a personalized space, living for example in public institutions such as prisons, it should come as no surprise to find that they tend to lose respect for the institution and even for themselves, thus often engaging in defacement and vandalism. "Cleanliness" and "dirtiness," moreover, are signs that appertain to spatial contexts. In a home "dirt" is really no more than displaced matter. If earth is found in a garden it is hardly considered to be dirt; however if found on a kitchen floor it takes on that very meaning. We define a kitchen as a kind of "dirt-free" or "dirt-removal" space. So, we find "dirty" kitchens repellent. We can tolerate "dirty" bedrooms much more because they do not involve food and because they are out of the line of sight (Douglas 1966).

Some buildings are perceived to be artistic texts. This is why the aesthetic response to them is varied. They differ from, say, sculpture only in the fact that the observer can be inside the art text (the building). The aesthetic response to buildings is affected by construction materials used, by the way they have been assembled, by the lighting conditions, by the form and style of windows, doors, floor design, and ceiling height. Movement through the spaces within a building also has narrative force, since the parts of a building are interpreted as being as structured as are the parts of a sentence or a story. Buildings are thus "read" as narrative texts with specific meanings. This is why one listens with great interest to a tour guide's story as he or she takes us through an historically-significant building.

The various elements of the building text are signifiers. Consider, for instance, how the height of a building can convey a specific kind of meaning. The cities built during the medieval period had one outstanding architectural feature—the tallest building noticeable along their skyline was the bell tower of the church or the church itself. The spires on medieval churches rose majestically upwards to the sky, reflecting semiotically the fact that there is something overpowering about looking up at tall buildings, making one feel small and insignificant by comparison. The height of churches thus came to symbolize the power and wealth of the Church. But, with the rise of secularism after the Renaissance, cities were gradually redesigned architecturally to reflect a new political order. The tallest buildings were the palaces of aristocrats and rich bourgeoisie—such as the buildings constructed in Urbino, Italy. Today, the tallest buildings in sprawling urban centers are certainly not churches or palaces. The tallest structures in cities like Dallas, Toronto, Montreal, New York, Chicago, Los Angeles are owned by large corporations and banks. Wealth and power now reside literally and symbolically in these institutions. Inside these mammoth buildings there is an architectural structure that mirrors the social hierarchical structure within it—the jobs and positions with the lowest value are at the bottom of the building; the more important ones are at the top. This architectural symbolism is the reason why we use such expressions as "you must work your way *up*," "she has finally made it to the *top*," "I have to climb the *ladder* of success," etc.

From the fourth century until after the Renaissance, Christianity influenced architectural trends, prompting the building of many new churches. Byzantine churches, domed and decorated with mosaics, proliferated throughout the Byzantine Empire. The Italian architect Filippo Brunelleschi (1377-1446) was among the first to revive the classical forms, championing a new architecture based on mathematics, proportion, and perspective. In 1418 he was commissioned to build the dome of the unfinished Florence Cathedral. His design for the dome was a great innovation, both artistically and technically. Saint Peter's Basilica in the Vatican was the most important of many sixteenth-century architectural projects. Toward the middle part of the century such leading Italian architects as Michelangelo, Baldassare Peruzzi, Giulio Romano, and Giacomo da Vignola started the trend of using the classical Roman elements in ways that became known as the *mannerist* style, characterized by arches, columns, and entablatures that enshrined the techniques of perspective and depth in western architecture. The best known architect of the period was the sculptor Gianlorenzo Bernini (1598-1680), designer of the great oval piazza in front of St. Peter's Basilica.

In the eighteenth century a new style arose, called *rococo*, reflecting a new affluence and elegance in society at large. But little less than a century later, with the advent of the Industrial Revolution, a new world order came into existence, accompanied by architectural trends that set the stage for the growth of industrialized building trends and the widespread use of cast iron and steel. At the beginning of the twentieth century, the so-called *Bauhaus school* (based in Weimar, Germany, around 1919-1925), brought together architects, painters, and designers from several countries to formulate the goals of the visual arts in the modern age, under its first director Walter Gropius (1883-1969). The Bauhaus style prevailed throughout the 1940s, 1950s, and most of the 1960s. Often referred to with the term *modernism*, its approach can be seen in the chaste elegance and subtle proportions of the Seagram Building (1958) in New York. Gropius wanted to rebuild the landscape by stripping it of its past symbolism, substituting a geometrically pure style that intentionally excluded references to the past. The Bauhaus School envisioned a working-class architectural landscape. Buildings were to be fashioned as box-like forms so as to eliminate all the symbols of traditional power. Out of this movement, modern office towers, housing projects, hotels, and other public buildings were built with the same basic cubic blueprint.

Between 1965 and 1970, architects started to reject modernism, which they found to be too monolithic and formulaic, promoting a new style that came to be known as *postmodern*. The postmodern architects wanted to inject individuality, intimacy, complexity, humor, and irony into building design. The American architect Robert Venturi (1925-2018), for instance, defended the new vernacular architecture—gas stations, fast-food restaurants, etc.—and attacked the modernist establishment with incisive criticism. By the early 1980s, postmodernism had become the dominant trend in American architecture and an important one in Europe as well. Its success in the US owed much to the influence of Philip C. Johnson (1906-2005). His AT&T Building (1984) in New York City instantly became a paragon of postmodern design:

AT & T Building (Wikimedia, Davide Shankbone 2007)

The building stands out from modernist skyscrapers in many ways, such as in the triangular roof, which also has a circular indentation carved in the middle, longer windows at the top, etc. Such elements have since been effectively used to build everything from office towers to private houses.

Architecture is all about imposing order on space. It is based on the general principle that when things look right, they feel right. In China this principle has even been given expression in the form of the "art of placement," which interprets the forces of Nature and of the cosmos to enhance well-being through design. Born out of the *I Ching*, the art of *Feng-Shui*, as it is called, is a mixture of geometry, geography, architecture, and psychology. Practitioners use an octagonal template called the *ba-gua* to assess an area as large as the floor of a building or as small as a desktop. The orientation, layout and placement of objects within an area are considered to be significant. While some may dismiss such arts as the products of superstition, I see in them a profound sense of spatial pattern which, in one form or other, we assume to be interconnected with destiny and the human condition.

The origin of cities is traced to mixed tribal settlements that came onto the scene around 6000-plus years ago. To protect themselves and their food supplies against predatory nomads, animals, and changes in climate, the people in these settlements built their dwellings within a walled area or a naturally fortified place, such as the acropolis of ancient Greek cities. Because the availability of water was also a key consideration, these early settlements were usually located around, near, or along a river. Gradually, the expanding configuration of buildings and spaces of the settlement created the need for a specialization of labor. Markets developed in which artisans could exchange their specialties for other kinds of goods. They became centers of commerce, learning, and technology.

The spread of the city concept in Europe was a result of the breakup of feudalism. At the beginning of the sixteenth century Europe had six or seven cities of 100,000 or more inhabitants; at the end of the century it had twice as many. During the seventeenth century, although the population of Europe remained stationary, that of the cities increased. But it was not until the late nineteenth century that the process of urbanization—more and more people moving into cities at the expense of rural districts—became a general trend. Its principal causes were the development of the factory system, improvements in transportation, and the mechanization of agriculture, which reduced the need for farm labor. Many modern cities were, in fact, planned as industrial centers near sources of raw materials. In 1890, barely 16 percent of the population of the US lived in cities of 100,000 or more. In 1990 just over one-fourth of the population did so, and three-fourths of the total population lived in cities and towns of 2500 or more.

City design reflects cultural values, beliefs, and emphases. In ancient Greece, religious and civic citadels were oriented in such a way as to give a sense of aesthetic balance to the inhabitants—streets were arranged in a grid pattern and housing was integrated with commercial and defense structures. In the Renaissance, the design of cities around piazzas was in sharp contrast to the narrow, irregular streets of medieval cities. Renaissance city planners stressed wide, regular radial streets forming concentric circles around a central point, with other streets radiating out from that point like spokes of a wheel. To this day, the downtown core is known as *centro* in Italy, reflecting this Renaissance view of cities as circles.

After the Industrial Revolution the concept of the grid started to gain a foothold on city designs. The grid conveys rationalization, efficiency of movement, and precision. This is evident in New York City's plan of 1811, which divided Manhattan into identical rectangular blocks that were even named in terms of the gird system—1st and 7th, 2nd and 31st, and so on. Since the middle part of the twentieth century, many new grid-type designs have emerged. And hotels and other recreational buildings (e.g. casinos) are taking on some of the symbols of power that were once associated exclusively with the banks and the corporations. The city of Las Vegas is a classic example of a city designed to cater to our modern-day craving for recreation and consumption. The tall hotel towers that mark its landscape are symbols of a world of fast money, quick recreational fixes, and consumerist delights.

Epilogue

Cultural codes influence beliefs, attitudes, worldview, and even sensory perception to varying degrees. As a concrete example, consider the phenomenon of optical illusions, which make it obvious that perception is not governed just by the physiology of vision alone, but is also the product of culturally-based inferences that we have learned to make about figures operating at an unconscious level. These influence how our eyes interpret figures drawn on surfaces. It is unlikely that the brain was designed by evolution to be duped by the eyes. The brain and the eyes are, simply put, out of whack and the phenomenon can only be explained by influence from human culture and drawing activities and the codes on which they are implanted.

One of the earliest documented optical illusions, called the *Duck-Rabbit Illusion*, was the one by Polish psychologist Joseph Jastrow (1863-1944), published in the German humor magazine, *Fliegende Blätter* on October 23, 1892. It is perceived by our mind as either a duck or a rabbit at different instances of viewing:

The Jastrow Illusion (Wikimedia Commons)

The illusion is caused because of graphical similarities in the picture that our visual perception interprets ambiguously, much like our verbal perception interprets some lexical forms ambiguously. Interestingly, when we resolve (or actually "see") the ambiguity, our brain experiences a pleasant jolt similar to the Aha Effect of solving some kinds of puzzles (Danesi 2019). Perhaps the two most broadly-known and discussed illusions are the Müller-Lyer Illusion, named after the German psychologist Franz Carl Müller-Lyer (1857-1916) who invented it in 1889. A version is shown below.

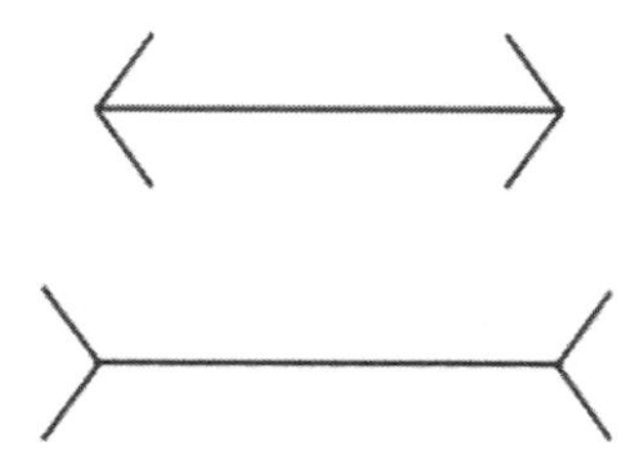

The Müller-Lyer Illusion (Wikimedia Commons)

Most people see the bottom line as longer than the top one, even though the two are equal in length. The source of the illusion is the different orientation of the two arrowheads. One plausible explanation for this is that we tend to interpret arrowheads that jut out as lengthening something, and vice versa, those pointing inwards as shortening something. Whatever the cause, the fact remains that these illusions would not occur without drawing practices or codes. The factor behind the illusions is cultural, not biological. They are caused, more specifically, by visual codes that shape drawing practices (as already discussed). The point is that the human brain is affected by culture.

Codes assign meaning to signs and texts, organizing sign systems to help us organize, explore, and record meaningful events, practices, and traditions. These govern all aspects of human life. In order to make contact with someone successfully we must know the appropriate body and verbal language codes. These provide the meaningful forms and actions (words, expressions, how the hands are to be used in the contact ritual, the length of the contact, and so on) and rules for combining them that make contact rituals successful or meaning-bearing. Similarly, writing, music, painting, and other kinds of codes provide and specify the ways in which tones, harmonies, colors, figures, and so on can be selected and combined to produce symphonies, portraits, and so forth. These ways are not invented on the spot. They are shaped by historical processes and, thus, are subject to change. When we invent a new code, the world has either changed or will change in tandem. What remains in codability, though, that is its formation on the basis of semiotic principles, such as iconicity, indexicality, oppositional structure, and so on. So, while the actual codes may change and our perceptual mechanisms along with them, their semiotic structure remains intact, adapting itself to new conditions and needs.

6
Conceptual Metaphors

Midway between the unintelligible and the commonplace, it is metaphor which most produces knowledge.

Aristotle (384-322 BCE)

Prologue

In a key 1962 book, *Models and Metaphors*, the American philosopher Max Black introduced a distinction that has become fundamental to linguistics and semiotics, namely that a specific metaphorical utterance, such as *That person is a snake*, is not an isolated one, but an exemplar of a more general conceptual strategy that links people and animals, or simply, *people are animals*. Since then, the former is called *linguistic metaphor* and the latter a *conceptual metaphor*. A watershed 1977 study (Pollio, Barlow, Fine, and Pollio 1977) then showed that conceptual metaphors pervaded common everyday speech. Titled *Psychology and the Poetics of Growth: Figurative Language in Psychology, Psychotherapy, and Education,* it found that speakers of English uttered, on average, 3000 novel metaphors and 7000 idioms (frozen metaphors) per week. It became obvious that metaphor could hardly be characterized as a deviation from literal speech, or a mere stylistic accessory to literal conversation. Two collections of studies published shortly thereafter, *Metaphor and Thought* (Ortony 1979) and *Cognition and Figurative Language* (Honeck and Hoffman 1980), and a groundbreaking book by George Lakoff and Mark Johnson, *Metaphors We Live By* (1980), set the stage for what came to be known as *conceptual metaphor theory* (CMT).

Lakoff and Johnson laid out the notions, analytical techniques, and overall research agenda upon which CMT was subsequently elaborated. Essentially, CMT sees an utterance such as *That person is a snake* as a manifestation of a mode of thinking, not as an isolated example of rhetorical style, but as an instantiation of a thought process that goes on unconsciously as we talk and think. The *person* could have been portrayed as any other animal, such as a *gorilla*, a *pig*, a *puppy*, and so forth. The result would have been a different metaphorical portrait of the person's personality. In other words, each linguistic metaphor realizes the *people are animals* concept. *People* is called the target domain and *animals* the source domain. The source domain is the set of animal concepts that allow us to grasp the target domain of human personality. The source for understanding the latter is not, however, limited to our experience of animals; it can be anything from a substance (*That person is a softie*) to electricity (*That person is always wired*). Each linguistic metaphor implies a different psychology behind our evaluation of human personality.

There are two other figures of speech that are considered to be cognitively different from metaphor in CMT—metonymy and irony. Metonymy is the process of representing a concept with something that is associated with it: *She loves Hemingway* (= the writings of Hemingway); *The automobile is destroying our health* (= the collection of automobiles); and so on. In parallel with the notion of conceptual metaphor, the term conceptual metonym has been adopted to refer to generalized concepts based on metonymy rather than metaphor: *the face for the person* (as in *He's nothing more than another pretty face); a body part for the person* (as in *Get your butt over here!*); and so on (Danesi 2004). Irony is limited in CMT to designating a strategy whereby words are used to convey a meaning contrary to their literal sense—for example *That person loves being tortured* would be interpreted as ironic if it were referring to someone experiencing unwelcome pain. The intent of the speaker, including tone of voice and other prosodic features, the speaker's relation to the listener, and the context are all factors that establish the ironic meaning of an utterance. If the above sentence were uttered about a masochist, then it would hardly have an ironic meaning.

All three figurative processes (metaphor, metonymy, irony) have semiotic structure—that is, they show that something—in this case an utterance with two referents—stands for something else, another referent, either by mapping one domain onto another (conceptual metaphor), using one domain to stand for another (metonymy), or using one domain contrastively for another (irony). In effect, CMT is a semiotic theory, even though it is rarely acknowledged as such.

CMT

This chapter will deal with conceptual metaphor theory—a branch of semiotics sometimes called *metaphorology*, which includes the study of other tropes. This is a critical topic in the field today, since it transcends language, constituting a semiotic feature in all types of codes. As in other chapters, however, we have had to be highly selective, since the field of CMT has become a truly broad one.

Background

From ancient times, the use of figures of speech, or *tropes*, has been seen primarily as a rhetorical strategy employed by orators and poets to strengthen and embellish their speeches and compositions. In this tradition, metaphor is defined as the use of a word or phrase denoting one kind of idea in place of another word or phrase for the purpose of suggesting a likeness between the two.

Aristotle (1952) was the one who discovered metaphor, coining the term *metaphor*—itself a metaphor (*meta* "beyond" + *pherein* "to carry"). The Greek philosopher saw the power of metaphorical reasoning in its ability to shed light on abstract concepts. However, he affirmed that, as conceptually-powerful as it was, its primary function was rhetorical, a way for sprucing up more prosaic and literal ways of communicating. Remarkably, this latter position became the rule by which metaphor came to be judged in western philosophy subsequently. But as twentieth century studies, such as the ones mentioned above showed, Aristotle's original view was in effect the correct one. Defining a single linguistic metaphor semiotically poses an interesting dilemma. In the metaphor above, *That person is a snake*, there are two referents, not one, which are linked to each other as follows:

- There is the primary referent, *professor*, which is known as the *topic* (or *tenor*) of the metaphor.
- Then there is a second referent, *snake*, which is known as the *vehicle* of the metaphor, which is chosen to say something about the topic.
- The linkage between the two creates a new meaning, called the *ground*, which is much more than the simple sum of the meanings of topic and vehicle.

Thus, a metaphor is a complex sign. First, the whole metaphor is itself a sign, showing the typical structure of standing for something other than itself—in the case above, personality, character, etc. But each part is itself a word-sign—*person* and *sign*. So, it is a linkage that produces an amalgam or blend, as it is now called (Fauconnier and Turner 2002). Note, moreover, that it is not the denotative meaning of the vehicle that is embedded into the metaphor, but rather its connotative meaning. There is no denotative metaphor, unless it is used over time to become a frozen metaphor and thus perceived as literal, having lost its metaphorical structure. An example is *point* in a phrase such as *I do not see your point.* It is used so often for "idea," that we hardly ever realize that it is a geometric metaphor, along with other such metaphors: *Yours is a circular idea; That is a square idea;* etc.

Metaphor reveals an unconscious tendency of the human mind to think of certain referents as interconnected. The question now becomes: Is there any psychological motivation for this? In the case of *That person is a snake*, the probable reason for correlating two apparently unrelated referents seems to be the *de facto* perception that humans and animals are interconnected in the natural scheme of things. It reveals a knack for seeking out and establishing similarities among things, interconnecting them semiotically. Among the first to point this out was the seventeenth-century Italian philosopher Giambattista Vico (Bergin and Fisch 1984). Before Vico, metaphor was viewed as a manifestation of analogy—an inductive form of reasoning whereby it is assumed that if two or more entities are similar in one or more respects, then a probability exists that they will be similar in other respects. For Vico, on the other hand, metaphor revealed how humans go about creating analogies. Paradoxically, and significantly, metaphor is so fundamental to how we form abstractions such as analogies, that it is impossible to talk about them without resorting to metaphor.

Aristotle saw metaphor as a product of proportional reasoning. For example, in the metaphor *Old age is the evening of life*, a proportion can be set up as follows: A = *old age*, B = *life*, C = *evening*, D = *day*; and, thus, the metaphor shows the following conceptual structure: A is to B as C is to D. The reasoning involved can be broken down as follows—the period of childhood is to life as the morning is to the day; the period of adulthood is to life as the afternoon is to the day; hence, old age is to life as the evening is to the day. This proportion, incidentally, pervades mythical and literary traditions, as Aristotle certainly knew. It is found, for example, in the legend of the Sphinx—the mythical creature with the head and breasts of a woman, the body of a lion, a serpent tail, and the wings of a bird who guarded entrance to the ancient city of Thebes. When Oedipus approached the city of Thebes, so the story goes, the gigantic Sphinx confronted him, posing the following riddle to him: "What is it that has four feet in the morning, two at noon, and three at night?" Failure to answer it correctly meant instant death—a fate that had befallen all who had ventured to Thebes before Oedipus. The fearless Oedipus answered: "Man, who crawls on all fours as a baby, then walks on two legs, and finally needs a cane in old age." Upon hearing the correct answer, the Sphinx killed itself, and Oedipus entered Thebes as a hero for having gotten rid of the terrible monster that had kept the city enslaved for a long period of time. However, the whole event revealed the fulfillment of an ominous self-fulfilling prophecy, since it lead to tragedy and personal disaster, as an oracle had forecasted when Oedipus was born. The Riddle of the Sphinx provides us with an early model of how metaphorical cognition manifests itself in human affairs.

It is somewhat ironic that a proto-founder of semiotics, John Locke (Chapter 1), did not see metaphor as a means of understanding. He saw as a "fault" in thinking and even speaking in his *Essay Concerning Humane Understanding* (Locke 1690: 34):

> If we would speak of things as they are, we must allow that all the art of rhetoric, besides order and clearness, all the artificial and figurative application of words eloquence hath invented, are for nothing else but to insinuate wrong ideas, move the passions, and thereby mislead the judgment; and so indeed are perfect cheats: and therefore, however laudable or allowable oratory may render them in harangues and popular addresses, they are certainly, in all discourses that pretend to inform or instruct, wholly to be avoided; and where truth and knowledge are concerned, cannot but be thought a great fault, either of language or person that makes use of them.

The philosopher Thomas Hobbes (1656) also inveighed against metaphor, characterizing it as an obstacle to communication, a source of ambiguity and obscurity, and thus, a kind of speech tic to be eliminated from true philosophical and scientific discourse. Hobbes came to form this view of metaphor because he believed that the laws of arithmetic mirrored the laws of human thought, and thus that the only meaningful form of philosophical discourse was of the same "literal" kind as the one used to explicate mathematical notions.

Such views were based on the belief that literal meaning is the default form of semantic systems, whereby forms (words, phrases, sentences, etc.) encode referents in a straightforward one-to-one fashion, that is, denotatively as an initial tendency. However, already in the medieval period, Thomas Aquinas went contrary to the literalist grain by claiming, in his *Summa Theologica*, that the writers of Holy Scripture presented "spiritual truths" under the "likeness of material things" because that was the only way in which humans could grasp such truths, thus implying that metaphor was a tool of cognition, not just a feature of rhetorical flourish (quoted in Davis and Hersh 1986: 250):

> It is befitting Holy Scripture to put forward divine and spiritual truths by means of comparisons with material things. For God provides for everything according to the capacity of its nature. Now it is natural to man to attain to intellectual truths through sensible things, because all our knowledge originates from sense. Hence in Holy Scripture spiritual truths are fittingly taught under the likeness of material things.

As mentioned previously, it was Vico who first sparked interest in metaphor as a crucial form of thought in the eighteenth century, emphasizing that metaphor was evidence of how "knowledge originates from sense," as Aquinas had so aptly put it. He saw it as a manifestation of "poetic logic" a form of thinking that links experiences to create previously unknown thoughts: "It is another property of the human mind that whenever men can form no idea of distant and unknown things, they judge them by what is familiar and at hand" (Bergin and Fisch 1984: 122). The two parts of the metaphor—topic and vehicle—suggest each other phenomenologically—that is, by saying that *life is a stage* we are also implying that *stages are life.* Vico's view of metaphor was, at first, largely ignored by his contemporaries. Mainstream philosophers of the era continued to insist that metaphor was no more than a decorative accessory to literal language. The exceptions to this mindset were Immanuel Kant, who mentioned in his *Critique of Pure Reason* (1781) that figurative language was evidence of how the mind attempted to understand unfamiliar things, and Friedrich Nietzsche (1873), who came to see metaphor as humanity's greatest flaw, because of its subliminal power to persuade people into believing it on its own terms.

Metaphor starred receiving serious attention in the first part of the twentieth century. In his now classic 1936 book, *The Philosophy of Rhetoric*, I. A. Richards (1893-1979) started a revolution in research on metaphor by arguing persuasively that it hardly could be classified as a replacement of literal meaning for communicative or stylistic purposes, but rather that it was part of a psychologically powerful meaning system that could never be encompassed by literal paraphrases. He was the one who named the parts of the metaphor (above) as the *tenor* (*topic*), *vehicle*, and *ground.* Richards then claimed that the linkage was hardly a matter of mere comparison or substitution, but rather an entailment based on perception of relationship. In strict psychological terms, the meaning inherent in the metaphor *life is a stage* is perceived as a categorical "interaction" between *life* and *stages*. There is, of course, more to *life* than *stages*, and *stages* may have functions other than to represent *life*. But these two categories of human experience overlap considerably in some domains of thought.

As mentioned at the start of this chapter, it was Max Black (1962) who formalized interactionist theory, claiming that the kind of conceptual linkages that metaphor permits not only underlies common conceptualizations, but is also the creative backbone of science. It is an example of what Peirce (1931-1958) referred to as an *abduction* or "informed hunch." Eventually, this type of treatment of metaphor led to Lakoff and Johnson's 1980 book that established CMT. There are a few caveats that must be made vis-à-vis CMT. First, whether or not all abstract concepts are structured metaphorically is a question that is open to research and debate. Second, even if this were so, it must not be forgotten that there are aspects of language that are not metaphorical. Metaphor is an iconic process; metonymy and indexical one; and irony a symbolic one (as will be discussed below. But despite these cautions, the current research on the comprehension and production of metaphor within CMT has made it no longer tenable to assign figurative meaning to some subordinate category with respect to literal meaning. In fact, metaphor is so common as an unconscious semiotic process in language and other codes that we hardly ever realize how it influences our perceptions, beliefs, actions, and behaviors.

Conceptual Metaphor Theory

Interactionist theory, originating with Richards and elaborated by Black (above) led gradually to the doorstep of Lakoff and Johnson's, *Metaphors We Live By* (1980), setting the stage for conceptual metaphor theory, by laying out the basic theoretical framework and the notions for researching metaphor in discourse and all other codes. As mentioned briefly above, they envisioned a metaphorical statement like *That person is a snake* as a token of a conceptual formula, namely *people are animals*. In this formula, they termed *people* as the target domain and *animals* as the source domain—animal referents that allow us to grasp human personality. So, portraying someone as a *monkey* or *eagle*, for instance, are not simple, unconnected, metaphorical utterances. They are specific expressions that are guided by the conceptual formula, which Lakoff and Johnson called a *conceptual metaphor*.

Metaphor allows us to grasp abstractions concretely. By thinking of *life* as a *stage*, for example, we can gain a concrete understanding of what this concept entails, since we have presumably had experience with what takes place on stages. With its characters, plots, and other theatrical accouterments, the stage is a metaphorical sign system that stands for life. From this representamen, we can expand the system with derivative metaphors such as *My life is a comedy* or *My life is a farce*, from which we can draw inferences about a person's actual life. This is a simplified explanation, of course, of the nature of metaphorical cognition. There is much more implicature involved between the referential domains in a metaphor. However, for the present purposes, it is sufficient to say that the referents embedded in conceptual metaphors are interconnected or suggestive of each other (Danesi 2017).

CMT has made it obvious that expressions such as *That person is a snake* or *life is a stage* are not disconnected ones, uttered simply for rhetorical emphasis or flourish—they are systematic, not exceptional or idiomatic. Moreover, it has shown that the same conceptual formula manifests itself throughout cultural codes. Depicting people as animals in the artistic and narrative domains is a product of the same form of thinking evident in the verbal instantiations of *people are animals*. This is why stories for children focusing on human personality often involve animal characters or why mythic stories of creatures that are half human and half animal are understandable in metaphorical ways.

The conceptual metaphor itself (*people are animals*) is, in effect, a compressed sign structure standing for the larger conceptualization of people as animals. The source domain can be anything that is linked to it in some experiential way: for example, *tactility* (*My friend is a softie*), *electricity* (*My friend is always wired*), *matter* (*My friend is a rock*), and so on. As can be seen, each one implies a different model of personality that finds its way into the system of culture as a recurrent metaphorical code. As such, metaphor is an iconic process, since it envisages resemblances among referents and then unites them through metaphor.

The psychological source of conceptual metaphors is traced to a mental mechanism called the *image schema* (Lakoff 1987, Johnson 1987, Lakoff and Johnson 1999). This is a mental percept that converts experiences (such as perceived animal behaviors) into source domains for understanding abstractions (such as human personality). Whatever its neural substrate, or its cultural source, the image schema manifests itself systematically in oppositions that constitute the source domains of metaphorical constructs. For example, the experience of orientation—*up*-versus-*down, back*-versus-*front, near*-versus-*far*, etc.—leads to the formation of an image schema underlying how we conceptualize such abstractions as *happiness* (*Lately my spirits are up*), *responsibility* (*You have to face up to your problems*), among many others. The common experience of how containers work and what they allow us to do underlies such concepts as *mind* (*My mind is full of good memories*), *emotions* (*My heart is filled with hope*), and so on. Obviously, it is impossible to determine which came first—the metaphor or the image schema. Perhaps this is a moot question, since the occurrence of a metaphor implies a specific image schema and vice versa—which is, in itself, a definition of iconicity (as discussed previously).

Idealized Cognitive Models

The systematicity of conceptual metaphorical thinking manifests itself not only through the creation of specific metaphors, but also in the production of higher-order metaphorical concepts that link different source domains, which Lakoff and Johnson call *idealized cognitive models* (ICMs). For example, conceptual metaphors delivering the notion of *ideation* (how ideas, theories, and other such abstract constructs are understood) include the following source domains (among others): *sight* (*I cannot see what you are saying*), *geometry* (*The views of Plato and Descartes are parallel in many ways*), *plants* (*That theory has deep roots in philosophy*), *buildings* (*Your theory is well constructed*), *food* (*That is an appetizing idea*), *fashion* (*His theory went out of style years ago*), and *commodities* (*You must package your ideas differently*). An ICM results from sensing a semiotic connectivity among these domains. Some of the source domains seem to cross cultural boundaries; others seem to be culture-specific. That is to say, it is likely that languages across the world commonly use source domains such as *sight* and *food* in the construction of ICMs for delivering the concept of *ideation*, but only those cultures that have traditions of Euclidean geometry and marketplace economics are likely to use source domains such as the *geometry* and *commodities* ones. This shows how universal tendencies in the brain interact with specific experiences *in situ* to produce cognition.

To see what all this implies, let us consider the target domain of *ideation* with the conceptual metaphors that produce it:

Conceptual metaphor I: *Ideas are food substances*

1. His ideas left a *sour taste* in my mouth.
2. They always find it hard to *digest* that person's policies.
3. She is *voracious* reader; but can't *chew* all that at the same time.
4. That professor is always *spoon-feeding* his students.
5. Your thoughts have a *sweet taste* to them.

Conceptual metaphor II: *Ideas are persons*

6. Freud is the *father* of modern psychology, isn't he?
7. Some ancient philosophical ideas continue to *live on* today.
8. Artificial Intelligence is still in its *infancy*, despite all its achievements.
9. Maybe we should *resurrect* older stories.
10. That professor *breathed* new life into the study of logic.

Conceptual metaphor III: *Ideas are fashion*

11. Postmodernism in architecture went out of *style* several years ago.
12. Quantum physics is at the *avant-garde* of science.
13. Those ideas are no longer in *vogue.*
14. The field of semiotics has become truly *chic*, academically.
15. That idea is an old *hat.*

Conceptual metaphor IV: *Ideas are buildings*

16. That idea is implanted on *solid* theoretical *ground.*
17. The *cornerstone* ideas of modern-day biology are due to Darwin.
18. That is only a *framework* for a new theory.
19. That theory is starting to *crumble* under the weight of criticism.
20. That theory is *built* solidly.

Conceptual metaphor V: *Ideas are plants*

21. That idea has many *ramifications.*
22. How many *branches* of knowledge are there?
23. That theory has deep historical *roots*.
24. That idea has produced many *offshoots*.
25. That is a new *budding* idea.

Conceptual metaphor VI: *Ideas are commodities*

26. That idea is *worthless.*
27. You must *package* your ideas more attractively.
28. You will not be able to *sell* your ideas easily in this day and age.
29. I guess he didn't *buy* my ideas after all.
30. You cannot put a *price* on that idea.

Conceptual metaphor VII: *Ideas are geometrical figures*

31. That idea is rather *square.*
32. His ideas are *parallel* to mine.
33. Her ideas are *diametrically opposite* to mine.
34. What's the *point* of your idea?
35. What you said is an example of *circular* reasoning.

Conceptual metaphor VIII: *Ideas can be seen*

36. I don't *see* what that theory is all about.
37. I can't quite *visualize* what you mean by that idea.
38. Let me take a *look* at that theory more closely.
39. I *view* what you say very seriously.
40. I took a quick *glance* at your ideas, and I really like them.

Now, the constant mapping of these eight conceptual metaphors onto speech produces, cumulatively, an ICM of *ideation* emerges that can be accessed separately, in tandem, or alternatively to discuss *ideas, theories,* etc. of various kinds, and to represent them in different but interconnected ways. So, for example, a sentence such as *I see that your idea has many ramifications, given that it is on solid ground* can be described as having been constructed by enlisting three of the above conceptual formulas: IV, V, and VIII. If we examine common conversations, it will become evident that large portions of them revolve around ICMs, with single expressions in conversations caught in a network of conceptual metaphors that are interconnected thematically to specific target domains.

Metonymy and Irony

As mentioned at the start of this chapter, in CMT, there are two figures of speech that are treated differently from metaphor—metonymy and irony. Metonymy, and its counterpart synecdoche, are viewed as revealing a *pars pro toto* reasoning: *She loves Hemingway* (= the writings of Hemingway). In parallel with the notion of conceptual metaphor, the term conceptual metonym can be adopted to refer to generalized metonymic concepts (Danesi 2004). Conceptual metonyms are distributed in nonverbal domains as well, producing their own kinds of derived or interconnected sign forms. For example, the *face* is a common metonym for personality (*There are many faces in the audience; His face tells it all*). The *face* is also a symbol of personality—as can be seen, for example, in the use of theatrical masks, in portraits that focus on the face, and so on. Metonymy is an indexical strategy, since it relates parts to wholes, indicating how they are related to each other existentially (in real life or in the imagination). Below are common manifestations of the conceptual metonyms in common expressions:

The face is the person

1. He's just another pretty *face*.
2. There are an awful lot of *faces* in the audience.
3. We need some new *faces* around here.
4. You can read his thoughts on his *face*.

A body part is the person

5. Get your *butt* over here!
6. The Yankees need a *stronger arm* in right field.
7. We don't hire *long hairs.*

The producer for the product

8. I'll have a *Pepsi*.
9. We bought a *BMW*.
10. He's got a *Rembrandt* in his house.

The object used for the user

11. My *violin* is sick today.
12. The *meat and potatoes* is a lousy tipper.
13. The *buses* are on strike.

The institution for the people in the institution

14. *Shell* has raised its prices again.
15. The *White House* thinks that the congressional law is wrong.
16. I don't approve of *Washington's* actions.

The place for the institution or a specific field

17. *Milan* is introducing new jackets this year.
18. *Wall Street* is in a panic.

19. *Silicon Valley* is introducing many new things this year.

Irony is constrained in CMT to designate a contrastive semiotic strategy—for example, *It is really hot today* would be interpreted as ironic if it is uttered by someone during the height of a very cold winter day. Only through familiarity with this use of language can the ironic meaning be grasped. This implies that irony is based on symbolic cognition, that is, on relating its meaning to something contrastively through cultural formulas that establish it in this way. There are three main types of irony, although this is a reductive typology, and used here for the sake of illustration since they show how it is tied to symbolicity:

1. *Verbal:* This implies the use of words to mean the opposite, in order to emphasize something or make an unexpected comparison: *What a great day* (uttered during a hurricane).
2. *Situational:* This signals the difference between what is expected (or what *should be*) and what happens (or *actually is*). An example would be the irony of being in an airplane where the pilot is afraid of flying.
3. *Dramatic:* This occurs when someone is aware of something that the interlocutor is not—a situation that happens frequently in drama. A famous example is in the play *Oedipus Rex* by Sophocles, in which the audience knows that the person killed by Oedipus, Laius, was his father, as Oedipus tries to figure out who the person was.

Blending Theory

The question that CMT begs is the following one: What process in the brain maps domains onto each other? The process is called *blending* (Fauconnier and Turner 2002)—when domains (vehicle and topics) are connected through some inferential or experiential sense, the brain blends them together through metaphor, which is the intended meaning of the blend and this can lead to new understanding:

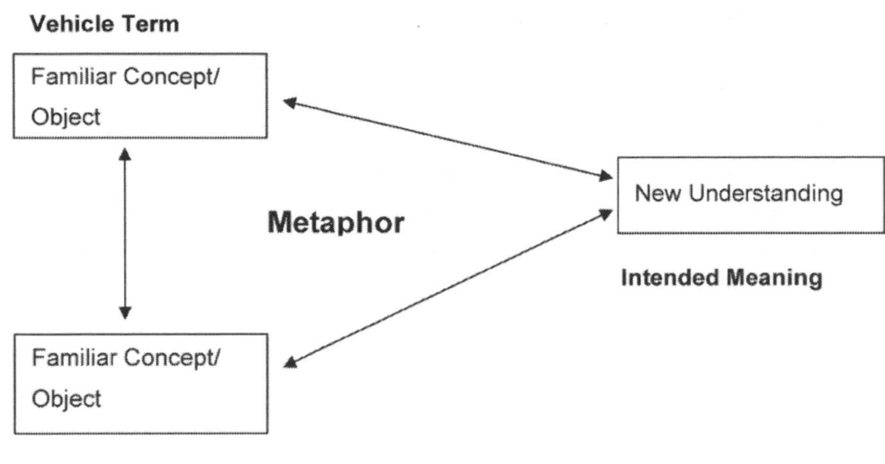

Metaphor as the Basis for New Understanding

A blend is formed, in effect, when the brain identifies two distinct inputs into separate mental spaces in different neural regions as the same entity in a third neural region—an identification rendered salient by the metaphor. But the blend contains more information than the sum of information bits contained in the two inputs, making it a powerful form of new knowledge. In the metaphor above, *That person is a snake*, the two distinct inputs are *person* (topic) and *snake* (vehicle). The blending process is guided by the inference that *people are animals*, constituting the final touch to the blend—a touch that keeps the two entities distinct in different neural regions, while identifying them simultaneously as a single entity in the third.

A conceptual metaphor results from a neural blend. In the linguistic metaphor *The professor is a bear* the *professor* and the *bear* are amalgamated by the conceptual metaphor *people are animals*. Each of the two parts is called a domain—*people* is the target domain because it is the general topic itself (the "target" of the conceptual metaphor); and *animals* is the source domain because it represents the class of vehicles, called the lexical field, that delivers the metaphor (the "source" of the metaphorical concept). Using the Lakoff-Johnson model, it is now easy to identify the presence of conceptual metaphors not only in language, but also in mathematics. The number line is a good example of what this entails. In this case, the target domain is *number* and the source domain is *linearity*. The latter comes presumably from the fact that we read numerals from left to right or in some languages, vice versa. So, the line is a blend of two input domains leading to a new way of understanding number and of representing. Thus the notion of number sense is relevant and interpretable only on the basis of specific cultural experience and knowledge. That is, only in cultures that use Euclidean geometry is it possible to make a general inference between geometrical objects such as lines and numerical ideas. Thus, conceptual metaphors are not just extrapolations; they derive from historical, cultural, and social emphases, experiences, and discourse practices.

What does talking about number as a figment of linearity imply? It means that we actually count and organize counting in this way. In a phrase, the conceptual metaphor both mirrors and the subsequently structures the actions we perform when we count. First, it reveals how the blend occurred; and second it then guided future activity in this domain of sense-making. For this reason, the number line has become a source of further mathematics, leading to more complex blends and thus producing emergent structure regularly. The number line results from blending experiences (inputs) to further conceptual abstractions, permitting us not only to recognize patterns within them, but also to anticipate their consequences and to make new inferences and deductions. Thus, blending theory suggests that the source domains (inputs) enlisted in delivering an abstract target domain were not chosen originally in an arbitrary fashion, but derived from the experience of events and, of course, from the subjective creativity of individuals who use domains creatively and associatively.

Metonymy and irony are also manifestations of blending. In the former case, the blend occurs when the brain extracts a part of something, amalgamating it to the whole. In the latter case, the brain extracts two opposite-meaning inputs, blending them together in such a way that their meanings are diverted to emphasize a contrastive meaning

Relevant research has shown that blending theory is not just a construct, but rather that it has psychological validity. A study by Fan-Pei et al. (2013), for example, looked at event-related potential (ERP) studies, which had suggested that literal mapping occurs during metaphor comprehension. However, the researchers found that their 18 participants read short novel metaphors (for example, *The girl is a lemon?*) or literal control sentences (for example, *The fruit is a lemon*) preceded by either a relevant or irrelevant word they found, using electroencephalography, that conceptual mapping across remote domains evoked larger amplitudes than mapping across close domains. The results thus suggested that there is a shared mechanism for both metaphorical and literal language comprehension, thus casting doubt on the literalist mapping theories. Moreover, once a blend is established, it leads to further blending.

Blending can be broken down into two main processes. The first one can be described as a "clustering" of source domains around a target domain. When the topic of *ideas* comes up in discourse, speakers of English deliver it by navigating conceptually through the various source domains that cluster around it according to need, whim, or situation. For example, the sentence *I can't see why your ideas are not catching on, given that they have deep roots and lie on solid ground* has been put together with three source domains (seeing, plants, and buildings) from the ICM of *ideas.*

Not all ICMs manifest a clustering structure. A second major type can thus be called "radiation," which inheres in different target domains being delivered by identical source domains. It can be envisioned as a single source domain "radiating outwards" to deliver different target domains. For example, the plant source domain above not only allows us to conceptualize ideas (*That idea has deep ramifications*), but also such other abstract concepts as love (*Our love has deep roots*), influence (*His influence is sprouting all over*), success (*His career has borne great fruit*), knowledge (*That discipline has many branches*), wisdom (*His wisdom has deep roots*), and friendship (*Their friendship is starting to bud just now*), among many others. Radiation can be defined more neursocientifically as the blending of abstract concepts that implicate each other through a specific experiential model or frame of reference (source domain). Radiation, by the way, explains why we talk of seemingly different things, such as wisdom and friendship, with the same metaphorical vehicles. Clustering, on the other hand, explains why we use different metaphorical vehicles. It thus allows people to connect source domains as they talk.

Epilogue

To conclude this chapter, it cannot be overemphasized that we do not detect the presence of metaphorical reasoning in common expressions because of repeated usage. For example, we no longer interpret the word *see* in sentences such as *I don't see what you mean, Do you see what I'm saying?* in metaphorical terms, because such uses of *see* have become so familiar to us. But the association between the biological act of seeing outside the body and the imaginary act of seeing within the mind was the original source of the conceptual metaphor *seeing is understanding or believing*, which permeates common discourse:

1. There is more to this than *meets the eye*.
2. I have a different *point of view*.
3. It all depends on how you *look* at it.
4. I take a *dim view* of the whole matter.
5. I never *see eye to eye* on things with you.
6. You have a different *worldview* than I do.

7. Your ideas have given me great *insight* into life.

This conceptual metaphor has been documented across societies as a fundamental source for understanding abstractions such as *thinking, belief, understanding, knowledge*, and the like. Interestingly, this basic or "root" metaphor leads to further (or derived) metaphorizing. Consider the *thinking is visual scanning* thought formula in English as evidence of this:

8. You must *look over* what you've written.
9. I must *look into* what you've told me a bit further.
10. She *saw right through* what you told her.
11. I'm going to *see* this thing completely *out*.
12. You should *look into* that philosophy further.

These also suggest that thoughts, like objects, can be moved, arranged, located, etc., or else seen, looked into, etc., a concept encoded by the *thoughts are objects* conceptual metaphor:

13. *Work* that idea *over* in your mind.
14. *Turn* that thought *over* in your mind.
15. You should *rearrange* your thoughts carefully.
16. *Put* your thoughts *in order,* before going forward with your plans.

As Walter Ong (1977: 134) has pointed out, the presence of such metaphorical formulas in human language suggests that "we would be incapacitated for dealing with knowledge and intellection without massive visualist conceptualization, that is, without conceiving of intelligence through models applying initially to vision." They also suggest that meaning is something "felt" or "experienced" as interconnected with other areas of experience. A 1955 study by the Gestalt psychologist Solomon Asch, for instance, showed that metaphors of sensation in several phylogenetically-unrelated languages used the same sensory source domains (*warm, cold, heavy*, etc.), although the choice of specific items from a domain varied as to their application to a target domain. For example, he found that *hot* stood for *rage* in Hebrew, *enthusiasm* in Chinese, *sexual arousal* in Thai, and *energy* in Hausa. As psycholinguist Roger Brown (1958: 146) aptly commented shortly after the publication of Asch's study, "there is an undoubted kinship of meanings" in different languages that "seem to involve activity and emotional arousal." Empirical work on metaphor proliferated in the 1970s and 1980s. By the early 1990s there was little doubt in the minds of many linguists and psychologists that metaphor was a guide to the workings of human abstract thinking.

The research in CMT has also shown that, unlike many aspects of language, metaphor emerges spontaneously. Children do not even have to be exposed to it to be able to use it to understand things in their environment. When children refer to the sun or the moon as a "ball" they do so without having ever heard it named as such. An identical form of metaphorical reasoning underlies the formation of color conceptual metaphors throughout the world, suggesting that many concepts (if not most) were originally forged as metaphors. Consider the concept of *red.* This color suggests "blood" and thus "vitality." This might why a *red heart* is commonly used as a symbol of love and passion. The source for this is probably the physiological fact that such emotions involve an increase in the heartbeat and thus in the blood pumped by the heart.

Before Lakoff and Johnson's trend-setting work, the study of metaphor fell within the field of rhetoric, where it was viewed as one of various tropes. But since the early 1980s the practice has been to use the term *metaphor* to refer to the study of all figurative language and to consider most of the other tropes as particular kinds of metaphor. Within this framework, *personification*, for instance, (*My cat speaks English*) would be seen as a particular kind of metaphor, one in which the target domain is an *animal* or *inanimate object* and the source domain *humans*. This kind of reasoning really reverses domains in the *people are animals* conceptual metaphor (*animals are people),* suggesting that rather than a mapping between domains, there really is an interaction or blending, as discussed above.

The relation between conceptual metaphors and culture cannot be overstated. More often than not, metaphors are guides to a culture's past. A common expression such as He *has fallen from grace* would have been recognized instantly in a previous era as referring to the Garden of Eden story in the Bible. Today we continue to use it with only a dim awareness (if any) of its Biblical origins. Expressions that portray life as a metaphorical journey—*I'm still a long way from my goal, There is no end in sight*, etc.—are similarly rooted in Biblical narrative. Proverbs too are extended metaphors that people employ to provide sound practical advice when it is required in certain situations: *You've got too many fires burning* (= advice to not do so many things at once); *Rome wasn't built in a day* (= advice to have patience); *Don't count your chickens before they're hatched* (= advice to be cautious); *An eye for an eye and a tooth for a tooth* (= equal treatment is required in love and war).

The study of the cultural and cognitive aspects of such metaphorical language has made it obvious that it can be considered a theory of mind, rather than just a theory of semantics (Fauconnier and Turner 2002). The CMT movement traces its inspiration to the 1930s, starting with I. A. Richards, as we have seen. It is now a powerful tool for investigating complex semiosis and how concepts are interrelated throughout cultural codes. This might seem to be an extravagant claim, but it really is not, especially if one assumes that metaphor is part of semiosis that aims to interconnect meanings that are distributed throughout the semiosphere though the process of blending.

7
The Arts

Art for art's sake? I should think so, and more so than ever at the present time. It is the one orderly product which our middling race has produced. It is the cry of a thousand sentinels, the echo from a thousand labyrinths, it is the lighthouse which cannot be hidden. It is the best evidence we can have of our dignity.

E. M. Forster (1879–1970)

Prologue

Art was excluded from the discussion of codes in Chapter 5. The reason was that it required special treatment, given both that the arts have been special targets of interest on the part of semioticians and because they have been instrumental in the origins and evolution of cultures across the world. This chapter will look at some of the arts from a semiotic perspective. Needless to say, we have had to restrict our commentary to a minimum, since each section in this chapter could have been elaborated into a tome of its own.

The artistic capacity—to draw and extract meaning from pictures, to make and enjoy music, to dance, to put on stage performances, among all the other creative-artistic practices that all cultures espouse—is a truly extraordinary endowment of the human species. The "art instinct" is innate in every human, allowing people to express and appreciate the entire range of feelings and emotions that differentiate humans from other life forms. It is indisputable evidence of the workings of what Vico (Bergin and Fisch 1984) called the *fantasia*—the creative imagination. Artistic traditions are passed on from generation to generation throughout the world as precious ones because they are perceived universally as transcending time, and as saying something true and profound about the human condition.

The field of semiotics that deals with art forms falls broadly under the rubric of *aesthetics*, and the study of the interpretation of art under *hermeneutics.* The two are concerned with how artistic texts—symphonies, paintings, plays, etc.—engender "feeling states" which are considered to be meaningful and revelatory of some inner truth. Each art is institutionalized and rendered meaningful by codability. So, for instance, a musical style or genre emerges as an art form when the sounds used are structured according to specific principles and structures of melody and harmony. The code is then applied to the creation of musical texts—songs, dances, etc. When the sense of music changes, then the code adapts accordingly. This leads to the creation of new musical forms and texts, which are then shaped into new aesthetic tools for interpreting musical products. However, for these to make sense, they must emanate from previous codes, as in a historical flow, unless there is a radical break from the past, as has happened in some of the contemporary arts (as will be discussed).

Art

Defining *art* is as impossible as defining *culture*—the two are often used as synonyms. Art is something that we all recognize, but which we cannot quite define or pin down to some meaning. The word *art* derives from the Latin *ars,* meaning "skill." This is perhaps it is used sometimes as a synonym for *skill*—the "art of gardening," the "art of chess," etc. In its broader meaning, however, it involves not only specialized skill, but also a creative imagination and a point of view about the world that is transferred to the artistic text.

Each art evokes specific cultural evaluations, according to time and place. In ancient and medieval times, for example, poets were praised for their words, whereas musicians, painters, sculptors, who used physical rather than creative verbal skills, were considered less important and, therefore, remained largely anonymous. This situation changed, starting in the Renaissance, when those skilled in the visual arts gradually gained greater recognition and social prestige, and thus the right to authorship and recognition. By the eighteenth century, a distinction was made between art that was aesthetic—art for its own sake—and art that was practical or ornamental—that is, a distinction was made between the *fine arts*—literature, music, dance, painting, sculpture, and architecture—and the decorative or *applied arts*—such as pottery, metalwork, furniture and carpet making, etc. However, since the mid-twentieth century, this distinction has become less rigid, as a greater appreciation of all types of art, including the applied arts, has given back to the word *art* its broader meaning.

Some scholars believe that art originally had a ritualistic and mythic function, mirroring the role and function of the early myths. In ancient cultures, art was created to be used as part of communal ceremonies or to adorn the public spaces. It was made by all members of the community, rather than by professional artists alone, to serve social functions or to record common ideas. In traditional native cultures of North America art continues, in fact, to be perceived as one aspect of community rituals that are designed to ensure a good harvest or to celebrate a significant life event such as a birth or a marriage. But even in modern western culture, art entails ritual. At a performance of a classical piece of music in a concert hall, for instance, there is ritualistic silence. At a rock concert, on the other hand, there is communal shouting and physical involvement. Hanging a painting in an art gallery invites an individualistic appreciation; but drawing something on a city wall, invites social participation (graffiti, commentary, modifications, etc.).

The first aesthetic theory of any scope was that of Plato, who believed that art was an imitation of ideal forms, which pre-existed as truths before the artist expressed them in some. So, the sculptor takes a clump of marble and gives it the imitative form of a human body. In this representation of the body, however, we discover many more things about it. The truth is already in the clump; it takes the sculptor to literally sculpt it. However, Plato also felt that art encouraged immorality, and especially music, which he saw as causing laziness and immoderacy. He thus suggested banishing some types of artists from society, to form his ideal "republic." Aristotle also saw art as imitation, but not in the same way that his teacher Plato did. The role of art, thought Aristotle, was to complete what Nature did not finish, separating the form from its content, such as the human bodily form from its manifestation in people, and then transferring that form onto some physical medium, such as canvas or marble. Thus, art was not pure imitation, but rather a particular representation of an aspect of referents that had the capacity to profoundly affect us and even transform us emotionally. In his *Poetics* (350 BCE), Aristotle argued that tragedy, for instance, so stimulates the emotions of pity and fear that by the end of the play the spectator is purged of them. This *catharsis*, as he called it, makes us emotionally healthier and thus more capable of happiness. The third-century philosopher Plotinus (205-270 CE), born in Egypt and trained in philosophy at Alexandria, also gave art great importance. In his view, art revealed the true nature of an object more accurately than ordinary verbal descriptions did, raising human understanding from the experience of the mundane to a contemplation of universal truths. According to Plotinus, the most precious moments of life were those instants when the soul is united, through art, with the divine.

Visual artists in the Middle Ages were considered to be primarily servants of the Church. The paintings of walls in churches, or of windows, were seen as visual narratives of religious events, symbols, and ideas. They were intended to reinforce ecclesiastical messages about the world. It was during the Renaissance that art reacquired its more secular functions. The Renaissance, moreover, saw little difference between the artist and the scientist. Indeed, many were both—Leonardo da Vinci was a painter, writer, and scientist, Michelangelo a visual artist and writer, to mention but two. It was only after the Enlightenment and the Romantic movements that an artificial split came about. The latter movement also assigned to artists an eccentric personality—namely, the view of artists as unique geniuses impelled by their own creative energies to free themselves from the shackles of society. In ancient times artists were laborers, paid by rulers for their services. Ancient Egyptian architects, for instance, were hired to build structures designed to glorify the pharaoh and life after death. In medieval Europe, as mentioned, visual artists and playwrights were hired by the Church to create texts designed to extol Christian themes. The choice to be an artist was a matter of social custom, not of some esoteric inclination at birth. Artists, like other people, customarily followed their fathers' profession. It was only after the eighteenth century that the choice to become an artist became an individual one—one that continues on to this day.

Why is art so effective emotionally, no matter who produces it or at which period of time it was produced? One of the best-known, and most widely-accepted theories for explaining the potency of art, favored by many semioticians, is the one put forward by the American philosopher Susanne Langer (1895-1985) during the middle part of the twentieth century (Langer 1948, 1957). We do not experience art, she emphasized, as individual bits and pieces (notes, shapes, words, etc.), but as a total emotional experience. It is only when we attempt to understand rationally why the art work had such an effect on us that the holistic experience is transformed by reasoning and language into one in which its parts can be taken apart, discussed, critiqued, etc. like the individual words in a sentence. But, no matter how many times we try to understand the aesthetic experience logically, it somehow escapes understanding, remains larger than the sum of its parts. One can analyze the opening movement of Beethoven's *Moonlight Sonata* as a series of harmonic progressions and melodic figures based on the key of C# minor. But the elements of melody and harmony come into focus as components of the work only during an analysis of the sonata's structure. When one hears it played as an artistic performance, on the other hand, one hardly focuses on these bits and pieces. One cannot help but experience the music holistically. And this is what makes it emotionally "moving."

Langer remarked, further, that because of its emotional qualities, great art transforms human beings and cultures permanently. It is truly a "mirror of the soul," to use a cliché. Humanity has never been the same since, for example, Michelangelo sculpted his *David,* Shakespeare wrote his *King Lear*, Mozart composed his *Requiem,* Beethoven composed his *Ninth Symphony*, Emily Dickenson her marvelous poetry, Jane Austin her penetrating novels, Maya Angelou her portraits of suffering in prose, Norval Morrisseau's revolutionary visual storytelling and so on and so forth. The meanings and the aesthetic effects in such great art works are constantly being experienced repeatedly to this day.

The Performing Arts

The word *performance* refers to the physical means employed for executing an art text (a song, a comedy routine, a play, etc.) before an audience. Performances are given spatial prominence usually through some platform, such a raised stage, and they typically involve props and paraphernalia such as costumes, masks, musical instruments, and materials of various kinds. The platform can be electronic today, such as a play or symphony being performed on radio, television, or YouTube. Performances are put on according to a socially defined tradition. They are prepared, scheduled, and set up in advance; they have a beginning and an end; they unfold in terms of a structured sequence of parts (for example, acts in a play, movements of a symphony, etc.); and they are coordinated for public participation. Performances are both reflective and constitutive of cultural meanings: they can shed light upon the values of the culture and critique them. If they are aesthetically powerful, they end up becoming part of history and may even transcend the cultures for which they were originally designed. This is why the works of Shakespeare or Molière are translated in other languages, Beethoven's symphonies are still performed in concert halls across the world, and so on.

The performing arts include theater, dancing, singing, instrumental music, mime, vaudeville, circus acts, pageantry, and puppetry. In this section we will focus on the theater, which can be defined as a performance put on by actors on a stage, generally following a script (the dialogical text that is recited by the actors), under the guidance of a director, with props to recreate situations on the stage. Since antiquity, theater has been perceived broadly as putting on display actions, themes, and events that we consider vital to our existence. It does so through the narrative medium. The dramatic text (the script) is usually verbal, but it can also be based purely on bodily movement. The latter type of theater is referred to more precisely as *pantomime,* which, rather than language, is based on facial expressions and bodily movements. In the open-air theaters of ancient Greece and Rome, where the audience could see more easily than it could hear, pantomime became an important integral aspect of verbal theater as well, leading to the use of stylized gestures and facial expressions to portray character in theatrical art generally. The term *theater* is used to describe both the performance itself and the place where it takes place. Stages have had distinctive forms in every era. Theaters today tend to be eclectic in design, incorporating elements of several styles. A theatrical performance, however, need not occur in an architectural structure designed as a theater, or even in a building. Many earlier forms of theater were performed in the streets, in open spaces, in market squares, in churches, or in rooms and buildings not intended for use as theaters. Much of contemporary experimental theater, too, rejects the formal constraints of the traditional stage performance, attempting to create the sense of auditorium through the actions of the performers and the natural features of the acting space.

Most scholars trace the origin of the theater to ancient ceremonial practices. These were intended as fertility or harvest rites, put on in order to appease the gods. Even in ancient Greece the first dramas revolved around tales of the gods. The plays of Aeschylus (c. 525-456 BCE), Sophocles (c. 497-405 BCE), and Euripides (c. 485-406 BCE), for example, were drawn from myth and legend, though their focus was not a simple performance of the mythic storyline, but rather a consideration of the tragedy of human actions as embedded in that storyline. The actors of those dramas wore masks, a practice that also had a ritualistic source. Masks shift the focus from individual actors to the characters they are portraying, clarifying aspects of theme and plot as well as imparting a sense of universality to the characters. In modern theater, make-up and facial expression have taken over from masks.

Comedy was developed in ancient Greece alongside tragedy for criticizing and satirizing both individuals and society in general. One of the first great comedic playwright was Aristophanes (c. 445-385 BCE), who became famous for satirizing both public figures and the gods, to the delight of large audiences. The comedic approach became even more popular in the Roman plays of Plautus (c. 250-184 BCE) and Terence (c. 185-159 BCR). But, with the fall of the Roman Empire in 476 CE, the Church saw comedy as too bawdy and scatological, discouraging it for many years, and promoting instead a liturgical form of theater based on Bible stories. By the fifteenth century, the latter had evolved into the *morality play*, which was a self-contained drama performed by professional actors, and which dealt, typically, with the theme of the individual's spiritual journey through life.

Interest in comedic theater was revived by the movement known as the *commedia dell'arte*, an improvised comedy genre that arose in sixteenth-century Italy and spread throughout Europe over the subsequent two hundred years. The six to twelve players in the *commedia* wore half-masks to portray the exaggerated features of a character. They did not use a script; rather, they improvised skits both on outdoor, impromptu stages and in conventional staging areas. Each actor played the role of a stereotypical character as, for instance, Harlequin, the clownish valet; the Doctor, who used meaningless Latin phrases and often suggested dangerous remedies for other characters' imagined illnesses; and Pulcinella, who concocted outrageous schemes to satisfy his animal-like cruelty and lust. Unlike traditional theater, *commedia* troupes featured skilled actresses rather than males playing the female characters. From the cast of stock characters, each troupe was able to put on hundreds of plays. *Commedia* actors also developed individual comic routines, called *iazzi*, which they could execute on demand, especially when it was felt that a sudden laugh was needed. For instance, a *commedia* performer might pretend to trip and tumble into a pail of bath water during the exit sequence. Many of the routines and ideas of the *commedia* live on in contemporary forms such as vaudeville, burlesque, and even television sitcoms.

By the mid-sixteenth century a new, dynamic secular theater had developed. The most important concept in its design was *verisimilitude*—the appearance of truth. Characters were common individuals. The plays had a single plot, which took place within a 24-hour period, and occurred only in one locale. In the Romantic nineteenth century, theater took another turn, concentrating on a search for the spiritual nature of humankind. One of the best examples is *Faust* (Part I, 1808; Part II, 1832), by the German playwright Johann Wolfgang von Goethe (1749-1832). Based on the classic legend of a man who sells his soul to the devil, the play depicts humankind's attempt to master all knowledge and power in its constant struggle with the universe.

As plays attracted larger and larger audiences, playwrights became more and more involved in writing about everyday life, focusing on the psychological realism of the characters and on social problems. They sought to present a "slice of life" on the stage. This new realistic trend in theater led to the notion of the *director* as the one who interprets the text, determines acting style, suggests scenery and costumes, and gives the overall production its overall quality—a tradition that continues on to this day.

By the first decades of the twentieth century, a reaction against realism erupted in the world of theater. Paralleling contemporaneous radical visual art and musical movements, a movement known as *absurdist* theater emerged. The emphasis of this new form of theater was on the absurdity of theater and of the human condition it glorified. The subtext in all absurdist drama was that of humanity as lost in an unknown and unknowable world, where all human actions are senseless and absurd. Absurdism reached its peak in the 1950s, but continues to influence drama to this day. The classic play in this genre was *Waiting for Godot,* published in 1952 by the Irish-born playwright and novelist, Samuel Beckett (1906-1989). *Godot* is a powerful indictment of the wretchedness of the human condition. It continues to have great appeal because, like the two tramps in the play, many people today seem to have become cynical about the meaning of human existence. The play perseveres in challenging the ingrained belief system that there is a meaning to life, insinuating that language, religion, and philosophy are no more than illusory screens we have set up to avoid the truth—that life is an absurd moment of consciousness on its way to extinction. But despite the play's nihilism, we seem paradoxically to discover meaning in it.

Waiting for Godot questions traditional assumptions about certainty and truth. It satirizes language, portraying as a collection of senseless words that can refer only to other words. It also deconstructs classic theater, which drew its stories and characters from myth or ancient history. The objective of the ancient dramas was to consider humanity's place in the world and the consequences of individual actions. The classical actors wore costumes of everyday dress and large masks. Movement and gesture were stately and formal. The plots emphasized supernatural elements, portraying how humans and the gods struggled, interacted, and ultimately derived meaning from each other. Similarly, medieval morality plays put on display principles of human conduct that informed the populace about what was meaningful to existence. Shakespeare's great tragedies continued in this vein. *Waiting for Godot* is a critique of this kind of theater. The ancient dramas portrayed a world full of metaphysical meanings Godot portrays a world in there is only a void. In the ancient dramas, human life was portrayed as having great meaning. In *Godot,* human beings fulfill no particular purpose in being alive—life is a meaningless collage of actions on a relentless course leading to death and to a return to nothingness. But Beckett's bleak portrait of the human condition somehow forces us to think about that very condition, paradoxically stimulating in us a profound reevaluation of the meaning of life.

Absurdist theater was deconstructionist, taking apart common beliefs and forcing people to reevaluate them. It continues to inform contemporary theatrical trends. In a play such as *American Buffalo* (1976) by David Mamet (b. 1947), for instance, little action occurs and the focus is on mundane characters and events. The language is fragmentary, as it is in everyday conversation. And the settings are indistinguishable from reality. The intense focus on seemingly meaningless fragments of reality creates a nightmarish effect on the audience.

Today, the functions of the theater have been largely replaced by cinema, although theater continues to attract a fairly large following. Musical theater has also emerged as a popular entertainment art form. Already in the 1920s musicals were transformed from a loosely connected series of songs, dances, and comic sketches to a story, sometimes serious, told through dialogue, song, and dance. Also, today, the theatrical practices in Asia—in India, China, Japan, and Southeast Asia—have started to attract great interest from the West. The central idea in Asian performance art is a blend of literature, dance, music, and spectacle. The West had actually discovered Asian theater in the late nineteenth century, a discovery that has gradually influenced many contemporary forms of acting, writing, and staging.

The technical semiotic study of the theater gains momentum starting in the 1970s, with works such as Anne Ubersfeld's *Reading Theatre* (1977), Aston and Savona's *Theatre as a Sign System* (1991), and de Toro's *Theatre Semiotics* (1995), among others. A semiotic analysis does not only take into account the actual text (script), but all the signifying structures that makeup the performance, including the staging aspects (performance text, costumes, props, sets, lights, etc.) and the kinesic aspects of the theater space in relation to the actors (body language, facial expression, etc.).

Thus, to write about the semiotics of the theater poses several issues, first of all one needs to define the language of the stage as being composed of various elements starting from space, together with the sonority, gestures, scenography and music. And the "theatrical miracle" is precisely the fusion of all these elements that create the spectacle. The danger, however, as Yuri Lotman maintains, is to treat these elements separately as this would be a serious mistake, precisely because the language of the scene is composed simultaneously of all the above mentioned elements, and another, in some respects perhaps the most important, the presence of an audience.

The latter element is a fundamental condition for the existence of a language of the scene unlike other artistic languages that do not require a human presence for their existence. One should also note that the language of the stage is necessarily impromptu, that is, it exists only at the moment in which it is preformed, seen and heard.

Another peculiarity of theatrical art is that the human element is at the very core of its existence. For this reason, as Agostino Lombardo maintains, a staging can live only in its perpetual transformation and die and then relive at every performance. So writing about the language of the stage, unlike poetic, literary, pictorial or cinematic language, means writing about something that existed, but that no longer lives and that can never be the same again, but always and only different at every performance, just like life. And because of its ephemeral nature it is no coincidence that theatre itself has been and is still used constantly as a metaphor for life.

Music

Music is an art form involving the organized use of sounds in terms of pitch, melodic properties, rhythm, and harmonic patterns. Music plays a role in all societies, and it exists in a large number of styles, each characteristic of a geographical region or a historical era. Indefinite border areas exist, however, between music and other sound-based arts such as poetry. For this reason, societies differ in their opinion as to the musicality of various sounds. Thus, chanting, half-spoken styles of singing, or sound texts created by a computer program may or may not be accepted as music by members of a given society or group. Often, it is the social context in which the sounds occur that determines whether or not they are to be regarded as music. Industrial noises, for instance, are not perceived as musical unless they are presented as part of a concert of experimental music in an auditorium, with a composer.

Various strata of musical art may exist. In western culture, the following three apply: (1) *classical music*, composed and performed by trained professionals originally under the patronage of aristocratic courts and religious establishments; (2) *folk music*, shared by the population at large; and (3) *popular music*, performed by professionals, disseminated through electronic media (radio, television, records, film) and consumed by a mass public. But the boundaries among these strata are not clear—melodies from the realm of classical music are sometimes adopted by the folk and pop communities, and vice versa.

Although an isolated cuneiform example of Hurrian (Hittite) music of 2000 BCE has been deciphered, the earliest precursor of western music known is that of the ancient Greeks and Romans, dating from about 500 BCE to 300 CE. Fewer than a dozen examples of Greek music survive, written in a notation that has still not been deciphered entirely. The rhythm of Greek music was closely associated with language, composed to duplicate the rhythms of the verbal text and especially of the various poetic meters. The internal structure of Greek music was based on a system of sound modes that combined a scale with special melodic contours and rhythmic patterns. Because each Greek mode incorporated rhythmic and melodic characteristics, listeners could easily distinguish between them. Greek theories on the nature and function of music are discussed by Pythagoras, Aristotle, and Plato. They believed that music originated with the god Apollo, the musician Orpheus, and other mythical figures, and that it reflected in microcosm the laws of harmony that rule the universe. They also believed that music influenced human thoughts and actions. Opinions differ as to the original motivation for, and the spiritual value of, music. In some African societies music is seen as the faculty that sets humans apart from other species; among some Native Americans it is thought to have originated as a way for spirits to communicate with human beings. In western society music is regarded generally as an art form. But in others it is considered to be of low value, and often restricted or even prohibited. This view is not unknown to America, where attempts in the 1950s to ban rock 'n' roll were based on the argument that it was an obscene and sinful form of musical expression. Some even called it "the devil's music."

The minimal unit, or signifier, of musical organization is the *tone*—a sound with specific pitch and duration. Musical texts are put together by combining individual tones to make melodies and harmonies, on the structural plan of regularly recurring beats. The makers of musical texts are known, appropriately enough, as composers, since the principal creative act in music is based on arranging sounds into sonorous texts known as compositions. Improvisation usually takes place on the basis of some previously determined structure, such as a tone or a group of chords; or it occurs within a set of traditional rules, as in the *ragas* of India or the *maqams* of the Middle East. Music is used frequently to accompany other activities. It is universally associated, for example, with dance. It is a major component in many types of religious services, secular rituals, and theater. In some societies it is also an activity carried out for its own sake. In Western society, for example, music is often listened to at concerts, on the radio, etc.

The power of music to transform people was brought out brilliantly by the1984 movie *Amadeus* directed by Milos Forman (1932-2018). The movie is based on the 1979 play by British playwright Peter Shaffer (1926-2016) about the purported eighteenth-century rivalry between Austrian composer Wolfgang Amadeus Mozart and Italian composer Antonio Salieri. The play plumbs the meaning of art, genius, and the central role of music in the spiritual life of human beings. The film captures these themes by juxtaposing the emotionally powerful music of Mozart against the backdrop of dramatized events in his life and the truly splendid commentaries of Salieri, who guides the audience through the musical repertoire with remarkable insight and perspicacity. Forman's camera shots, close-ups, angle shots, tracking shots, and zooming actions allow us to literally probe Mozart's moods (his passions, his tragedies, etc.) on his face as he conducts or plays his music, as well as those of his commentator Salieri (his envy, his deep understanding of Mozart's art, etc.) as he speaks through his confessor to us. Forman thus blends music, plot, and commentary through camera artistry to create a truly effective *mise-en-scène* that is narrative, drama, musical performance, and historical documentary at once. The movie conveys the power of music to transform human evolution. A world without the music of Mozart can be envisioned, but it would be a greatly impoverished one.

There is a recently-established tradition of the semiotic study of music, which comes under the rubric of *musical semiotics.* A widely-cited work in this area is the one by Kofi Agawu (2008) who sees the musical text as a looking both inward (to the music in itself) and outward (to what it does to interpretants). The founders of this branch are, however, Roland Barthes (1977), Eero Tarasti (1979, 1994) and Jean-Jacques Nattiez (1990). In all approaches, the concept of text and of connotation prevail, whereby the sounds and structures of music are seen as analogues of all semiotic structures, such as those in language. So, music has syntactic, semantic, and pragmatic components, which allow for the signs in a text to cohere meaningfully.

The Visual Arts

The question of the function of the visual arts in human life has become part of a general social debate, as contemporary art galleries routinely put controversial "bizarre" paintings and sculptures on display in many societies. One of the most famous versions of this debate was initiated by Andy Warhol (1928-1987), the American pop artist who produced paintings and silk-screen prints of commonplace objects, such as soup cans and photographs of celebrities. When asked *what*, for instance, his painting of a Campbell's Soup Can (1964) means, those who are not art critics, will tend to: (1) say that it means nothing, or (2) give responses such as "It is a symbol of our consumer society," "It represents the banality and triviality of contemporary life," and so on. The latter pattern of responses suggests that we tend to interpret certain texts as "works of art" because meanings and values are attributed to them by those who make them, by the society in which they live, and by those who look at them in later years. But, such "art" does not evoke the same response all over the world. The modern idea of visual art as something to be appreciated individualistically by viewing it in a gallery or museum hides the fact that art in its origins had a public function. Art works were meant to decorate the public square or to commemorate some meaningful event. The idea of "authored" art is a modern one that took shape in the late Renaissance. And only after the Romantic nineteenth century did the idea of the "art gallery" as the appropriate locus for appreciating art emerge as an *idée fixe.*

The visual arts are divided into several main areas, of which painting and sculpture are the main ones. Since the early part of the twentieth century, however, photography and cinema have been added to the list. The earliest photographs on record were made by the French physicist Nicéphore Niépce (1765-1833). Then in 1831 the French painter Louis Daguerre (1789-1851) succeeded in developing a positive photographic image. The first camera for public use was produced by the American George Eastman (1854-1932) in 1889. During the 1950s, new manufacturing processes greatly increased the speed, or light sensitivity, of both black-and-white and color film. The decade was also marked by the introduction of electronic devices called light amplifiers, which intensify dim illumination, making possible the recording on photographic film of even the faint light of very distant stars. Such advances in mechanical devices systematically raised the technical level of both amateur and professional photography. Today, digital cameras, which were introduced in the early 1990s, can produce an image almost instantly. These filmless cameras have a light-sensitive mechanism called a charge-coupled device (CCD). The lens focuses light on the CCD, which changes the light into electronic signals. The images can be viewed immediately on cameras equipped with a liquid crystal display (LCD) screen.

Photography became an art form almost from the instant it was invented. Indeed, from the 1860s through the 1890s it was conceived of as an alternative to drawing and painting, allowing for greater fidelity. In other words, photography was viewed as a shortcut to traditional visual art. The Swedish photographer Oscar Gustave Rejlander (1813-1875) and the English photographer Henry Peach Robinson (1834-1901), for instance, emulated painting forms with their cameras. Like the painter, they claimed, the photographer inevitably makes a selection of what is to be recorded. This selection may be planned ahead of time or calculated on the spot. Lighting, focus, and camera angle may be manipulated to alter the appearance of the image; the developing and printing processes may be modified to produce desired results; or the photograph may be combined with other media to produce a composite art form.

Photography has become much more than an ersatz form of painting today. It now constitutes one of the mementos we utilize to remember people, events, and things. The photographs that adorn our tables and walls are, in effect, visual mementos and testimonials of who we are. Photographs capture a fleeting and irretrievable moment in time, extracting it from the flux of change that characterizes human life. Such captured moments have strong appeal because they provide eyewitness evidence, so to speak, that we do indeed exist in some enduring form, at least in the photographic space. This is why in Michelangelo Antonioni's 1966 movie masterpiece, *Blow-Up*, the search for clues to a crime in a blow-up of a photograph is a metaphor for the search for clues to our own existence in our photographic images. However, the reliability of photographs in reproducing "reality" is not always there. In fact, the more the protagonist of the film enlarges the photograph he took to look for clues, the less revealing it becomes.

The study of visual art in semiotics comes under the rubric of visual semiotics, sometimes called pictorial semiotics. As already discussed, the technique is to decode a visual text into its sign structures and processes in order to flesh out any inherent meanings in them. Suffice it to say here that the study of the visual arts has always formed an intrinsic part of semiotics.

Cinema

The example of *Blow-Up* leads to the topic of *cinema*, which became the major art form of the twentieth century, and continues today to be prominent. to which most people today respond most strongly and to which they look for recreation, inspiration, and insight. Movies are aesthetically powerful because they juxtapose dialogue, music, scenery, and action in a visual-narrative way. Semiotically speaking, a film can be defined as a text which, at the level of the signifier, consists of a chain of images that represent real-life activities. At the level of the signified, films are metaphorical mirrors of life. The topic of cinema is, clearly, a central one for semiotics because movie genres constitute signification systems to which most people today respond and to which they look for recreation, inspiration, and insight at the level of the interpretant.

Most cinema historians trace the origin of cinema to the year 1896, when the French magician Georges Méliès made a series of films that explored the narrative potential of the new medium. In 1899, in a studio on the outskirts of Paris, Méliès reconstructed a ten-part version of the trial of French army officer Alfred Dreyfus and filmed *Cinderella* (1900) in 20 scenes. He is chiefly remembered, however, for his clever fantasies, such as *A Trip to the Moon* (1902), in which he exploited the new possibilities for offering perspective that the movie camera afforded. His short films were an instant hit with the public and were shown internationally. Although considered little more than curiosities today, they are significant precursors of an art form that was in its infancy at the time.

The cinematic fantasies of Méliès influenced the American inventor Edwin S. Porter, often called the father of the silent film, when he produced the first major American silent film, *The Great Train Robbery*, in 1903. Only eight minutes long, it greatly influenced the development of motion pictures because of its intercutting of scenes shot at different times and in different places to form a unified narrative, culminating in a suspenseful chase. With the production of D. W. Griffith's racist film, *The Birth of a Nation* (1915), small theaters sprang up throughout the United States, and cinema emerged as a *de facto* art form and even, as Griffith's movie showed, a means to promote ideologies. Most films of the time were short comedies, adventure stories, or filmed records of performances by leading actors of the day. Between 1915 and 1920, grandiose movie palaces proliferated throughout the United States. The film industry moved gradually to Hollywood. Hundreds of films a year poured from the Hollywood studios to satisfy the ever-increasing craving of a fanatic movie-going public. The vast majority of them were Westerns, slapstick comedies, and elegant romantic melodramas such as Cecil B. DeMille's *Male and Female* (1919). In the 1920s movies starring the comedian Charlie Chaplin ushered in the golden age of silent film. After World War I, motion-picture production became a major American industry, generating millions of dollars for successful studios. American films became international in character and dominated the world market. Artists responsible for the most successful European films were imported by American studios, and their techniques were adapted and assimilated by Hollywood.

The transition from silent to sound films was so rapid that many films released in 1928 and 1929 had begun production as silent films but were hastily turned into sound films, or "talkies" as they were called, to meet the growing demand. Gangster films and musicals dominated the new "talking screen" of the early 1930s. The vogue of filming popular novels reached a peak in the late 1930s with expensively mounted productions of classic novels, including one of the most popular films in motion-picture history, *Gone with the Wind* (1939).

The trend toward escapism and fantasy in motion pictures was strong throughout the 1930s. A cycle of classic horror films, including *Dracula* (1931), *Frankenstein* (1931), and *The Mummy* (1932), spawned a series of sequels and spin-offs that lasted throughout the decade. One of the most enduring films of the era was the musical fantasy *The Wizard of Oz* (1939), based on a book by L. Frank Baum—a children's movie with a frightful theme that reflected the emerging cynicism of society at large, namely, that all human aspirations are ultimately make-believe, that the Wizard at the end of the road of life is really a charlatan. The fun of living is getting to Oz, not finding out the truth about Oz; by living we find out our own truths, including friendship, intelligence, and courage. One American filmmaker who came to Hollywood from radio in 1940 was the writer-director-actor Orson Welles, who experimented with new camera angles and sound effects that greatly extended the representational power of film. His *Citizen Kane* (1941) and *The Magnificent Ambersons* (1942) influenced the subsequent work of virtually every major filmmaker in the world. From the late 1940s to the mid-1970s, Italian cinema achieved an intimacy and depth of emotion that radically transformed cinematic art, starting with Roberto Rossellini's *Open City* (1945) and Vittorio De Sica's *The Bicycle Thief* (1949) to Fellini's *8 ½* (1963) and Lina Wertmuller's *Swept Away* (1975).

One of the most distinctive and original directors to emerge in post-World War II international cinema was Sweden's Ingmar Bergman (1918-2007), who brought an intense philosophical and intellectual depth to his films, treating the themes of personal isolation, sexual conflict, and religious obsession. In his film *The Seventh Seal* (1956) he probed the mystery of life and spirituality through the trials of a medieval knight playing a game of chess with Death. In *Wild Strawberries* (1957) he created a series of poetic flashbacks reviewing the life of an elderly professor. He dissected the human condition starkly in a series of films—*Persona* (1966), *Cries and Whispers* (1972), *Scenes from a Marriage* (1973), and *Autumn Sonata* (1978)—which excoriated the futile penchant in the human species to search for meaning in existence.

In the 1950s and 1960s the color movies gradually replaced the black-and-white film. But some filmmakers still prefer the latter, striving for "naked" realism. Such black and white films as *Psycho* (1960) by Alfred Hitchcock, *The Last Picture Show* (1971) by Peter Bogdanovich, *Raging Bull* (1980) by Martin Scorsese, *Zelig* (1983) and *Shadows and Fog* (1992) by Woody Allen, and *Schindler's List* (1994) by Steven Spielberg have become classics in the genre. Of the many directors of the last part of the twentieth century, perhaps no one has been as successful at exploiting the film medium as a versatile art form as has Steven Spielberg (b. 1947). His *Jaws* (1975), about a killer shark that terrorizes a small beach community, became the model for a number of films in which fear-inspiring creatures threatened helpless victims. His *Close Encounters of the Third Kind* (1977) and *E.T.* (1982) capitalized on a widespread fascination with the possibility of extraterrestrial life. His other multimillion-dollar blockbusters include *Raiders of the Lost Ark* (1981), *Indiana Jones and the Temple of Doom* (1984), and *Indiana Jones and the Last Crusade* (1989), all imitative of the serial cliffhangers of the 1930s. Most of Spielberg's films rely heavily on high-tech special effects, especially his *Jurassic Park* (1993), which features frighteningly realistic computer-generated dinosaurs. Within the first four weeks of its release, *Jurassic Park* became one of the highest-grossing films up to that time, only to be surpassed by *Titanic* (1998) a few years later and some current-day ones.

The 1980s and 1990s saw a revolution in the home-video market, with major releases being made available for home viewing almost immediately after they left the movie theater. This development, combined with the advent of cable television, which features relatively current films on special channels, seemed to threaten the long-term survival of movie theaters and created a climate similar to that of the early 1950s, when television began to challenge the popularity of motion pictures. As a result, film companies increasingly favored large spectacles with fantastic special effects in order to lure the public away from home videos and back to the big screen. But despite the challenge from video, the traditional movie theater has remained as popular as ever—a testament to the power of cinema as a "social art form," much like the theater once was. Although there are now various platforms, such as YouTube, for delivering films, the idea of cinema as a cultural code that subsumes all other performative codes is still an extant one in the twenty-first century. In fact, it has proliferated with independent movie-makers now proliferating. Online cinema and the multiplication of TV platforms that produce and offer movies on demand has had an impact on movie goers. In fact, except for action movies, attendance in theatres has drastically dropped.

As a final word on cinema, it should be mentioned that it was a source for= the promotion of *postmodernism* as an artistic-philosophical movement. As mentioned in Chapter 5, the term was coined originally by architects to designate a style that was meant to break away from an earlier modernist style (skyscrapers, tall apartment buildings, etc.) that had degenerated into sterile and monotonous formulas. Postmodern architects called for greater individuality, complexity, and eccentricity in design, along with allusions to historical symbols and patterns. Shortly after its adoption in architecture, the notion of postmodernism started to catch on more broadly, becoming a more general idea in philosophy and the arts. A well-known example of postmodern cinema is Godfrey Reggio's brilliant 1983 film *Koyaanisqatsi*—a film without words that unfolds through a series of discontinuous, narrativeless images. It is worth revisiting here briefly as an illustrative case-in-point. The film has no distinctive characters, plot, dialogue, commentary: in a word, nothing recognizable as a narrative. The camera juxtaposes contrasting images of cars on freeways, atomic blasts, litter on urban streets, people shopping in malls, housing complexes, buildings being demolished, etc. We see the world as the TV camera sees it. And it is a turgid, gloomy world indeed with no identifiable purpose or meaning. People move around like mindless robots. To bring out the insanity of a world characterized by countless cars, decaying buildings, and crowds bustling aimlessly about, Reggio incorporates the mesmerizing music of Philip Glass (b. 1937) into the movie's visual structure. The music acts as a guide to understanding the images, interpreting them tonally. We can feel the senselessness of human actions in such a world in the contrasting melodies and rhythms of Glass' music. His slow rhythms tire us with their heaviness, and his fast tempi—which accompany a demented chorus of singers chanting in the background—assault our senses. When the filmic-musical frenzy finally ends, we feel an enormous sense of relief.

In a certain sense, the whole film can be conceived of as a musical sonata with an opening part or exposition, a middle developmental section, and a final recapitulation with coda. The film starts off with a glimpse into a vastly different world—the world of the Hopi peoples of the southwestern US. This is a world firmly implanted in a holistic view of existence, a view that does not separate humans from Nature. Glass' choral music in this exposition is spiritual, sacred, and profound. It inspires reverence for the bond that links the human spirit to the physical world. This stands in dark contrast to the development of the filmic sonata—a cornucopia of dissonant images of a decaying, senseless, industrialized world. Then we are taken back, at the end, to the Hopi world. As in any recapitulation, the opening profound strains of the choir come back, hauntingly, awesomely, and with a warning this time (the coda), which is projected onto the screen:

koyaanisqatsi (from the Hopi language)

1. crazy life
2. life in turmoil
3. life out of balance
4. life disintegrating
5. a state of life that calls for another way of living

Today, postmodern movies no longer resonate in the same way they did in the latter part of the twentieth century. Nevertheless, postmodernism has left its mark in cinema. An example of its legacy is *The Matrix* (1999) and its sequel *The Matrix Reloaded* (2003), both of which struck a resounding chord with young audiences at the time brought up in a world dominated by computers. The movies exposed the artificial world of the computer screen, with intertextual allusions to the Bible. They also had a subtext—the search for a higher state of consciousness, free of objects, is ultimately what satisfies humanity. It also raises an ancient philosophical question in a kind of "neo-postmodern" style: What is truth? It is, what we make of it in our minds, seems to be the answer. The horror comes when we "lose the mind" that creates the truth.

A technical branch, called film semiotics, is traced to Christian Metz's *Film Language: A Semiotics of the Cinema* (1974) in which he compares the parts of cinema to minimal units similar to the phonemes of language. From this he concludes that filmic language is a mirror of actual language. By and large, however, the semiotic analysis of movies is an extension of literary semiotics, which is based on the structure of texts and their interconnections to cultural processes. The film is thus studied as a text with the same kinds of properties of literary texts. Eco's, *The Role of the Reader: Explorations in the Semiotics of Texts* (1979) has frequently been applied to the study of filmic texts. Eco shows that determining where the meaning of a text lies—in the author (director) or the reader (viewer)—depends on the nature of the text itself. To oversimplify Eco's argument, if we view a Hitchcock thriller, it is unlikely that we will see it as a comedic text. We grasp the purpose of genre and thus allow the text tom work on us through that genre. In his 1989 book, the *Open Work*, Eco shows that there are two main kinds of texts, called respectively *closed* and *open*. The closed text leads to a singular or fairly limited range of interpretations already built into the text by its maker (for example, detective stories). An open work, on the other hand, allows readers to make up their own minds as to what it means. Openness is, for Eco, the textual condition that leads to a free play of associations and, thus, to an aesthetic appreciation of it. Nevertheless, even in open texts, in reality the nature of the text itself and the author's intentions constrain the range of interpretations. When a given interpretation falls outside this range, we tend to see it as erroneous or implausible.

Epilogue

Perhaps nothing else differentiates human beings from all other species like art does. It is an innate faculty that allows us, from infancy on, to extract meaning from drawings, music, performances, and the like. It is a testament that we are, after all, spiritual beings searching for an explanation to the universe. Whereas science asks questions and seeks answers to the meaning of life with a blend of imaginative and logical thinking, art probes the meaning of life through the emotions. This is why the experience of art is called an aesthetic experience, and the experience of science an intellectual experience. But it would be a mistake to see the two types of probes as categorically different. Both are used by human beings to probe the same questions, in different ways.

Each major era of human civilization has practiced the arts, with specific arts dominating specific periods—theater and sculpture in antiquity, painting in the medieval and Renaissance periods, music in the seventeenth to the end of the twentieth century, etc. The question now becomes: Is there some dominant art form that characterizes the contemporary world, based on the Internet? One immediate answer that comes to mind is eclecticism—an admixture of arts and stylistic devices, such as memes, that is truly an unprecedented amalgam, with no major art form predominating. We may be in a holding pattern, waiting for our technologies to lead us to new forms of aesthetics. One thing is for certain, the art instinct will not disappear, and in fact is showing its presence everywhere even today, albeit not in many traditionally coded ways.

Digital documents can store the equivalent information of myriad paper books. Cyber-libraries are replacing traditional libraries and online bookstores are outdoing physical ones. However, at the present time, an audience for traditional print books continues to exist, because it seems that people simply enjoy reading and buying them. Purchasing books at a bookstore is a diverting and distracting experience in itself—something that bookstore chains have come to realize, as witnessed by the fact that they have joined forces with coffee chains and other businesses. The market for paper-based print materials such as magazines and newspapers also continues to exist, even though digital versions are replacing the paper versions. This kind of eclecticism can be seen for movies, theater, and the other arts.

The growth of social media technology in the mid-2000s also allowed everyone to express their artistic talents though cyberspace. Social media systems such as Facebook, Twitter, and Instagram have allowed anyone to interact with anyone else in the world, and they have become platforms for visual artists, musicians, writers, etc. to showcase themselves. There is a new "stage" for the artists—cyberspace. Clearly, the advent of the Internet has had, and continues to have, enormous implications for how we carry out interpersonal, group, and mass communications, as well as how we develop our artistic talents. The Internet Galaxy is expanding human potential literally at the speed of light—hopefully it will not get lost in the light.

8
The Mind

The mind is not a vessel to be filled but a fire to be kindled.

Plutarch (c. 46-120 CE))

Prologue

Semiotics is defined broadly as a science of signs. It studies the structure, formation, uses, and typologies of signs and sign systems, including texts and codes. But ultimately, studying signs is tantamount to studying the mind that makes them, uses them, and is guided by them—which is, as discussed, semiosis. So, in a fundamental sense, semiotics is a study of the mind, as Saussure himself understood when he located semiology as a branch of psychology (Saussure 1916).

We hardly realize the presence of unconscious semiotic mechanisms that manifest themselves in the words and phrases used during conversations, in written texts, in kinesic and proxemic behaviors, and so on. Traditionally, the study of these mechanisms has come under the rubric of psychology. But then, as Saussure indicated, semiotics is a branch of psychology providing it with unique analytical tools for investigating the mind through semiosis. The semiotic approach is, however, an interdisciplinary one itself, aiming to understand how the mechanisms of thought are intertwined with verbal and nonverbal signs, and thus carries out its examination of the mind with insights derived from linguistics, psychology, anthropology, cultural studies and other human sciences and humanities. This chapter provides a schematic overview of the study of mind, starting with philosophy (itself linked to semiotics since antiquity, as discussed previously), and then profiling major approaches in psychology and Evolutionary Psychology. In each section, we will glean the relevant semiotic insights, or else apply the work in the different fields to the study of semiosis in a general way. The next chapter will then deal with human attempts to "construct" the mind, focusing on cybernetics and Artificial Intelligence as tools for doing so. Given the world in which we live, these are extremely important topics on which semiotics can help shed important light.

Interest in the enigma of the human mind is as old as recorded history. The Greek historian Herodotus claimed, in his *Historia,* that Egyptians thought differently from Greeks because they wrote from right to left, rather than from left to right, as did the Greeks. Herodotus seems to have understood two implicit things with this assertion which prefigure the discipline of semiotics: first, access to how the mind works is via its semiotic artifacts, such as writing; and second, the mind is not a rigid entity; it is shaped by situational factors, including cultural ones. A similar view was articulated by the fourteenth century Algerian scholar Ibn Khaldun, who wrote a truly fascinating treatise in which he noted that the subtle mental and behavioral differences that existed between nomadic and city-dwelling Bedouins were due to their differences in vocabulary and in how they used language to think about reality.

Philosophy

As John Deely (2001) has cogently argued, semiotics and philosophy emerged in tandem in antiquity, although, as we saw in Chapter 1, semiotics came eventually to awareness to philosophers, such as John Locke (1690), as a tool of philosophy, rather than a synonym for it. The ancient philosophers were among the first to discuss the relation between the body, the senses, and mentation, using a dialectic method—a method of posing questions and seeking answers in order to discover truths. One of the first to use dialectal reasoning was Zeno of Elea (fifth century BCE). Although the universe may appear diversified to our mind, Zeno argued, it exists as a single, undifferentiated substance.

Socrates (c. 470-399 BCE) taught that everyone was born with a full understanding of truth, and that this could be accessed through conscious reflection. His view was an early example of what is now called innatism, which holds that we are born with inherent knowledge that is drawn out through specific observations or experiences. In the *Meno*, a Socratic dialogue written by Plato) Socrates leads an individual to successfully grasp a complicated geometrical problem by getting him to reflect upon the truths hidden within him through a series of questions designed to elicit specific answers. Plato went further in stressing that every human being comes equipped at birth with innate "ideal forms" of understanding. These can be exemplified with geometry. A triangle, for instance, is an "ideal form" which is inherent in the mind. When geometers define a triangle as three straight lines that are connected to form three angles, they are referring, in effect, to the innate concept of "triangularity." An object may thus be called a "triangle" insofar as it resembles this innate concept. Plato thus separated physical experience from the mind, claiming that the body exists in the physical world, whereas the mind exists in the immortal world of ideas.

Plato's own pupil, Aristotle, criticized his teacher's dualism, maintaining that the mind cannot be separated from the body's activities and feelings. Aristotle also provided the first theory of logical thinking with his concept of the *syllogism*, a mode of thinking based on connecting premises, such as the following to each other, which lead inescapably to a conclusion:

1. All mammals are warm-blooded.
2. All cats are mammals.
3. Therefore, all cats are warm-blooded.

We perceive this as valid because the premises are connected logically. The skeletal structure of the logic involved can be shown as follows:

1. All A are B.
2. All C are A.
3. Therefore, all C are B.

One does not need to use syllogistic argumentation to accept this as true, though. Common sense tells us that this is so. However, common sense does not show us the validity of the logic behind the reasoning involved. In effect, the syllogism was the first theory of the rational mind. Among the first to discuss a possible relationship between the syllogism and the actual make-up of the mind were the so-called Stoics, around 308 BCE, who argued, additionally, that our signs—words and symbols—revealed how human thinking unfolded. For centuries thereafter, in the medieval period, little was written about the mind by philosophers, who concentrated instead on theological matters. It was in the Renaissance that debates about the nature of mind separate from religious views emerged. English philosopher and statesman, Francis Bacon (1561-1626) criticized Aristotelian logic on the grounds that it was futile for the discovery of how we gain knowledge of reality—it was just an exercise in reasoning. By the seventeenth and eighteenth centuries, philosophers such as Thomas Hobbes (1588-1679), René Descartes (1596-1650), Benedict Spinoza (1632-1677), David Hume (1711-1776), John Locke (1632-1704), and George Berkeley (1685-1753), among others, revisited the Platonic mind-body problem from different perspectives. In his book, *De Homine* (1633), Descartes gave the problem a new formulation, known as dualism, which maintains that the two are distinct entities. Descartes suggested that the body worked like a machine that was animated by "animal spirits" flowing through the nervous system and that the pineal gland was the "seat of thought" and thus the location of the mind. When the gland became aware of the animal spirits it stimulated conscious sensations. The mind could thus double back on the body by instigating the flow of the animal spirits to a particular part, activating it as the case may require. Contemporary neuroscience has largely dismissed Descartes' "error," as psychologist Antonio Damasio (1994) termed it. But Cartesian dualism is still a subtle factor in some models of the mind, as we shall see in the next chapter.

The mind-body problem became a central one in subsequent centuries. Immanuel Kant (1724-1804), for instance, claimed to have solved it by suggesting that the mind imposed form and order on all its sensory experiences, and that this unfolded *a priori* by reflection, and thus that the body and the mind were cooperative contributors to thinking (Kant 1790). Georg Wilhelm Friedrich Hegel (1770-1831) argued that logic governed human actions, rather than impulses and sensory intuitions, which required a different model of mentality for understanding their relation to logic (Hegel 1907). Friedrich Nietzsche (1844-1900) led the Romantic revolt against the view that reason ??? Edmund Husserl (1859-1938) went further than any of his predecessors in stressing the bodily basis of all cognition. Husserl's approach is known as *phenomenology*, which aims to understand the bodily structures of experience as they present themselves to consciousness (Husserl 1890). Alfred North Whitehead (1861-1947) revived the Platonic theory of forms (Whitehead 1929), while Martin Heidegger (1889-1976) combined the phenomenological approach of Husserl to understand how the mind comes to perceive and classify the world of objects (Heidegger 1976).

In traditional philosophy, the main debate has revolved around the mind as either a separate entity from the body or a derivative of sensation. In effect, it studied semiosis indirectly, or directly in the case of Charles Peirce (1931-1958), as we saw. Although this is somewhat reductive, it is also correct to say that human semiosis requires the interaction of body and mind. We will return to this below.

Psychology

It was toward the end of the nineteenth century when, as Flanagan (1984: xi) has aptly remarked, the perception was forged that the musings of philosophers were to be viewed as no more than "harmless amusements of fundamentally unrealistic minds," and that a scientific approach to the mind, was required. The new science was *psychology*—a term that had existed previously, but was revived with a precise new designation, namely as a science of mind.

It was Wilhelm Wundt (1832–1920) who founded the first "laboratory" of experimental psychology in 1879 in Leipzig, following up on Darwin's suggestion that humans and animals are linked by evolution and that consciousness can be studied as an organic principle of life, rather than as some enigmatic "animal spirit," as Descartes called it (Wundt 1880, 1901). Wundt's laboratory inspired universities in Europe and America to set up similar programs in psychology. Among his students were Edward Titchener (1867-1927) and James Cattell (1860-1944), both of whom are now considered early founders of the discipline, alongside Wundt. One of the most important insights put forward by Wundt was that the mind was not only a product of evolution, but also of culture, which, as we have argued throughout this book, is a fundamental axiom of semiotics.

In 1895, Conway Lloyd Morgan published the first textbook of psychology, *Introduction to Comparative Psychology*, in which he summarized the goals and methods of the fledgling science. A few years later, Edward Lee Thorndike, wrote a highly influential treatise, *Animal Intelligence* (1898), that outlined the methods for conducting laboratory experiments with animals. At the turn of the twentieth century, Ivan Pavlov (1902) introduced the theory of classical conditioning. As is well known, Pavlov presented a piece of meat to a hungry dog, producing the expected response of salivation. He called this the "unconditioned response," since it is part of instinctual behavior. Then Pavlov rang a bell at the same time that he presented the meat stimulus a number of times. He discovered that the dog eventually salivated only to the ringing of the bell, without the presence of the meat stimulus. Clearly, the bell ringing, which would not have triggered the salivation instinctively, had brought about a "conditioned response" in the dog. In follow-up work, it was assumed that if certain activities and behaviors occurred in animals, then they had parallels in humans, albeit in more complicated ways. In other words, the tacit goal of early psychology was to figure out the nature of human intelligence via experiments with other species—a viewpoint was taken up somewhat by Evolutionary Psychology (below). In the twentieth century, psychology underwent three main revolutions—behaviorism, Gestalt psychology, and cognitivism. Based on Pavlov's work, behaviorism became the main school of psychology from the 1920s to the 1960s. The movement was actually founded before Pavlov by William James (1890) and then developed by Edward Thorndike (1905), John B. Watson (1913), Edward Tolman (1932), and B. F. Skinner (1938). Thorndike continued the comparative method, introducing the notion of "instrumental conditioning" with his maze experiments that became a hallmark of behaviorism generally. Thorndike's mazes, called "puzzle boxes," allowed him to observe how an animal, such as a cat, devised a way out of the box in order to reap the reward of food. The box could only be opened by the animal with a latch, which would eventually discover its function through trial and error. From these experiments, Thorndike put forth a "Law of Effect" which claimed that any behavior that is followed by a reward is likely to be repeated, whereas any behavior followed by unpleasant consequences is likely to be discontinued.

William James introduced the notion of "stream of consciousness," as a flow of personal thoughts that occurs below the threshold of consciousness. This led outside of psychology to a style of fiction designed to reveal a character's feelings and thoughts as they unfolded in everyday actions. Major exponents of this style were American novelist William Faulkner (1897-1962), British writer Virginia Woolf (1882-1941), and Irish writer James Joyce (1882-1941), who brought the technique to its apex in *Ulysses* (1922) and *Finnegans Wake* (1939). Consciousness thus stems from the combination of separate thoughts, much like the meaning of a sentence inheres not in its separate words, but in the syntax that unites them.

Edward Tolman also used mazes with rats to examine how reinforcement through rewards unfolded. He discovered that the rats used more than trial and error to find their way to the maze to the food reward. He suggested that they developed a "cognitive map," of the box after an initial trial-and-error period, even when no rewards were to be attained at the end. In other words, Tolman discovered that animals extract ideas from experience and use them to conduct subsequent tasks. He called this kind of behavior "latent," since it occurs without any reinforcement of the behavior that was learned previously. B. F. Skinner developed behaviorist theory further by adding the individual's interactions with the environment as crucial determinants to learning and thinking. Like previous behaviorists, Skinner also used boxes to carry out experiments. Called "Skinner boxes," these were enclosed containers where an animal could press a bar or key in order to obtain food or water as a reward. Calling this "operant conditioning," Skinner concluded from his experiments that some form of reinforcement was crucial in learning new behaviors.

At the same time that behaviorism was spreading as a mainstream paradigm in the early twentieth century, psychoanalysis, spearheaded by Sigmund Freud (1856-1939), emerged to examine the stream-of-consciousness notion more concretely. Freud renamed it the "unconscious," defining it as the region of the mind containing our hidden wishes, memories, fears, feelings, and ingrained ideas that are prevented from gaining expression by the conscious part of the mind (Freud 1901). So, they manifest themselves instead by their influence in dreams, works of art, and symbols. Freud devised his term in contrast to the term *subconscious,* which was coined by French psychologist Pierre Janet (1893), which he thought was too vague. Freud suggested that the unconscious had a biological origin and that culture was a collective system that emerged to regulate and constrain unconscious sexual urges. The Swiss psychologist Carl Jung (1983) saw Freud's interpretation of the unconscious as too narrow. He accepted Freud's basic idea, but he divided the unconscious into two regions: a *personal unconscious*, containing the feelings and thoughts developed by an individual that are directive of particular life schemes, and a *collective unconscious*, containing the feelings and thoughts developed cumulatively by the species that are directive of its overall evolution. Jung described the latter as a "receptacle" of primordial images shared by all humanity that have become such an intrinsic part of the psyche as to be beyond reflection. So, they gain expression instead in the symbols, myths, tales, rituals, etc. that are found in cultures across the world. He called these *archetypes*. Both Freud and Jung have been of special interest to semiotics, because both deal with the origin, evolution, and formation of symbols. Archetypes are thus based on oppositional structure: *male*-versus-*female*, *hero*-versus-*trickster*, etc.

Another line of psychological inquiry that became especially relevant to semiotics was Gestalt psychology, which emerged between 1910 and the mid-1940s. It was developed early on by Max Wertheimer (1923), Kurt Koffka (1921), and Wolfgang Köhler (1925). The Gestalt psychologists emphasized the study of mind and experience as a unified whole, not as the result of isolated stimuli and responses, emphasizing the relation between the perception of form to knowledge—a fundamental principle of semiotics as well. Two Gestalt principles in particular, known as closure and figure-ground perception, are now basic ones within psychology and semiotics generally. The former explains why we perceive a fragmented circle as a complete circle and the latter why we tend to regard any kind of pattern as a figure against a background (such as words on a page).

In the late 1950s and early 1960s, Gestalt psychology ignited a related, but autonomous, movement, called cognitivism. The term *cognition*, rather than *mind* or *behavior*, was introduced in order to eliminate the artificial distinction maintained by behaviorists between inner (mental) and observable (behavioral) processes. A key early work in cognitive psychology was George Miller's 1956 study, which showed that the ability to process bits of information was limited to between 5 and 9 equally-weighted choices. The implication was that there is a limit to how much novel information we can grasp and remember, if there are no previous cognitive maps for it, as Tolman called them. Another key work was Edward Tulving's (1972) division of memory into episodic and semantic systems. The former specifies and stores past events as "episodes." It is useful for getting on with the practical matters of life—recognizing faces, friends, family members, telephone numbers, etc. The semantic memory system, on the other hand, is involved in providing concepts in the form of language and other symbol systems.

One of the first cognitive psychologists to study the development of mind in childhood was the French psychologist Jean Piaget (1969, Piaget and Inhelder 1969). The main stages of development that Piaget posited—sensory-motor, concrete operations, formal-logical thinking—are now accepted broadly as the primary milestones that follow in sequence in the cognitive growth of the child, and these have been sued by semioticians to map the progress of semiosic patterns as well. But the psychologist who is perceived broadly as a founder of psychological semiotics, is the Russian psychologist Lev Vygotsky (1961), who worked on childhood development in the 1930s. It was the translation of his book, *Language and Thought*, in 1961 that made his ideas known more broadly. Vygotsky proposed developmental stages that go from external (physical and social) actions toward internal cognitive constructions and interior speech. His definition of speech as a "microcosm of consciousness" is particularly reflective of this.

As cognitive psychology became mainstream, it started adopting insights and terms from the emerging science of AI. Cognitivists began to study the mind by seeking parallels between the functions of the human brain and those of the computer. Ulrich Neisser (1967: 6) put it as follows:

> The task of the psychologist in trying to understand human cognition is analogous to that of a man trying to discover how a computer has been programmed. In particular, if the program seems to store and reuse information, he would like to know by what "routines" or "procedures" this is done. Given this purpose, he will not care much whether his particular computer stores information in magnetic cores or in thin films; he wants to understand the program, not the "hardware." By the same token, it would not help the psychologist to know that memory is carried by RNA as opposed to some other medium. He wants to understand its utilization, not its incarnation.

Neisser realized, however, that the computer metaphor, if brought to an extreme, would actually lead psychology astray. So, only a few pages later he issued the following warning (Neisser 1967: 9): "Unlike men, artificially intelligent programs tend to be single-minded, undistractable, and unemotional; in my opinion, none does even remote justice to the complexity of mental processes." As cognitive psychology progressed throughout the 1970s, eventually it came to be transformed by the insights coming out of AI, leading to the emergence of *cognitive science*, as a new science of the mind, as will be discussed in the next chapter.

Neuroscience

Early on in the nineteenth century, psychology formed a partnership with the science of brain functioning, which later came to be called *neuroscience*. It was the Hippocratic physicians around 400 BCE who developed the first scientific notions of brain structure. The Greek physician Galen (c. 130-200 CE) subsequently claimed that the brain was the primary organ for all human sensations and emotions and that it carried out its functions in specific ways. The first attempts to develop a classification system for assigning mental functions to specific cerebral sites, however, had to await the fifteenth century and sixteenth centuries. Unfortunately, most of those attempts were based on speculation rather than on empirical evidence. It was believed, for instance, that the functions were localized in different ventricles—the internal cavities of brain tissue. Known as *phrenology*, this type of speculation was discarded in 1861, when the French anthropologist and neurologist Pierre-Paul Broca (1824-1880) published a paper linking a specific area in the left hemisphere of the brain to aphasia. Broca noticed a destructive lesion in the left frontal lobe during the autopsy of a patient who had lost the ability to articulate words during his lifetime, even though he had not suffered any paralysis of his speech organs. Broca concluded that the capacity to articulate speech was thus traceable to that specific cerebral site—which shortly thereafter came to bear his name (*Broca's area*). That was the watershed discovery that established, once and for all, a direct link between a mental capacity and a specific area of the brain. For the sake of historical accuracy, it should be mentioned that the military surgeon Marc Dax had presented similar evidence in 1836 at the Congrès Méridional de Montpellier, relating a destructive lesion in the left hemisphere (LH) to language loss. However, his paper was never published. And in the same year of 1836, a Scottish physician named John Abercrombie published a paper in which he associated LH damage with verbal deficits. However, it is Broca to whom history has conferred the distinction of being the first to make an empirically-based connection between an area of the brain and a cognitive function.

Right after Broca's discovery, the study of aphasias became the basis for mapping the brain's cognitive sites. If damage to a specific cerebral site brought about a specific type of impairment, then the site could be inferred to control the function in question in healthy brains. Thirteen years after Broca's discovery, in 1874, the German neurologist Carl Wernicke (1848-1904) published further evidence linking the LH to language. Wernicke documented cases in which damage to another area of the LH consistently produced a recognizable pattern of impairment to the faculty of speech comprehension. Damage to the left temporal lobe impairs the ability to find words and name objects and things—a syndrome known as *anomic aphasia*. Then, in 1892 the physiologist Jules Déjerine published findings showing that reading and writing deficits resulted primarily from damage to areas surrounding both Broca's and Wernicke's areas.

In 1929, the American psychologist Karl Lashley (1890-1958) claimed that while the origin of a particular function can perhaps be traced to a specific brain site, its overall modality (manifestation and characteristics) involved other sites. In the 1930s, Vygotsky argued, further, that language in a restricted sense—that is, as sounds, words, and grammatical categories—did indeed have a primary locus in the LH; but as a communicative-expressive modality it was more likely to arise from various synaptic connections that were distributed throughout the brain. Vygotsky suggested, moreover, that the whole brain, not just one hemisphere, was endowed at birth with a unique kind of "plasticity" that rendered it highly sensitive and adaptive to stimuli during childhood. Therefore, he put forward the intriguing proposal that neural processes were constantly being subjected to modifying influences from rearing and other kinds of environmental factors. The brain, Vygotsky argued, was hardly a "hard-wired" mechanism; on the contrary, it was a highly adaptable and plastic organ.

During the 1950s, the so-called split-brain patient studies—known more technically as commisurotomy patients—involving epilepsy victims who had had their two hemispheres separated by surgical section of the corpus callosum in order to attenuate the seizures they tended to suffer. Each of their hemispheres could thus be "investigated," in isolation by simply presenting stimuli in an asymmetrical fashion. The studies provided a detailed breakdown of the main functions according to hemisphere. And by extension, they suggested that in the "intact brain" both hemispheres were needed in a neurologically-cooperative way to produce complex thinking. By the mid-1970s, neuroscientists started developing a host of non-clinical techniques to investigate the brains of normal subjects. Today, technologies such as *Positron emission tomography* (PET) and *functional magnetic resonance imaging* (fMRI) have enabled neuroscientists to observe the brain directly while people carry out cognitive tasks. These are particularly useful because they do not require any physical contact with the brain. They produce images that show which parts of the brain are active while a person carries out a particular mental or physical function. The PET and fMRI studies are now confirming that language processing is extremely complex, rather than involving a series of subsystems (phonology, grammar, etc.) located in specific parts of the brain. The neuronal structures involved are spread widely throughout the brain, primarily by neurotransmitters, and it now appears certain that different types of language tasks activate different areas of the brain in many sequences and patterns. It has also become apparent that language is regulated, additionally, by the emotional areas of the brain. The limbic system—which includes portions of the temporal lobes, parts of the hypothalamus and thalamus, and other structures—has been found to play a larger role than previously thought in the processing of certain kinds of speech (Damasio 1994).

Without going into details of current work in neuroscience that have implications for semiotics, suffice it to say that it has led to an understanding of how semiosis unfolds in the brain. Recalling blending theory in Chapter 6, for example, neuroscience has shown how different areas of the brain interact to produce cognitive states, manifested by metaphor. It has shown, in other words, that the body is in the mind, as Johnson (1987) has aptly put it, namely that signs and their formation involve areas that regulate sensory processes. In effect, semiosis is a "whole-brain" process.

Evolutionary Psychology

In the 1970s a movement emerged, called *Evolutionary Psychology* (EP) by Michael Ghiselin in 1973—a term that was spread broadly a little later by Jerome Barkow, Leda Cosmides, and John Tooby in their 1992 book, *The Adapted Mind: Evolutionary Psychology and the Generation of Culture.* EP is now a major branch of psychology, aiming to study how evolution has shaped the human mind and human behavior. Within EP, biology and culture are seen as co-partners in human evolution. EP is actually an offshoot of *sociobiology*, defined as the study of the biological aspects of social behavior in animals and humans.

The key figure behind sociobiology was the North American biologist E. O. Wilson (1975, 1979, 1984), known for his work tracing the effects of natural selection on biological communities, especially on populations of insects, and for extending the idea of natural selection to human cultures. Wilson maintains that social behaviors in humans are genetically based and that evolutionary processes favor those behaviors that enhance reproductive success and survival. Thus, characteristics such as heroism, altruism, aggressiveness, and dominance should be understood as evolutionary outcomes, not in terms of social or cultural processes. Moreover, Wilson sees the creative capacities undergirding language, art, scientific thinking, myth, etc. as originating in genetic responses that help the human organism survive and continue the species. As he has stated rather bluntly, "no matter how far culture may take us, the genes have culture on a leash" (Wilson and Harris 1981: 464).

Largely in response to sociobiology, the movement in semiotics known as *biosemiotics*, which traces its roots to von Uexküll (1909), as discussed previously, but which came into distinct disciplinary focus in the 1980s and 1990s (Kull 1999). According to the biosemiotics movement, sociobiology has ignored the role of semiosis in the development of mind and of culture, as an interaction between the biosphere and the semiosphere. Conscious social behaviors are, of course, partially based in biology; but they are not totally so. Genetic factors alone do not completely define human beings. They tell us nothing about why humans create their meaningful experiences and pose the questions they do about life.

According to the basic sociobiological paradigm, an organism inherits tendencies to develop certain types of behavior, which increase the organism's chances of transmitting its genes to the next generation. For example, Wilson used the case of a worker bee who will sting an intruder to protect the hive—an act that kills the worker bee but protects the queen bee, which has many of the same genes. The queen bee will thus be better able to pass on these genes to her offspring. So, the more closely two animals are related genetically, the more likely one is to sacrifice itself to protect the other. Wilson speculates that such self-sacrificing behavior in human beings may also have a genetic basis—it allows humans to carry out acts of sacrifice and altruism in the service of species survival. But, as biosemioticians maintain, by and large, there is no genetic evidence that social and psychological evolution is guided strictly by survival mechanisms—this model is speculation.

EP differentiates itself from sociobiology, by focusing on the evolutionary history of mind states, proposing in some ways that there may not even be a mind, which is a philosophical construct. EP focuses on genetic processes as generative of mental and cultural forms of existence. It views the mind as having the same modular structure of the body, with different adaptations serving different functions. It is based on four core principles (Buss 2004):

1. The brain is an information-processing device that translates external inputs into behavioral outputs.
2. The brain's adaptive mechanisms are the result of natural and sexual selection.
3. The brain has evolved specialized mechanisms to solve recurring problems of survival, which have remained part of the triune brain.
4. Most neural processes are unconscious and these enter automatically into the resolution of the problems.

There is no need to enter into the many debates that EP has spawned, nor whether it is just speculation, rather than science. Suffice it to say here that the above principles are valid insofar as they explain the connection between inputs and the brain. However, the mind is more than the brain. And semiosis is the link between the two. Biosemiotics takes many of its insights from the ideas of Peirce. One of these is how evolution is characterized by three modes, which he called tychasm, anancasm, and agapasm (Peirce 1931-1958, volume 6: 302-303):

> Three modes of evolution have thus been brought before us: evolution by fortuitous variation, evolution by mechanical necessity, and evolution by creative love. We may term them tychastic evolution, or tychasm, anancastic evolution, or anancasm, and agapastic evolution, or agapasm…All three modes of evolution are composed of the same general elements. Agapasm exhibits them the most clearly. The good result is here brought to pass, first, by the bestowal of spontaneous energy by the parent upon the offspring, and, second, by the disposition of the latter to catch the general idea of those about it and thus to subserve the general purpose.

Tychism holds that absolute chance is a real factor operative in evolution. This stands in contrast to positions such as the EP one, which fall into the doctrine of necessity, which claims that "the state of things existing at any time, together with certain immutable laws, completely determine the state of things at every other time." Peirce attacks this idea asserting: "To postulate a proposition is no more than to hope it is true" (Peirce 1931-1958, volume 6: 339-360). Of course, Peirce does not deny that there are laws in the universe; rather, that there are regularities and irregularities, but the law themselves develop from chance. Peirce explains the difference between anancasm and agapism as follows (Peirce 1931-1958, volume 6: 312-313):

> Anancastic evolution advances by successive strides with pauses between. The reason is that, in this process, a habit of thought, having been overthrown, is supplanted by the next strongest. Now this next strongest is sure to be widely disparate from the first, and as often as not is its direct contrary. It reminds one of our old rule of making the second candidate vice-president. This character, therefore, clearly distinguishes anancasm from tychasm. The character which distinguishes it from agapasm is its purposelessness. But external and internal anancasm have to be examined separately. Development under the pressure of external circumstances, or cataclasmine evolution, is in most cases unmistakable enough.

To examine evolution, paradoxically, a theory is required, because it cannot be investigated empirically in any real way; but the theory is itself part of evolution—hence its tychistic nature. As von Uexküll (1909) cogently argued, it is unlikely that we will ever be able to "know" how we ourselves have developed our ability to "know."

Meme Theory

Within sociobiology, the notion of *memes,* devised by Richard Dawkins (1976, 1985, 1987, 1998), has been used as a means to understand the evolution of mind. A meme is a unit of information that is passed on in cultural environments in order to enhance survivability and promote progress by replacing the functions of genes (chapter 1). Memes are replicating patterns of information (ideas, laws, clothing fashions, artworks, tunes, and so on) and of behavior (marriage rites, courtship rituals, religious ceremonies, and so on) that people inherit directly from their cultural environments. Like genes, memes involve no intentionality on the part of the receiving human being, who takes them in unreflectively from birth, passing them on just as unreflectively to subsequent generations through subsequent progeny. The *memetic code* has thus emerged in human life to complement the *genetic code,* directing human evolution in a co-evolutionary partnership. In a phrase, memes have emerged from evolution in order to help human beings cope with their particular form of consciousness, thus enhancing their collective ability to survive as a species. It is to be noted that many EP researchers avoid explicit use of the term *meme*, seeing it as non-scientific. But its meaning is everywhere to be found in EP science, named under various different rubrics, but all having in common the idea that the memetic code is, in fact, responsible for the transmission and entrenchment of concepts.

That said, the term meme as it is used today refers to ideas that do indeed circulate randomly—in cyberspace. Called an *internet meme*, it is a type of meme that is spread via the Internet and social media platforms, among other digital channels. The name is an apt one because meme theory involves replication which, with each replica being actually modified, produces a new memetic form, much like genetic transmission. So a meme can be changed for reasons of parody or as part of a mashup. It can also be combined with other memes to produce increasingly larger structures, in an intertextual way. The intertextuality in this case has nothing to do with established texts, but with memetic texts that have been created a-historically. So, an Internet meme may stay the same or evolve over time, by chance or through some modification. Internet memes spread extremely rapidly, forming a kind of semiotic backbone to the structure of the Internet—a backbone that is hardly based on the representation of established meanings. Some claim, therefore, that cyberspace and its meme structure might be changing—or mutating—human evolution, producing a form of consciousness where anything that appears in cyberspace is believable, whether or not it is real or true, at least for a short period of time. In this space, information becomes a premium in itself, diminishing the capacity to decode it critically or reflectively.

The increasing use of irony in memetic propagation has resulted in new bizarre forms of postmodern art, implying that new memes cannot be understood without reference to previous memes—producing an art of the immediate moment. The implications for the future of semiosis and meaning-making are significant. The difference between the notion of code in semiotics and a memetic code involves meaningfulness. Memes have a short life, whereas ideas from the arts, science, etc., if found to be meaningful, will transcend the instantaneity of trending factors, Memetic theory might explain the "contagious" spread of something through the Internet, but it fails to explain why memes have a short life, whereas certain important ideas and movements do not.

Epilogue

Dawkins' (1976: 192) initial definition of meme is worth repeating here, by way of summing up the discussion in this chapter:

> I think that a new replicator has recently emerged on this very planet. It is still in its infancy, still drifting clumsily about in its primeval soup of human culture. We need a name for this new replicator, a noun that conveys the idea of a unit of cultural transmission, or a unit of imitation. 'Mimeme' comes from a suitable Greek root, but I want a monosyllable that sounds a bit like 'gene.' I hope my classicist friends will forgive me if I abbreviate mimeme to *meme*. If it is any consolation, it could alternatively be thought of as being related to 'memory,' or the French word *meme*.

Dawkins goes on to portray memes as parasites, viruses, or other "selfish" organisms—a figurative lexicon that is now includes terms such as *meme infection, allergy, immune-depressant*, and the like. What this shows is that in order to coin a concept, such as meme, it must one connected to other ones metaphorically, as discussed in Chapter 6. So, meme theory is its own conceptual metaphor theory of the mind. Memetic culture is hardly a real culture in the sense of a network of signs that cohere into the semiosphere, but rather an artificial culture that comes and goes at random.

The different approaches to the study of mind discussed rapidly here, and their implications for the study of semiosis, lead us back to Saussure's original notion that semiotics is a branch of psychology, and indeed may be its major theoretical tool. For semioticians, the age-old quest to understand the mind equals the quest to understand semiosis. Signs shape us in every way imaginable. But they do not imprison us cognitively or creatively. Even though particular kinds of signs influence how we perceive reality, they can also be used as "tools of discovery," revealing that, perhaps, we use signs as part of a system of awareness of what reality is all about that is unique to our species. The *raison d'être* of semiotics is, arguably, to investigate whether or not reality can exist independently of the signs that human beings create to represent and think about it. The languages, myths, narratives, rituals, art works, etc. that humans have invented are hardly simple products of genetic processes or of memetic codes—they are attempts to understand ourselves. As Charles Peirce often suggested, as a species, we are programmed to "think only in signs."

9
Artificial Minds

The development of full artificial intelligence could spell the end of the human race....It would take off on its own, and re-design itself at an ever increasing rate. Humans, who are limited by slow biological evolution, couldn't compete, and would be superseded.

Stephen Hawking (1942-2018)

Prologue

In the previous chapter, we looked at theories of the human mind, extracting implications for semiotics, arguing that semiotics is itself a theory of mind. Semiosis defines the mind; without it the mind would function like a computer, generating signs that it would not consciously recognize as bearing meanings. But, then, what would an artificial mind, built into a computer, be like? Is it possible to truly construct artificial minds?

These questions are no longer just speculative one. Artificial minds are everywhere today—in homes, in automobiles, in wearable devices, and in other technologies. The smartphone, for instance, is an Artificial Intelligence (AI) system in a box—a box that would have been considered magical not too long ago. It is even capable of making features in its interface resemble real-world objects, thus improving their recognizability and usability. AI-based technologies have become, in a word, intrinsic to modern life, used in everything from medicine to manufacturing. This aspect of AI can be called, simply, *practical*, since it is designed to help humans carry out asks efficiently and economically. The use of AI to simulate or reproduce the faculties of the human mind can instead be called, *theoretical*. It is this latter type that is of concern in this chapter, which will look at the implications that AI, cybernetics, and other mind-constructing efforts entail, and the kinds of philosophical movements into which they fall. As in the previous chapter, the goal here is to extract insights for semiotics as well as to evaluate trends in the field from a semiotic perspective.

Actually, several branches of semiotics have emerged to study artificial semiosis, called *computer semiotics, cybersemiotics,* and *finite semiotics*. The first one looks at computer programs and algorithms, in order to identify: (a) properties that make human semiosis unique, based on experience and historical forces and thus not programmable in its entirety (Andersen 1997); (b) the nature of human-computer interactions (2008); and (c) utilizing computer programming as a means for evaluating models of the sign (Tanaka-Ishii 2010). Cybersemiotics (Brier 2005) examines cybernetics in semiotic terms, especially as it relates to biosemiotics. And finite semiotics (Shackell 2018, 2019) looks at the broader issues of semiosis in terms of machine intelligence and the importance of rephrasing core concepts in semiotics in terms of computational theories of mind and research in AI.

Research in theoretical AI has become very sophisticated. It is even anticipated that in the next few decades it will generate a "super intelligence." In his 2005 book, *The Singularity is Near*, inventor Ray Kurzweil maintained that there will come a moment in time when AI will have progressed to a point that it will autonomously outperform human intelligence. That moment, known as the *technological singularity*, will occur when an upgradable software becomes self-sufficient without human intervention, thus becoming capable of self-improvements. Each new self-improvement will bring about an intelligence explosion that will, in turn, lead to a powerful artificial super-intelligence that will surpass human intelligence. Kurzweil predicts that the Singularity should occur around 2045, when AI technologies will be so advanced—he predicts—that they cannot be stopped by human intervention (see also Kurzweil 1999, 2012).

The idea of a singularity can actually be traced back to a comment made by mathematician John van Neumann, cited by Stanislas Ulam (1958: 5): "[The] ever accelerating progress of technology and changes in the mode of human life, which gives the appearance of approaching some essential singularity in the history of the race beyond which human affairs, as we know them, could not continue." Then, in a 1965 article, mathematician I. J. Good predicted that eventually an ultraintelligent machine would trigger an intelligence explosion (Good 1965: 31):

> Let an ultraintelligent machine be defined as a machine that can far surpass all the intellectual activities of any man however clever. Since the design of machines is one of these intellectual activities, an ultraintelligent machine could design even better machines; there would then unquestionably be an 'intelligence explosion,' and the intelligence of man would be left far behind. Thus the first ultraintelligent machine is the last invention that man need ever make.

In 1981, writer Vernor Vinge popularized Good's ideas, using the term *singularity* in his novella *True Names*. He followed this up with a 1993 article in which he maintained that the singularity would become a reality in the first part of the twenty-first century. Clearly, the research in artificial minds has deep implications for semiotics, since it raises the main questions of semiotics, philosophy, and psychology: What is the mind? What is meaning? What is intelligence? This chapter is to look at these questions in a general way.

Artificial Intelligence

The discussion of AI here will necessarily be reductive and highly selective, given the amplitude and range of the field today and its enormous implications for the future of humanity. Our goal here is simply to select a few themes that are of relevance to semiotics in a general way.

AI is implanted on two versions: (a) the creation of computer algorithms to test models of knowledge and of brain functioning, called the "weak" version, which aims to shed light on how the human mind does what it does indirectly, by observing how artificial simulations of it work or do not work; and (b) the "strong" version, which claims that all human mental faculties and activities, including perception, emotions, and social behavior, are not only representable in the form of algorithms, but that machines themselves can be built to think, feel, and socialize. The weak version of AI is really an exercise in semiotic analysis, since it focuses on modeling something in a particular way. Like the semiotician, AI researchers ask a fundamental question: How can we best represent or model phenomenon X? As a trivial, yet useful, example, consider how factoring in algebra could be modeled algorithmically—as, for instance, factoring the expression $2x + 4y + 16z$. The instructions to the computer would include sequential steps such as the following:

1. Check for factors in all symbols.
2. Define factors: numerals or letters that are recurrent
3. Extract the factors.
4. Move them to the front.
5. Add parenthesis to the remaining symbols in front and in back.

The operation of the instructions would then produce the required output: $2(x + 2y +$

8*z*). This is, needless to say, an outline model of factoring itself and a highly reduced one. Nonetheless, the idea of sequential structure, which (as discussed) is a syntagmatic function of sign and text creation, alongside steps in which specific symbol selections were involved (a paradigmatic function) by extension, is, all-told, a semiotic one. As such, the algorithm is a form of knowledge representation in a specific domain. The difference semiotics and AI is that in the former the focus is on how meaning and interpretation are involved in the modeling, whereas in the latter, the system simply follows input instructions, created by humans. The strong version involves algorithms that allow the machine to learn by itself from context. Without going into details here, suffice it to say that such AI is programmed to learn by induction (extracting patterns and applying them in new ways) and to function via *recursion.* In AI, recursion refers more technically to the process of repeating items in a self-similar way and, more precisely, to a method of defining functions in which the function being defined is applied within its own definition, but in such a way that no loop or infinite chain can occur. The so-called *recursion theorem* says that machines can be programmed to guarantee that recursively defined functions exist. Essentially, it asserts that machines can encode enough information to be able to reproduce their own programs or descriptions (Berlinski 2000).

AI has always been effective in breaking down the features of mental tasks, but the question of how these are assembled by natural intelligence to constitute meaningful wholes has always been a thorny problem. Moreover, humans do not learn only by induction, but primarily by abduction (as Peirce called it). And, they are able to put elements together into holistic meanings that are more than the sum of the elements. The meaning of a sentence, for example, is not perceived as the sum of the meanings of its individual words, but the holistic meaning that is extracted by their selection-combination patterns. Such thorny problems of equivalence between natural and artificial intelligence have become central to AI in search of making an "ultraintelligent" machine. As Max Black (1962) pointed out at the start of AI, the idea of trying to discover how a computer has been programmed in order to extrapolate how the mind works was the founding principle of AI. But Black expressed a simple caveat, reinforced later by physicist Roger Penrose (1989), namely that computers can never truly be intelligent because the laws of nature will not allow it. Natural intelligence is based on semiosis, which is the product of an interaction between the body, the mind, and the environment, as discussed throughout. In strong AI, the assumption is made that the mind can be extricated from the body and the environment, and work independently of them. This remains what Damasio (1994) has correctly called "Descartes' dream." How would we define artificial semiosis?

The advent of AI dovetailed initially with the discipline of Machine Translation—the use of computers to translate texts from one natural language to another. Machine Translation (MT) was, and still is, a testing ground for weak and strong versions of AI. It made an early crucial distinction between the *virtual* symbols in abstract systems or algorithms and the *actualized* symbols in language texts. The idea was to design algorithms capable of mimicking the actualized symbols in linguistic behavior. MT has thus been crucial in allowing programmers to develop representations of linguistic knowledge that do indeed mimic linguistic behavior. Although the computer cannot interpret its outputs (actual symbols) in human terms, it can model them in virtual terms. The interpretation of the difference is the task of the analyst. The problem of interpretation remains at the core of AI—how does the mind interpret verbal information, rather than just process it? The problem was articulated more precisely in the early stages of AI in terms of the inbuilt ambiguity of linguistic forms such as words. Linguist Yehoshua Bar-Hillel (1960) was among the first to use an example of linguistic ambiguity that came to be known as the *Bar-Hillel Paradox.* Bar-Hillel argued that humans use extra-linguistic information to make sense of messages and that computers may not be capable of ever accessing this in the same way that humans do. In other words, context is a determinant in how humans understand verbal signs and interpret their meanings. His example was the following one:

1. *The pen is in the box* (= the writing instrument is in the container)
2. *The box is in the pen* (= the container is inside another container [playpen])

Humans can instantly distinguish the different meanings of the two messages because they have access to outside information connected to the word *pen.* It brought out the importance of real-world context in determining the meaning of things. In order for a fully-automatic AI system to process Bar-Hillel's sentences correctly, it would have to have some rule subsystem in the algorithm that would indicate that *pens* as writing instruments are (typically) smaller than boxes; that boxes understood as containers are smaller than *pens* (typically again); and that it is impossible for a bigger object to be contained by a smaller one. In effect, the programmer would need to conduct both an "internal linguistic analysis" (ILA) of the grammatical and lexical aspects of sentences and then an "external linguistic analysis" (ELA) of the real world contexts that constrain the selection and concatenation of the rules within the ILA system. In other words, the relation between ILA and ELA is at the core of modeling language and other symbol systems. Advances in computer technology have actually made the resolution of Bar-Hillel's paradox rather straightforward. Without going into the technical details here, the point is the "guesswork" involved in AI systems is vastly different than the one involved in human understanding. Humans make their hunches on experiences based in context, algorithms involve probability models of usage in order to infer the appropriate meaning. The two are isomorphic systems, not identical ones.

As psychologist-semiotician Yair Neuman (2014: 61) has argued, this type of MT is actually a powerful semiotic tool, since it allows us to truly understand our culture-based peculiarities of meaning-making:

> The reason for using MT is twofold. First, there is no better way to understand the loss accompanying translation than by examining the most structured and formal attempt of translation known today. Second, instead of pointing at the problems and errors of MT, I suggest using it in order to better understand cultural peculiarities and discrepancies. The second suggestion is somewhat counterintuitive as we positively think of eliminating errors and solving problems. Sometimes, however, errors can be used for the better.

An important area of AI that overlaps with *cybernetics* (discussed below), comes under the rubric of Intelligence Amplification (IA). This is the use of AI to enhance natural intelligence by amplifying it through prosthetic technologies. Cybernetics was introduced in a 1948 book *Cybernetics, or Control and Communication in the Animal and Machine* by Norbert Wiener. William Ross Ashby then made the science known more broadly in his 1956 book, *Introduction to Cybernetics.* These two books were followed-up by J. C. R. Licklider (1960) and Douglas Engelbart (1962), who came to be designated as the founders of the IA movement.

IA has led to cyborg theory, or the view that physical and mental abilities can be extended beyond normal human limitations by mechanical elements built into the body. It espouses the view that the amalgamation of humans with machinery and artificial systems is bringing about a veritable paradigm shift in human evolution. A *cyborg* is a human whose functions are taken over in part by various electronic or electromechanical devices, or else whose anatomical or psychological capacities are bolstered by prosthetic technology. This theory is often inserted into a larger philosophical discourse called *posthumanism*, or the view that humans should no longer dominate the world but instead merge with animals and machines to create a new world order. The theorist initially associated with this philosophy is Donna Haraway (1989, 1991). Since the cyborg can have masculine, feminine, and mixed racial traits, it will rise, claims Haraway, to efface the "isms" of traditional human-centered worlds. She also claims that the cyborg will efface the belief in a Self contained inside the human body as well as the traditional notions of the uniqueness of human consciousness. She calls the cyborg a "posthuman subject" whose identity will undergo "continuous construction and reconstruction." In posthumanism, humans are just small organic particles in the overall scheme of things and thus there is a need to move beyond archaic concepts of human nature and to establish a society that is without the traditional prejudices and biases. Posthumanism will be discussed below.

The Singularity

Building an artificial mind with the capacity to outdo a human mind is, as mentioned, called reaching the *singularity.* It falls under the rubric of Seed AI, which traces its technical roots to *Machine Learning* (ML), a term coined by Arthur Samuel in 1959. One of the first feats of ML came in the 1990s when computer scientists at IBM developed a chess algorithm named Deep Blue that was capable of analyzing millions of chess positions every second. In 1996, world chess champion Garry Kasparov defeated the computer in a highly publicized match, 4 games to 2. He faced an improved version of Deep Blue a year later in a rematch. The enhanced computer was capable of processing two hundred million positions per second and to learn from the evolving configurations of the chess pieces, adjusting its program accordingly. Kasparov won the first game of the rematch, but after Deep Blue secured draws in games 3, 4, and 5 and victories in games 2 and 6, Kasparov was declared the loser, 2.5 games to 3.5. The event marked the first-ever defeat of a human world chess champion by a computer. Defeats of humans by machines in game-playing have become routine since then.

A major component for Seed AI is Natural Language Programming (NLP). An early NLP system was developed by Joseph Weizenbaum in 1966, which he called ELIZA. It was a program designed to mimic a dialogue with a psychotherapist. ELIZA's questions such as "Why do you say your head hurts?" in response to "My head hurts" were perceived by subjects as being so realistic that many believed that the machine was actually alive. But, as Weizenbaum wrote a decade later, ELIZA was a parodic imitation of psychoanalytic speech; it had no consciousness of what it was saying. ELIZA was the start of NLP. It was shortly after that sophisticated NLP algorithms emerged, with each one coming closer and closer to producing human speech that verged on verisimilitude. Human speech, however, is rarely precise—it is highly variable along social and geographical axes, which include slangs, dialects, and registers. To solve these dilemmas, current approaches to NLP use "learning-based" AI that examines patterns in data to improve a program's own understanding.

Deep Learning is another major input into Seed AI. It is a sub-branch of ML based on learning algorithms, as opposed to task-specific algorithms. It studies how computers can learn from huge amounts of data by using statistical techniques. An everyday example of a Deep Learning system is the one that distinguishes between spam and non-spam emails on servers, allocating the spam ones to a specific folder. Research in ML generally involves both "shallow" and "deep" approaches. The former uses plain statistical-probability analysis to determine the sense of, say, an ambiguous word on the basis of the words surrounding it in a text. Collocation theory is used in such shallow disambiguation. A collocation is a sequence of words that typically co-occur in speech more often than would be anticipated by random chance. Collocations are not idioms, which have fixed phraseology. Phrases such as *crystal clear, cosmetic surgery*, and *clean bill of health* are all collocations. Whether the collocation is derived from some syntactic (*make choices*) or lexical *(clear cut*) criterion, the principle underlying collocations—frequency of usage of words in tandem—always applies. And it is this principle that undergirds shallow algorithms. First, the algorithm identifies a key word in context and then determines the frequency of combination of other words with the key word in order to disambiguate the meaning of the phrase.

Research in Seed AI informs the theory of the singularity, which implies that at a certain point AI will become conscious of what it is doing (Bor 2012). But the use of the word *consciousness* is itself ambiguous. So, to avoid this ambiguity, Kurzweil (1999) used the designation "mind-beyond-machine," which alludes to the original Cartesian view that the mind is a machine that is activated by some animal spirit (Chapter 8). The difference in singularity theory is that the animal spirit is replaced by the algorithm. There are two obvious problems with this idea—one is that we still do not know what the mind really is in human terms and second there is no way to program human semiosis in the form of algorithms, sin e it requires an organic body. Moreover, at the emotional level of mind the brain produces "affective" models of reality, which are connected to the functions of the body, not to any algorithmic rules. Actually, there is now a sub-field aiming to study and develop computer systems and devices that can recognize and simulate human emotions. So-called Affective Computing (AC) software has been developed with the capacity to detect emotional states in people on the basis of the algorithmic analysis of facial expressions, muscle tension, postures, gestures, speech tones, pupil dilation, etc. The relevant technology includes sensors, cameras, big data, deep learning software, etc. The aim is to construct machines that can decode emotional states or influence them. This line of research has led to the building of so-called Empathy Machines, which are companion robots that display the ability to respond to human emotional states or language. To actually achieve empathy, however, a robot would have to be able to experience emotion and that means being able to recognize and comprehend it. It is also difficult to predict how an Empathy Machine will process, reproduce or simulate emotions. Incidents have been documented with Alexa (a commercially-available machine) that bring this out. Apparently, the machine started producing laughter for no reason. The technical diagnosis was that Alexa somehow processed the command, "Alexa laugh," when the user had not, in actual fact, uttered the statement.

Despite such obstacles, AI has continued to pursue the goal of replicating and optimistically passing human intelligence. This specific and focused approach now comes under the rubric of Artificial General Intelligence (AGI), which is the study of intelligence irrespective of its carrier—human, animal, or machine. Sirius and Cornell (2015: 14) define this field as follows:

> AGI describes research that aims to create machines capable of general intelligent action. The term was introduced in 2003 in order to avoid the perception that the field was about creating human-level or human-like intelligences, which is covered by the term "Strong AI." AGI allows for the inclusion of nonhuman as well as human models of general intelligence.

A goal of AGI is reverse engineering of the brain (Hawkins and Blakeslee 2004), which has led to projects such as the so-called OpenWorm project—an international open science project—that has produced the most advanced form of artificial life so far. It has modeled a nematode, a worm of the large phylum Nematoda consisting of 1000 cells and connecting neurons entirely in software. This "digital worm" wriggles around in realistic fashion as a real worm. Work on developing an even larger worm brain is ongoing.

One of the first attempts to reverse engineer a brain is Henry Markram's Blue Brain Project (Markram 2008). The brain is made up of electrical signals between neurons using the architecture of dendrites and axons. In the cortex, neurons are organized into columns, each one containing around 10,000 neurons that are intricately interconnected. These are called microcircuits, repeating millions of times across the cortex. The Blue Brain Project aims to recreate the microcircuitry of the cortex which then can presumably be used as the blueprint for a reverse-engineered brain. A related project is the Spaun Brain Simulation Project (see Eliasmith, Stewart, Choo, Bekolay, DeWolf, Tang, and Rasmussen 2012). The artificial brain in this case consists of around two and half million neurons, and it has an eye and an arm. Similar projects are starting up across the AI and IA worlds, including IBM's Blue Matter Project (Ananthanarayanan, Esser, Simon, and Modha 2009). Suffice it to say here that for any truly effective inroads to be made into AGI, a powerful form of computer technology would have to be used. One such technology is the quantum computer, which can operate at 100 million times as fast as current computers. A quantum computer makes use of the quantum states of subatomic particles to store information and to process it.

It is relevant to note that already in the 1930s, Alan Church provided a blueprint for determining what principles would be required to build a mind (Church 1935, 1936). Known as the Church-Turing thesis, the set of principles claimed that any mental process can be translated into an equivalent mechanical process with general recursive functions. The thesis was applied to cellular automata, substitution systems, combinators, and even quantum computing. There were conflicting points of view about the thesis from the outset. One states that it can be proved, even though a proof has not been as yet discovered, and another says that it serves mainly as a definition for computation. Support for the validity of the thesis comes from the fact that every realistic model of computation has been shown to be equivalent. The thesis has thus become the basis for the principle of computational equivalence (Wolfram 2002), which claims that there are only a small number of intermediate levels of computing power before a system is universal.

Cybernetics

The topics of Intelligence Augmentation, cyborg theory, the singularity, etc. are interconnected notions and movements. All can be traced back to one science—*cybernetics*, or the study of control and communication in humans, machines, and animals, founded by Norbert Wiener, as mentioned, although the ideas in it go back to antiquity. The underlying principle of cybernetics is that intelligence can be studied in itself, independently of any specific type—human (natural intelligence), animal (animal intelligence), or machine (artificial intelligence). Cybernetics aims to take intelligence out of its bearer or container, so to speak, whether it be a brain or an algorithm, in order to examine what its features are.

Examining cybernetic systems involves understanding how they communicate. Mechanical systems communicate via signals of various types; animals use sophisticated signals based on their specific biology; and human communication, which is the most complex and evolved, uses all kinds of signals and sign systems—it can unfold (as discussed in this book) through: (1) gesture (hands and bodily actions); (2) vocal organs (oral language) (3) writing (pictographic, alphabetic, etc.); (4) visuality (painting, sculpting, etc.); (5) mechanical means (radio, computers, etc.); (6) audio media (singing); (7) body signals (gestures, facial expressions, etc.). Communicative exchanges can be interpersonal (between human beings), group-based (between some individual or medium and groups), and mass-based involving communication systems that encompass entire societies. No other communication system, for now, can approach this level of complexity and versatility.

Cybernetics views communication in all systems as analogous. It is interested in the ways in which the elements in the systems are organized and what features of organization are cross-systemic. Because of the increasing sophistication of computers and the efforts to make them behave in humanlike ways, cybernetics today is closely allied with AI, robotics, and information science. As used in this science, the term *communication* refers, more narrowly, to the feedback and error-correction signals and mechanisms (biological or mechanical) that control the operation of communication. Such signals and mechanisms are called *servomechanisms*. Strictly defined, a servomechanism is a mechanism producing forces at a higher level of energy than the input level, where feedback is employed to make it automatic. Servomechanisms were first used in military and marine navigation equipment. Today they are used in automatic machine tools, satellite-tracking technologies, celestial-tracking systems, automatic navigation systems, and anti-aircraft control technologies. A primary task of cybernetics is to understand the guidance and control servomechanisms that govern the operation of social interaction and then to devise better ways of harnessing them.

The term *information* invariably comes up in any cybernetic discussion of communication and consciousness. Cyberneticians define it practically as any form of data that can be received by humans, animals, or machines in both differential and common ways. At one level, information is seen as something probabilistic—a ringing alarm signal carries more information than one that is silent, because the latter is the "expected state" of the alarm system and the former its "alerting state." This binary state carries the information load through an opposition—*off*-versus-*on*. It is relevant to note that in a schematic way this is consistent with the general notion of opposition.

Wiener developed cybernetics from observing that people and machines carried out their functions in purposeful and orderly ways, seeking stability in the enactment of these methods, albeit with different goals and in different ways. One of the most important characteristics shared by both systems (natural and artificial) is the notion of feedback, which involves the circling back of information to a control device (such as a thermostat or a human brain) which has the ability to adjust behavior or functioning accordingly. For instance, when a human being's body temperature is too high or too low, the body feeds this information back to the brain. The brain then reacts to correct the temperature or to suggest ways to look for a solution (such as seeking shade). A household thermostat functions in an analogous way, using feedback to adjust the operation of a furnace to maintain a fixed temperature. For Wiener, mechanisms for self-correction in machines serve the same purpose that the nervous system in humans serves in coordinating information to determine which actions will be performed. Their functions and purviews may differ, but their underlying *structure* is the same.

There are two main types of feedback. In an electronic-mechanical heating system, as just discussed, the feedback mechanism is the thermostat which controls the system, keeping it in balance—when a certain temperature is reached, a device in the thermostat sends information to the temperature-regulating system to shut down or start up. This self-correcting process is an example of what cyberneticians call *negative feedback*, whereby changes in output are fed back to the input source so that the change is reversed. In *positive feedback*, an increase in output is fed back to the source, expanding the output, thus creating a snowballing effect. An example is the screeching sound that occurs when a microphone is brought too close to its loudspeaker. Using the notion of feedback as transferable across systems, cybernetics has led to sophisticated attempts to build machines that simulate human behavior, including decision-making and analysis of data. Since the 1940s, cybernetics has influenced work in biochemistry, computer science, psychology, and communication science.

The question that is germane to the purposes of the present discussion is: What insights has cybernetics provided into the nature of the human mind? This very question was approached by Danish semiotician Søren Brier (2007), who claimed that the brain is more than a feedback device—it is a meaning-making organ that is unique among cybernetic systems. So, rather than providing insights into the human mind directly, it can be said that cybernetics has actually made it possible to single out the unique qualities of human semiosis (sign comprehension and production) by comparison with other systems. A corollary question is: Why does human intelligence transcends simple feedback mechanisms, and leads to discoveries, inventions, and creative systems of all types, including in mathematics and science? We could conceivably live without the Pythagorean theorem. It tells us what we know intuitively—that a diagonal distance is shorter than taking an L-shaped path to a given point. And perhaps this is why it emerged—it suggests that we seek efficiency and a minimization of effort in how to do things and how to classify the world. But in so doing we "squeeze out" of the theorem other ideas and hidden truths. To put it another way, the practical activity of measuring triangles contained too much information, a lot of which was superfluous. The theorem refines the information, throwing out from it that which is irrelevant. The ability to abstract theories and models from the world of information involves the optimal ability to throw away irrelevant information about the world in favor of new information that emerges at a higher level of analysis—not just react to it as if in a feedback system.

Aware of the far-reaching implications of his proposal, Wiener discussed both the pros and cons of making analogies between animals, machines and humans. This very discussion led, a little later, to the notion of *autopoiesis* (Maturana and Varela 1973), or the view that physical (organic) systems themselves adjust themselves to change. So, in the case of human systems, it is insufficient to study information transfers solely as probabilistic feedback signals. It is in the linkages made between words, meanings, and other interpretive structures that the human brain somehow is capable of gaining a unique form of understanding.

Two related areas of cybernetic research are robotics and automata theory, both of which dovetail with research in AI and computer engineering. Robotics can be defined simply as machines engineered to carry out activities that mimic human activities (or even replicate them). Engineers have developed sophisticated mobile robots equipped with cameras for sight and sensors for touch. One of the first mentions of robots (called automatons) is in Homer's *Iliad,* in which the god of metalwork, Hephaestus, created an army of robot servants. The term itself comes from the Czech word *robota*, meaning "drudgery," used for the first time with its modern designation by Czech writer, Karel Capek in his 1921 play, *R.U.R.*, in which he criticized technology and social conformity by creating a race of manufactured people (robots) who take over the world. One of the first robots, named Elektro, was made in 1937 by the Westinghouse Electric Corporation. Elektro was humanoid in appearance—it could walk and move its arms and head by voice command, speak around 700 words (through a record player built into it), and smoke cigarettes. But Elektro did not have advanced AI, and thus could not learn to adapt to its environment and learn to do new tasks through Deep Learning mechanisms (previous chapter).

A typical robot today is programmed with a set of algorithmic instructions that specify precisely what it must do and how to do so. The instructions are stored in the robot's computer control center, which, in turn, sends commands to the motorized joints, which move various parts of the robot, constituting servomechanism and feedback systems. Most robot algorithms are based on data mining information which is converted into knowledge network systems to produce knowledge representation (discussed in the previous chapter). In some instances, the algorithm attempts to generalize from certain inputs in order to generate, speculatively, an output for previously unseen inputs. In other cases, the algorithm operates on input where the desired output is unknown, with the objective being to discover structure in the information. Essentially, robot algorithms are designed to predict new outputs from specific test cases. They mimic the same kinds of inductive learning patterns by the human brain, that is, the extraction of patterns on the basis of specific cases. The goal has been (and achieved in many cases) robots which acquire skills through autonomous exploration of specific cases and through interaction with human teachers.

A basic design principle of robots is called "degrees of freedom," which refers to the different ways that the robot can move—up and down, in and out, side to side, tilt, rotate, etc. Part of the relevant algorithm is designed so that the robot can achieve such degrees of freedom, using camera images of the environment to determine movement. Robots can also use satellite navigation systems to move around and to perform actions such as picking things up, moving them around, etc. House robots (housebots) are now designed to use language through a speaker, take voice commands, and to use a Wi-Fi computer for adapting information to the state of events. In effect, modern robots are part of a growing "smart technology," which aims to make machines as humanlike as possible, in effect realizing one of the aims of cybernetics. Such technology has resulted in highly publicized feats. For instance, in 2001 surgeons in the city of New York operated on a patient in Strasbourg, France by manipulating remote-controlled arms and equipment via the Internet. Robot systems in Strasbourg copied the movements and carried out the surgery successfully. Robotic body parts can nowadays replace real parts that have been injured or lost. The wearer controls them by thinking, sending the resulting nerve signals connected to the neurology of thought to skin sensors which control toe robotic body parts.

Robotics is now a branch of Automata Theory, the science studying the principles of automation. For example, many modern cities use automated systems to coordinate their traffic lights and thus to enhance the smooth flow of traffic. Sensors in the pavement near a traffic light assess the number and speed of vehicles on the street, sending the data to a central computer, which then decides how to time each traffic light in the area and sends signals to the traffic lights. All automata work on the feedback principle (discussed above); that is, the information processed by the sensors of an automaton is fed directly back to the system, enabling the machine to adjust its operation as needed. Feedback makes automation different from mechanization (the use of machinery to replace human workers). A mechanized industrial robot, for example, does not use feedback and therefore cannot adapt its operation to changing conditions. Automated systems, instead, compare the actual output with the desired output. So, as mentioned, in a heating system, the thermostat compares the thermometer reading with the temperature for which the thermostat has been set. If the actual output of the system differs from the desired output, the system sends an error signal to a controller, which decides how to correct the error. The thermostat in a heating system functions as a controller. In most advanced automata systems, the controller is a sophisticated computer.

Research on data mining techniques is now part and parcel in the construction of robots or any automata system. By compiling and sifting through large quantities of data on the Internet, and other databases, the goal is to extract useable patterns in it: for example, mined demographic data can be used to predict the shopping habits of a targeted market segment. The techniques include the automatic grouping of documents or files, categorizing them into directories, and analyzing patterns and interrelationships within them. One particular technique, called *filtering*, involves making profiles of people's interests and then comparing these against related information from various

Web sources. Needless to say, the breadth and scope of the current automata techniques available with the new technologies are mind-boggling, since it is now possible to collate disparate facts about individuals and generate profiles of various kinds (psychographic, sociographic, etc.) about them based on those facts in a matter of seconds. The social and existential dangers were already noticeable in the middle part of the twentieth century. Psychologist Carl Jung (1983), for instance, feared that modern societies were losing the view of the individual as a unique human being, turning the person into a "unit" that can be easily categorized, manipulated, and exploited. Existential philosophers saw information mining as a "panopticon" tool, the circular prison envisaged by philosopher Jeremy Bentham in the eighteenth century where the prisoners cannot tell if they are being observed, so they must assume that they always are. As the early cyberneticians also suspected, without controlling the growth of cybernetic machines, humans might be subject to unwanted consequences. It is, in fact, obvious that the world of the data-mining and smart technologies is changing traditional concepts of identity, privacy, and individualism, as we become more and more inured to practices such as data-mining.

Of special interest to cybernetics has always been the creation of robots that can both interact with humans and thus, indirectly, provide insight into the nature of intelligence. The type of robot that has a capacity to interact meaningfully with humans is called a *cobot.* In contrast with traditional robots, which are designed to operate autonomously or with limited guidance, cobots show a high degree of AI that gives them the ability to respond to situations through learning algorithms that are stored in their memory system which can accessed to construct responsive activities. Interestingly, cobots have been found to develop word-to-meaning mappings without grammatical rules—a very important finding to say the least. Suffice it to say here that research on cobots is allowing us to understand how the mechanisms of language operate; however, so far it has told us virtually nothing about how the human brain extracts meaning from language and then applies it to discover the world in new, not automatic, ways.

Posthumanism

The advent of cybernetics and of AI, which dovetailed in the 1950s, has been the inspiration of new views of humanity that started emerging in subsequent decades. One of these is *posthumanism*, which, as mentioned briefly above, is a term used broadly to refer to the belief that an era is coming in which humans no longer dominate the world but instead have merged with their machines and with animals to create a new world order that pits humans not at the center of the universe but as equal partners with other intelligences. As also mentioned previously, the posthumanist movement was given impetus by Donna Haraway (1991), who saw the rise of AI and robots as the spark for eliminating all distinctions among humans, animals, and machines.

Posthumanists believe that human beings can be ameliorated through technological amalgamation. In posthumanism, humans are just small organic particles in the overall scheme of things and thus there is a need to move beyond archaic concepts of human nature and to establish a society that is without the traditional prejudices and biases. Posthumanism has developed several principles, of which the following are the major ones:

- A cyborg humanity can move beyond archaic concepts of human nature and establish a society that includes other species and machines.
- A new definition of reality is required, which sees the individual human brain as a part in broader or global consciousness that will guide future evolution.
- There is a need to obliterate all traditional distinctions based on age, gender, race, class, and so on—all of which are irrelevant to the cyborg.
- All traditional notions of religiosity and spirituality need to be eliminated or revamped.

As Haraway (1989: 377) put it, the hope of posthumanism is: "that the always oblique and sometimes perverse focusing would facilitate revisionings of fundamental, persistent western narratives about difference, especially racial and sexual difference." A cyborg, in Haraway's perspective, is a hybrid creation, merging human and machine parts and systems into an integrated whole. Although it has always been a creature of science fiction, the advanced technologies of today are making it more and more likely that the merger will become reality. The cyborg will completely efface the artificial oppositional dichotomies of the past (*male*-versus-*female*, *young*-versus-old, etc.). Haraway introduced the notion of multiple subjectivities as part of cyborg theory. She sees them as constituting a split of the notion of Selfhood. So, a cyborg is "the one who can interrogate positionings and be accountable, the one who can construct and join rational conversations and fantastic imaginings that change history. Splitting, in this context should be about heterogeneous multiplicities that are simultaneously necessary and incapable of being squashed into isomorphic slots or cumulative lists" (Haraway 1991: 193). Haraway's split refers to the merging of humans and machines, positing that human consciousness unfolds in terms of "multiple agents" operating within a combination of competing forces within the body. She calls this the posthuman subject: "the posthuman subject is an amalgam, a collection of heterogeneous components, a material-informational entity whose boundaries undergo continuous construction and reconstruction" (Haraway 1989: 3).

Posthumanism has precedents. One of these is movement known as *cosmism*, which originated in the late 1800s in Russia, but expanded recently by Ben Goertzel and Giulio Prisco (see Goertzel 2010). Cosmism is the view that all minds are interconnected and constitute one huge form of consciousness. Goertzel and Prisco have put forward several revised principles of cosmism:

- Humans are merging with technology, constituting a new evolutionary phase of the species.
- The dichotomy between natural and artificial intelligence will become irrelevant at the time of the Singularity, leading to augmented intelligence.
- AI will become sentient and self-aware, and displace biological evolution.
- Humans will eventually populate other planets and cosmic worlds.
- Science will eventually eliminate the faults in biology, such as mortality and aging.

One of the subtexts in cosmism is that eventually we will be able to upload everything, including the human mind. Notions such as Selfhood will become obsolete as individual minds merge cosmically to produce one huge form of consciousness—a situation that seems to have actually occurred in our wired world, as will be discusses in the next chapter.

Transhumanism

"We live invested in an electric information environment that is quite as imperceptible to us as water is to fish" (McLuhan 1968: 5). With this observation, the late communications theorist Marshall McLuhan warned that we tend to be unaware of the effects of the electronic environment in which we live. Like fish in water, we do not realize that it is the water that determines how we live and how we are shaped by it. If some fish can live out of water, then their whole inner world, and even anatomy, would be vastly different. In a cybernetic environment information is scattered broadly through real and electronic space. This type of environment favors mindsets such as posthumanism and cosmism. Another one is called *transhumanism*.

This is the belief that the human race can evolve beyond its current physical and mental limitations by means of science and technology. Although it has roots in the nineteenth century, in its modern day version transhumanism is traced to a 1957 book by biologist Julian Huxley, where he defines it as follows (Huxley 1957: 14):

> Up till now human life has generally been, as Hobbes described it, "nasty, brutish and short;" the great majority of human beings (if they have not already died young) have been afflicted with misery; we can justifiably hold the belief that these lands of possibility exist, and that the present limitations and miserable frustrations of our existence could be in large measure surmounted. The human species can, if it wishes, transcend itself—not just sporadically, an individual here in one way, an individual there in another way, but in its entirety, as humanity.

An important theme in transhumanism is that of cellular automata, or sets of units in a mathematical model that is based on simple rules governing their replication and destruction. These are used to model complex systems composed of simple units such as living things or parallel processors. This whole area can be traced to mathematician John Conway's brilliant 1970 *Game of Life*, which consists of cells inhabited by dots (alive) or nothing (dead) (see Conway 2000). A dot stays alive if it has two or three neighbors, but dies if it is crowded (four or more neighbors) or too lonely (one or no neighbors). When an empty cell borders three dots a new dot is "born." The game, like life itself, unfolds as an array of sequences of reproducing patterns. Without going into details here, it is sufficient to point out that Conway's game has had implications for algorithm design and for the theory of cellular automata. Martin Gardner (1970) made the game known widely through his *Scientific American* column, providing the following assessment:

> The game made Conway instantly famous, but it also opened up a whole new field of mathematical research, the field of cellular automata. Because of Life's analogies with the rise, fall and alterations of a society of living organisms, it belongs to a growing class of what are called "simulation games" (games that resemble real life processes).

Conway was influenced by John von Neumann's (1958) notion of "universal constructors," or structures that could build copies or models of themselves. In Conway's game, von Neumann's models are reduced to four basic ones:

1. those that do not involve explosive growth;
2. those that possess few initial patterns with unpredictable outcomes;
3. those that have potential for emerging universal constructors;
4. those that enfold simple rules of construction.

To cite Sirius and Cornell (2015: 22):

> The Game of Life is "Turing complete:" it can simulate any real-world computer or computer language. It is used in cryptography. As a model it's helpful for anyone researching synthetic biology. Some physicists even believe that our universe is best described as a cellular automaton.

As an aside, it can be mentioned that Hermann Hesse's marvelous novel, *Magister Ludi* (1943), is a fictional counterpart to Conway's game. In the narrative, the meaning of life is revealed gradually to a Master of the Game, via the insights he derives from playing an archetypal bead game that involves repeating patterns, not unlike those found in Conway's game.

A basic input science to the philosophical make-up of transhumanism is that of Augmented Reality (AR), or the overlaying of digital systems and information onto the real world. AR is based on large datasets that can be analyzed computationally to reveal patterns, trends, and associations, especially relating to human behavior and interactions. The use of such data has enormous implications for privacy and the threat of manipulation by those who compile such data, such as government agencies, advertisers, and the like. However, since Big Data can predict behavior and to spot trends. it can also be used for benevolent purposes, such as preventing crime and diseases.

Movements such as posthumanism and transhumanism are tied to developments in technology—through which we are now evolving as a species. This topic will be discussed further in the next chapter. To live in this new world order, new languages have become necessary—languages that allude to the new forms of semiosis and culture that are emerging. Posthumanism and transhumanism are two such languages.

Epilogue

Cybernetics is a specific instantiation of anthropologist Gregory Bateson's (1972) goal to understand the relation between the human brain and nature, using scientific rather than philosophical theories. This has become a major theme not only in the sciences of intelligence themselves, but also in semiotics, as discussed at the start of this chapter.

In the end, the question of artificial intelligence is, semiotically, a moot one, since if a machine can truly think consciously, then we will not be able to enter its "mind" and understand its thoughts. What is germane and instructive to the foregoing discussion is that AI—in its strong version—aims to take the mind out of the body and study it in the machine, and as a subsidiary goal to get the machine to think independently. This takes us back to biologist Jacob von Uexküll's (1909) view of semiosis (discussed several times already). The key to understanding the nature of mind lies in the anatomical structure of an organism. Animals with widely divergent anatomies do not live in the same kind of mind world, because each species filters information according to its own particular *Bauplan*—the mental modeling system that allows it to interpret the world in a biologically-determined way. A machine also has a *Bauplan*—the human-made computer program. But this is not grounded in the body, but in wires and electrical impulses. The computer and the human being have, in effect, widely divergent "anatomies" and, as von Uexküll would have it today, do not "live" in the same kind of mind world. The Embodied Cognition movement within semiotics and other cognitive sciences, which started with Maturana and Varela's 1973 book, *Autopoiesis and Cognition*, is based on this premise, namely that human thought is shaped by aspects of the body beyond perception and cognition. In a phrase, intelligent behavior emerges from the interplay among brain, body, and world, and constructing a body is something that can only be approximated through prosthetics not in any real way.

10
Media

It is the medium that shapes and controls the scale and form of human association and action.

Marshall McLuhan (1911-1980)

Prologue

Herbert Marshall McLuhan (1911-1980) was a University of Toronto professor who studied the role of technology and the mass media in shaping (or reshaping) human life, starting in the early 1950s (McLuhan 1951). His views of how our tools and our communication media extend our body and mind, allowing us to do more than would be possible through our biological legacy, is actually a fundamental principle of semiotic science as a whole—namely, signs and sign systems are semiotic models of our senses, perceptions, feelings, thoughts, etc., which allow us to probe reality much more effectively than through our instincts. McLuhan never used the word *semiotics* in his writings. But there is little doubt that many of his ideas are fundamentally semiotic. So, a point-of-arrival for considering the implications of using semiotics to understand the contemporary world is to take a look at some of McLuhan's most relevant semiotic ideas, including the global village, the medium is the message, the four laws of media, and a few more. These form the basis for applying semiotic analysis insightfully to our wired world (the global village) and to investigate how semiosis is unfolding within it.

McLuhan's ideas provide, in effect, a semiotic lens through which we can better understand the communicative, expressive, and intellectual phenomena that are unfolding in the "global village"—his term for the world perceived as a single community linked by telecommunications. McLuhan was among the first to emphasize that the structuring of content that the new electronic media allowed re-shaped how we think about content—hence, his phrase "the medium is the message." This has changed traditional concepts of what a text is, what constitutes a sign, what authorship means, etc. (McLuhan 1951, 1962, 1964). In a phrase, McLuhan provided perceptive semiotic snapshots of the contemporary world at the same time that he used these to criticize it. He left it up to readers to collate the snapshots into an overarching understanding of that world on their own terms.

The starting point for relating McLuhan to semiotic theory is his notion that the tools we make extend human faculties. Throughout history, tools have allowed us not only to carve up and modify the environment for reasons of physical survival, but also to encode, preserve, and facilitate the transmission of information. In other words, tools are not only objects, but also sign structures documenting how human history unfolds in the eras in which they emerge. In fact, if there is one predominant insight to be gleaned from reading McLuhan, it is that each major change in tool-making technologies invariably brings about an evolutionary change in human life. For example, around 1000 BCE, the invention of alphabets and phonetic writing, which extended the previous pictographic forms of writing, marked a radical break away from oral cultures toward literacy-based ones. For McLuhan, a "tool" was both a physical and mental invention. With the rise and spread of mechanical print technology in the mid-1400s, writing became an increasingly expanding mode for encoding and disseminating information and knowledge. This brought about what he called the "Print Age," an era of history shaped by the structure of written knowledge. People started to see themselves as separate from the tribe or communal form of social living because of the simple fact that they read by themselves, forming opinions on their own without the guidance of some leader and without the pressures of groupthink. Over time, this encouraged individualism, abstract thinking, and the valorizing of literacy over tribal ritual and magic. As he so eloquently put it in a posthumous publication: "Literacy, the visual technology, dissolved the tribal magic by means of its stress on fragmentation and specialization and created the individual" (McLuhan 1998: 23).

Before his death, McLuhan predicted the demise of the Print Age and a return to a quasi-communal form of life, but on a global scale, brought about by the ability of electronic media to unite people from across the world in a tribalistic way, as if they lived in an imaginary village. He called this the "Electronic Age" and the village the "electronic global village." With the arrival of the Internet, social media, and digitization technologies, decades after his death, that village has become a reality.

The Global Village

The current world of digital communication technologies impels all of us to become more involved with one another, no matter what language we speak, what culture we come from, where we live physically, and who we are. We are all denizens of the same global village, which we navigate virtually every day through cyberspace. Everything from purchasing goods, accessing and recording information, seeking recreation and even enacting courtship rituals takes place through that virtual world, producing a strange kind of disembodied consciousness, which retrieves features of orally-based tribal life but in virtual (imaginary) ways. The new media have, indeed, become the new message—to paraphrase McLuhan. They have offset the individualistic and privatizing forces of the Print Age, devalorizing many of its previous sacrosanct tenets, such as the authorship and the primacy of canonical texts—texts such as those by Shakespeare and Homer, among others, that in the Print Age were intertextually primary ones. Even sources of authoritatively-coded knowledge, such as print encyclopedias, have now become open to the participation and collaboration of everyone, not just individual experts—as can be seen by the spread of the various "wikis" on the Internet, which, going against all traditions of the past, allow for the collaborative editing of content by users. The advent of the global village signals, fundamentally, that the world has morphed into a paradigmatically different one from any social system of the past. There is no turning back the clock, to employ a cliché that McLuhan himself used often in his lectures at the University of Toronto.

Real-space villages and communities involve boundaries—geographical, linguistic, and cultural—that keep them separate from other villages and locales. But in the global village, made-up of interactive social networks, these are no longer requirements. Thus, a new interactional dynamic has emerged uniting people in virtual ways, which now influences major events in everyone's lives. Election outcomes, for example, are influenced as much by the chatter on Facebook, Twitter, Instagram, and YouTube as they are by debates in real-world auditoriums and by advertising via the traditional mass media (television, print, and radio). In effect, the medium in which information is recorded and transmitted is decisive in determining social patterns: to put it more concretely, an oral tribal culture is vastly different in organization and outlook than an alphabetic one; so too an electronic culture is vastly different than either an oral or alphabetic culture. Because people the world over can now see themselves as participants in events going on in some other part of the world by navigating through websites and social media, they tend to feel interconnected. As McLuhan put it in 1962: "The human family now exists under conditions of a global village. We live in a single constricted space resonant with tribal drums."

The *global village* has crystallized because, as McLuhan claimed, the major media in which information is recorded and transmitted are decisive in shaping trends and in charting future progress, since they extend human faculties (biological, mental, institutional), re-calibrating these faculties and, thus, leading to a different (and disembodied) understanding of Otherness. By simply switching on our television sets to satellite-transmitted programs, visiting websites, using social media, and the like, we tend to feel connected to others in an abstract, rather than real, fashion. Our interactions with, and perceptions of, people are being shaped more and more how we interact with them on screens rather than in face-to-face environments. Moreover, given the frequency and rapidity of communicative events in the global village, we now tend to valorize information on its own without interpretation. The danger, as McLuhan understood, was in fact that in the global village, we are tempted to amputate interpretation from information, seeing the latter as important in and of itself.

McLuhan foresaw the danger that the modern mass media were making us mere "spectators," inclined to abrogate our responsibility to think and act independently, thus debilitating true democracy and meaningful discourse. This was already foreseen at the threshold of the Electronic Age by journalist Walter Lippmann (1922). However, as things have turned out, the same media that induce spectatorship, can also engender independent thought, since social media allow everyone to express their opinions freely and, in fact, challenge the status quo. Overall, mass communications technologies define an age. Such inventions as the telephone, the phonograph, the radio, motion pictures, the automobile, television, the airplane, the computer, mobile devices, and the like have lent substantive support to this key McLuhanian notion. The proof is compelling—we have become addictively dependent on our modern technologies to carry out everyday communicative, interactive, creative, and intellectual activities. We have, in effect, become enmeshed in our own tools, even if this is sometimes to our detriment. McLuhan claimed that, while new technologies enhance many aspects of human life, they also have hidden negative effects. Since the middle part of the twentieth century, industrialist technologics and their entrepreneurial agendas have led to a global consumerist lifestyle and worldview that is threatening ecological systems and the quality of human life itself. As McLuhan himself often intimated, we must come to recognize the negative by-products of technology, in order to counteract them.

Laws of Media

One of the paradigms put forward by McLuhan that has particular relevance to semiotics is the one in which he expounds his four laws of media—amplification, obsolescence, reversal, and retrieval. The gist of these laws is that a new technology or invention will at first amplify some sensory, intellectual, or other human psycho-biological faculty. While one area is amplified, another is lessened or rendered obsolescent, until it is used to maximum capacity whence it reverses its characteristics and is retrieved in another medium. A well-known, and now classic, example given by McLuhan is that of print technology, briefly mentioned above. Initially, it amplified the concept of individualism because the spread of print materials encouraged private reading, and this led to the view that the subjective interpretations of texts was a basic right of all people, thus rendering group-based consciousness obsolete until it changed from a single printed text to mass produced texts, leading to mutual readings, albeit typically displaced in time and space. This allowed for the retrieval of a quasi or secondary communal form of identity—that is, reading the same text connected readers in an imaginary way.

These four laws can certainly be applied to understanding the contemporary Digital Age, which has amplified all aspects of communication and information access, rendering traditional print media obsolescent. But the latter are still around, having converged with digital media in new ways. Obsolescence does not mean elimination. There is always a historical flow to ideas, media, technologies, and the sign systems that ensue from them. There is no sudden or abrupt interruption to the flow. So, in a basic sense, these laws can be used to describe how changes in signifying structures both mirror and lead to changes in expressivity, cognition, and worldview. A new sign system, such as contemporary emoji writing, does indeed amplify the ways in which we write messages (bolstering them visually), thus rendering purely phonetic writing obsolete (in some ways). However, this is leading to a retrieval, and even revival, of standard writing practices in various domains of social life, from the academic to the intellectual, as people realize the power of traditional literacy in many areas of contemporary life (Danesi 2016). The connection with print technology has been rechanneled, not severed.

The foregoing discussion can be encapsulated in a phrase —tools and artifacts (physical and mental) are extensions of ourselves. Bicycles and cars extend the locomotive capacities of the human foot, axes and knives the ability of the hands, nails, and teeth, houses our body's heat-control system, clothing our skin, the computer our central nervous system, and so on. These extensions are real and tangible—literally. By holding a book in our hands, we are effectively holding thoughts and information in our palms.

Extension works at different levels or orders. So, for example, the hand-ax can be called a first-order extension. It is made from materials from the natural environment directly, shaping them into a particular object. Knives are second-order extensions, because they are made from axes or by extending the principles used to create axes previously. The higher the order of the extension, the more removed is the tool or artifact from physical reality. So, there is an extensional continuity among tools and artifacts—the invention of one does not eliminate the other; it extends it in various ways. This process has been called meta-extension here. Extensions do not cut the thread of technological history, therefore, because of the semiotic value of previous tools. So, if some object does indeed become obsolete, such as the typewriter, then it is eliminated from everyday usage but not forgotten, since typewriters are now museum pieces. Museums are repositories of previous tools and artifacts and displayed according to their historical values and previous social functions. Moreover, various structural features of typewriters are still present in computer keyboards and in other digital components, such as printers. Indeed, the first PCs were actually called "word processors," since they simply extended the functions of typewriting words considerably, adding the capacity for correction, change, memory storage within the device itself.

The notion of the *tetrad* was introduced, as a synthetic model to represent the operation of the four laws, posthumously by McLuhan's late son, Eric (McLuhan and McLuhan 1988). The tetrad is meant to show concretely how the four laws operate simultaneously albeit in different degrees and at different times. It provides a framework for determining what changes tools, artifacts, and new media bring about in tandem. For example, applying the four laws to the Internet will show how that medium amplifies, obsolesces, retrieves, and reverses various features, traits, and so on:

Amplifies	Obsolesces
• Networking among denizens of cyberspace • Decentralization of information sources • Speed and range of information searches • Access to the Global Village • Access to connected intelligence systems • Virtual communities • e-systems (e-trade, e-books, etc.) • Self-publishing • Access to materials and information of all kinds	• Previous restrictions of time and space in communications • National boundaries • Face-to-face communication • Single-source propaganda • Privacy • Copyright • Censorship • Print monopolies • Retail merchandising • Paper print technologies • Reading print materials such as books for various purposes such as leisure
Reverses into	**Retrieves**
• Obsession with information itself • Information overload • Loss of affect • Disorders of a new kind (addiction to technology) • Loss of values associated with literacy • Loss of sense of importance associated with traditional academic humanistic disciplines	• Writing and reading in new ways • Tribalism • Secondary orality (see below) • Local activism • New forms of interaction that actually retrieve the need to form cliques and groups

Internet Tetrad

The different quadrants are organically intertwined, thus explaining, in a fundamental sense, how the human brain deals with the new media and how it adapts to them in a specific environment.

The foregoing discussion raises a fundamental semiotic question: Are signs and sign structures tools extending sensory-anatomical-neural features, allowing us to do things that would be impossible otherwise? If so, this would require tweaking semiotic theory, somewhat along the lines suggested by the biosemiotic movement, starting with the work of Jakob von Uexküll (1909), as discussed a number of times in this book. Von Uexküll suggested that the world of objects and information (the *Umwelt)* is perceived in a particular way by a species via the particular neural-anatomical structures with which it is endowed by Nature, and this allows the species to construct its own necessary models of that world (the *Innenwelt*) so as to be able to understand it on its own terms and thus cope with it. In the case of humans, the modeling process is a sophisticated one that involves abstract sign-modeling. This is perhaps why humans do not simply react to stimuli; they interact inventively, creatively, and symbolically with them. They change stimuli into sign models of the world that then can be used to further explore that world.

This means, ultimately, that humans are in charge of their own evolution. This might seem to be a preposterous idea to some, but in recent decades, biologists have come increasingly to adopt von Uexküll's basic perspective, calling human evolution "autopoietic." The term was introduced by Maturana and Varela in their famous 1973 book, *Autopoiesis and Cognition*, where they claim that an organism participates in its own evolution, since it has the ability to produce, or at least shape, its various biochemical agents and structures, in order to ensure their efficient and economical operation. In the case of humans, autopoiesis seems to know no bounds. So, in a fundamental sense, technology is autopoietic, allowing humans to shape their own evolution, in partnership with Nature. So, the McLuhanian view of tools and technology is hardly a moot or trivial one—it might provide a critical framework for understanding the relation between non-genetic semiosis and biological life.

Essentially, McLuhan argued that we create tools, at first, to extend ourselves—to see farther, to run faster, to think more quickly, and so on. Once we have the necessary tools for doing so, we extend them further and further to create sophisticated tool systems and technologies. As a consequence, our own evolution is guided autopoietically, that is, through the conditions, activities, and meanings generated by the very tools we have made, rather than through strictly biological processes. We are, in effect, makers of our own world, or as he aptly remarked, we live in "a man-made environment that transfers the evolutionary process from biology to technology" (McLuhan 1968: 85).

There are various kinds of extensions: physical (the wheel extends the foot), intellectual (the alphabet extends the ability to record knowledge efficiently), symbolic (numeral systems extend the ability to count), mechanical (the printing press extends the use of writing), mnemonic (the book and now the computer allows for greater storage of information than single brains can ever expect to store), and so on. As we invent new and more powerful technologies, so too do we change our modes of knowledge-making, of understanding the world, of transmitting information, of interacting socially, and so on. These changes add up cumulatively to new forms of consciousness. In the Print Age, the book was the main tool for conducting knowledge enterprises and learning. It was a synchronic one for the era—it was a tool that humans knew how to use efficiently and effectively for various reasons. It also formed the basis of how we processed information and grasped knowledge. As the Print Age gave way to the Electronic Age and then to the Digital Age, the tools for knowledge-making and communicating also changed; also we derive a different sense of our own bodies, the organic substances that have been extended. As McLuhan (1970: 180) put it (posthumously), "When the evolutionary process shifts from biology to software technology the body becomes the old hardware environment. The human body is now a probe, a laboratory for experiments." But print communication has not disappeared. The lesson is that human evolution is guided by the forces of technological innovations but such innovations do not cut the chains in the historical chronicle that we ourselves have fashioned.

Extension always had positive and negative effects. While it enhances biological, mental, and institutional structures, it also may lead to "amputations," as McLuhan called them. So, for instance, the ax made it possible to cut wood more effectively, but it also became a weapon of killing, literally allowing humans to amputate each other more effectively. The automobile extended the body's locomotive abilities, allowing us to go farther and faster than walking and running would allow. However, it has also led to the loss of physical locomotion capacities that might have evolved biologically more so than they have—that is, it has led to the amputation of walking and the healthy aspects connected with it. We are thus no longer a walking culture, but an automobile culture. Nevertheless, we truly are an inventive species, counteracting amputation effects in ingenious ways. So, we have retrieved walking with walking clubs, jogging, running competitions, and so on. The Internet extends the reach of communication and information access, but in so doing it has amputated the art of calligraphy and personal signatures as a means to convey personality, as well as the desire to check facts through primary sources. It has also amputated previous voice technologies like the telephone. Nevertheless, we have retrieved writing in various other ways, such as courses on writing and graphology; and, of course, cell phones and smart phones have retrieved telephony in a new and more versatile way.

We praise extensions and minimize or even forget the amputations they produce. McLuhan suggested, however, that we do so at our own peril. This paradoxical nature of extension can be seen throughout history. Take, again, the example of contemporary digital forms of communication. Losing the kinds of literacy and numeracy skills that the print book introduced into human life is clearly a risky amputation. While the World Wide Web has greatly enhanced the ability to access information and create sophisticated texts, the peril is that it may have amputated reading for reflection and contemplation. There is retrieval of these important mental attributes in various forms, of course, but the value placed on reading for meaning, rather than for informational or recreational purposes, may be somewhat amputated. However, books have not disappeared, nor has reading culture. In some ways, reading and writing modalities have become more eclectic, perhaps more so than at any other time in the past, given the new media for books (ebooks, and the like). That is the paradox of technological extensions—they take us forward (amplification) and back (retrieval) at the same time.

McLuhan also feared what he called "over-extensions," whereby a technology like the automobile, when over-extended, leads to atrophy, pollution, and fatalities that challenge its benefits. Indeed, the dangers of over-extension might outweigh the benefits, including a tendency to instill superficial values into human life. We praise extensions and minimize or even forget the amputations they produce. McLuhan suggested, however, that we do so at our own peril. This paradoxical nature of extension can be seen throughout history.

Any new medium can thus be seen to have a vertical-horizontal modality; that is, it looks forward and back at the same time, amalgamating these two temporal dimensions into a flow that moves vertically and horizontally along a historical axis that resembles the Cartesian coordinate system—hence the configuration of the tetrad in the form of such a system with its four quadrants. The social-evolutionary implications are obvious—there is no future without the past and the past itself is constantly being retrieved in the present. So, to extend the analogy with the coordinate system, we can "plot" on the tetrad's quadrants any "point" in relation to other points in it. So, when people talk about the obsession with information that the Internet has brought about, this can be mapped onto other points in the tetrad—namely the advent and appeal of new information sources, while at the same time retrieving the penchant for reading.

McLuhan always emphasized that the individuals who understood the meanings of a new medium insightfully were not the scientists who invented it, but rather artists, creative individuals, and younger people who tap into it almost instinctively. So, a technology such as moving pictures (movies) was at first adopted by creative individuals (directors) who established a new popular art form—*cinema* at the turn of the twentieth century. Any component of popular culture can be explained in this way. A new art form is at first connected to some new technology and appropriated by individuals who exploit it to produce new forms of art and expression. The perfect example of this is the pop art movement, which actually used commercial objects of technology as its subject matter. The James Bond set of movies has also always tapped into changing social realities connected with technologies. The 2015 movie, *Spectre,* dealt with a villain who wanted to dominate the world by manipulating all information sources and using them ruthlessly to thwart individual freedoms—a theme that reflects an unconscious fear in virtually everyone today with respect to the new information-based world order. New media invariably involve us and affect us organically, that is, throughout our body and mind. McLuhan (1961) put it as follows: "Media are means of extending and enlarging our organic sense lives into our environment." We literally live in the new media of cyberspace experiencing them as extensions of our organs.

During the 1970s, the Digital Age started fomenting as newspapers and other print publications began to use the computer to create their texts. The same digitization process occurred eventually across all other traditional media—leading to the convergence of all media into one huge system of digital mass communications. McLuhan pointed out, again perceptively, that the content of one medium is always another medium. In the Web 2.0 world, we now experience media content as a two-way process, not the one-way process that characterized virtually all previous stages. It is useful to cite Jenkins (2006), who breaks down the contemporary meaning of convergence into various categories, given that convergence is a critical notion in the Digital Age:

1. *Technological convergence*, or the digitization of all content and the manufacturing of devices that contain recording and video functions, so that anyone can record, videotape, and upload content.
2. *Economic convergence*, whereby mega-media companies buy up content more and more turning the mass media system into a conglomerate.
3. *Social convergence*, which involves channel switching, multimodal navigation and multitasking, a system of behavior that now affects all aspects of life.
4. *Cultural convergence*, or participatory culture unfolding in such media as social networking sites.
5. *Global convergence*, which is the admixture of hybrid cultural products arising from global exchanges.

Convergence of the mass media has led to various critical questions, including how these may be effacing traditional cultures across the globe. No wonder, then, that the concept of extension is becoming a focus of study in various academic disciplines. As argued here, it dovetails with the basic definition of semiosis. McLuhan's ideas are this of rather profound importance to the study of the relation between semiosis and technology. There is little doubt, in my mind at least, that alongside the names of Saussure and Peirce the name of McLuhan must be added to the modern history of sign study.

Figure-Ground

McLuhan used the concept of figure-ground to illustrate how the tetrad works cognitively. The "figure" is any consciously recognizable element of a structure or situation, and the "ground" is the part that goes unnoticed but which encodes meaning and sense and must thus be figured out and interpreted. A figure is literally in the foreground of our attention while the ground occupies the background. When a new medium is introduced, its content is part of the foreground, while its new environment is part of the background. To understand how it works, one must attempt to get to the background.

The idea comes initially, of course, from visual art study, relating to the perception of images via the distinction of objects from a background from which they appear to stand out, especially where this distinction leads to ambiguity. The relation between the figure and the ground and its potential for ambiguity is seen in classic optical illusions (discussed briefly in Chapter 5), such as the so-called Rubin face, named after Danish psychologist Edgar Rubin, who first described it in 1921:

The Rubin Optical Illusion

This shows how the figure-ground relation works cognitively, since at one time we see two faces and at another a vase, and this occurs automatically without any way of controlling the back and forth shift in image perception. In semiotic terms, this relation constitutes an opposition (discussed previously). As we saw, opposition is, generically speaking, a relation between two (or more) forms which are differentiated from each other but are unified because of sharing some conceptual domain—one cannot be thought of without the other.

McLuhan argued that an extension or amplification constitutes the figural part of a conceptual opposition, much like an optical illusion, bringing the future into the present. So, at times we perceive its future uses, and at others its current practical ones. Every new medium is therefore a kind of optical illusion. Indeed, with every new technological innovation we all sense the future as "having arrived" through it and the past as having been rendered obsolete. Right below this figure in the reversal quadrant of the tetrad is the ground on which this figural perception can be seen to exist, whereby we sense a reversal. So, for example, we might perceive new digital devices as literally allowing us to see the future of communications, at the same time as we learn how the devices fit in with the present. Retrieval involves the figural perception of the new tool as somehow allowing us to recapture our historical past. It brings, as mentioned, the past into the present. Obsolescence is, in this model, a ground, whereby we sense that the weakening of some faculty allows us to evaluate the past in terms of the present. It thus takes the present into the past:

AMPLIFICATION *FIGURE* A human attribute is amplified and the perception occurs that through it we have brought the future into the present.	OBSOLESCENCE *GROUND* A faculty or medium is rendered obsolete, and is perceived as the past. So, the new medium is sensed as taking the present into the past.
REVERSAL *GROUND* When a new tool or medium is pushed to maximum capacity, we sense that it is literally grounded in the present but anticipates the future. It is perceived as taking the present into the future.	RETRIEVAL *FIGURE* A human attribute is amplified and the perception occurs that through it we have brought the future into the present.

Figure-Ground Relations

This figure-ground relation was a mainstay theme of research in Gestalt psychology, as is well known. And it was the basis upon which Freud developed his theory of mind, dovetailing with artistic movements such as Surrealism and Cubism. As McLuhan put it: "While Poe and the Symbolists were exploring the irrational in literature, Freud had begun to explore the resonant figure/ground double-plot of the conscious and unconscious" (McLuhan and McLuhan 1988: 52). Indeed, Cubism, as McLuhan went on to observe, is really a grounding of acoustic space in visual form (McLuhan and McLuhan 1988: 55).

One system where McLuhan identified the figure-ground opposition as being intrinsic to its very constitution and *raison d'être* was language: "Language always preserves a play or figure/ground relation between experience and perception and its replay in expression" (McLuhan and McLuhan 1988: 121), thus anticipating the contemporary research on metaphor, which is highly supportive of the figure-ground view of language and thus of its metaphorical structure: "All words, in every language, are metaphors" (McLuhan and McLuhan 1988: 121). Given the importance of the current research on metaphor to the McLuhanian notion of figure-ground, it is worthwhile taking a rapid overview here of its main ideas and findings. The finding that stands out, above any other, is that metaphor is an amplification of human thinking and sense-making, and when a new metaphor enters the lexicon it renders previous forms of discourse obsolete—rendering them clichés.

Metaphor, as we saw (Chapter 6), amplifies the mind to think beyond the senses and concrete stimuli. Modern-day scientific interest in metaphor as a trace to the nature of human cognition, rather than as a mere figure of speech, is due to the pivotal work of the early psychologists in the latter part of the nineteenth century. Overall, the findings are highly supportive of the figure-ground nature of language put forth by McLuhan. A tetrad can, in fact, be drawn up to show how metaphor works as a cognitive tool:

AMPLIFICATION *FIGURE* A metaphor blends information in an open-ended fashion, allowing us to see things that are not present and thus to anticipate future events.	OBSOLESCENCE *GROUND* It renders previous language to describe some phenomenon obsolete, thus allowing us to see it as clichéd.
REVERSAL *GROUND* The metaphor is coined in the present but its open-ended nature allows us to anticipate the future. It takes the present into the future.	RETRIEVAL *FIGURE* Human cognition is amplified, allowing us to see the future in the present by re-evaluating past forms of language and thought.

Tetrad for Metaphor

Findings show that metaphor evokes synesthesia. When we speak of *warm, soft, cold, harsh* colors, we are evoking different senses in tandem. This is strong indirect evidence that metaphorical se This is strong indirect evidence that metaphorical semiosis is intermodal, involving more than one sensory modality at once. As McLuhan (2011: 166) put it: “Languages are environments to which the child relates synesthetically.” Incidentally, language can also produce aesthetic effects, or the activation of all the sensory modalities in a holistic way. This occurs when we read poetic works which utilize various tropes in tandem, including metaphor, allusion, metonymy, onomatopoeia, and so on.

Economy and Efficiency

A major theoretical implication of the four laws is that they can be used to understand an unconscious psycho-biological "law" of evolution and semiosis that can be called the "E-E" law—an abbreviation "Economy and Efficiency." Basically, it stipulates that each new system introduced by new technology and/or symbolism is more economical and efficient than previous ones. Consider the development of positional numeral systems in mathematics. This constitutes a new mental technology (a meta-extension) that has spurred discovery and innovation within mathematics itself. The decimal system has made it possible to represent mathematical operations in economical ways, that is, in ways that make quantitative information more manageable than, say, the Roman numeral system. This new symbolic toolbox has allowed mathematics to evolve more rapidly—ten digits (symbols) are all that are needed to represent numbers ad infinitum. The binary system is even more economical and efficient, operating on a binary dichotomy that seems to inhere in all kinds of natural and mechanical systems. It is consistent with the on-off structure of electrical circuits and thus the basis for computer hardware and the overall design of computational systems. In contrast to non-positional systems of notation, these are efficient, mirroring perhaps the E-E propensities of the human brain. In language this propensity for "doing a lot with very little" has, as is well known, been designated the principle of *double articulation*, a term introduced by the French linguist André Martinet (1955).

A small number of phonemes in a language (usually around 50-60) is sufficient to make words endlessly in that language. The construction of words is guided by rules of word formation and syntax, of course, but these are hardly innate structures, as Noam Chomsky has always maintained (mentioned previously); grammatical and mathematical rules are our reversal responses to the amplifications that symbolic and mediated changes bring about, rendering them more stable over stretches of time. Moreover, the rules are our descriptions of what is anatomically possible and what is not. For example, in English the phoneme /p/ *(p)* can be combined with, say, the phoneme /f/ *(f)* (*helpful, upflow, stepfather*) within words ad infinitum, but the two cannot be combined in initial or final position, as they can in German, its sister language *(Pferd* "horse," *Knopf* "button"). However, /p/ can be combined with /r/ or /l/ in any environment to make words ad infinitum. Now, in no language known, can initial /p/ be combined with /k/ or /x/, because the anatomy of the organs of phonation cannot be used to articulate resulting clusters in an effortless way. In other words, our anatomy blocks the formation of certain phonic structures. So, all our rules do is acknowledge these facts.

Without double articulation and anatomically-based rules of formation, it would require an enormous amount of effort and memory to create words with distinct sounds each time that we need some word for encoding some novel referent; it would require the creation of huge vocabularies, countless new phonemes, and thus an enormous memory system to remember them. The E-E law guarantees that such a situation would never occur. The E-E law also explains how specific symbolic systems emerge. For example, the use of exponential symbolism was devised initially to be an abbreviation strategy to facilitate the cumbersomeness of reading repeated multiplications of the same digit, such as:

$$10 \times 10 \times 10 \times 10 \times 10 \times 10 \times 10 \times 10 \times 10 \times 10 \times 10 \times 10$$

The brain seems to boggle at such complex information-processing tasks. But the use of 12 as a superscript symbol, standing for the times a number is to be used as a factor, greatly simplifies such tasks:

$$10 \times 10 \times 10 \times 10 \times 10 \times 10 \times 10 \times 10 \times 10 \times 10 \times 10 \times 10 = 10^{12}$$

In other words, exponential notation saves space and reduces the time and cognitive energy required to process the same information. It reflects the E-E law perfectly. Now, a simple invention such as this invariably produces a domino effect, leading to new inventions and new discoveries. In other words, this simple notational device did much more than just make multiplication less effortful to process. Right after its introduction it took on a life of its own. In fact, subsequent to its invention mathematicians started to play with exponential notation in an abstract way, discovering new facts about numbers. For example, they discovered that $n^0 = 1$, thus enucleating a property of zero that was previously unknown. They also developed a new set of arithmetical laws, such as the following:

$$(n^a)\,(n^b) = n^{a+b}$$
$$(n^a)\,(m^a) = (nm)^a$$
$$(n^a) \div (n^b) = n^{a-b}\ (n \neq 0)$$
$$(n^a)^b = n^{ab}$$
$$n^{-a} = 1/n^a$$

Exponential notation also became the basis for the theory of logarithms, which also started out as a means of doing arithmetic more efficiently and with more economical means. Logarithms have been used in many areas of mathematics, in science, and in statistics, allowing for all kinds of discoveries to occur in these domains as well. They are a concrete illustration of how the domino effect works. The relevant point is that a simple notational device invented to make a certain type of multiplication easier to read was the source of all kinds of new discoveries, directly or indirectly.

The minimal requirement for double articulation in mathematics is two symbols. This is the case with the binary digit system, where all numbers can be represented with 0 and 1. As mentioned already, this type of system is incredibly productive; it is a domino that has set off a true cascade of ideas and applications. For example, it was used in the Morse Code as dashes and dots (mentioned several times previously), and of course it is the basic principle underlying how computer architecture works (where on-versus-off are the two basic states). Binary symbol systems constitute a skeletal set of elements (two) from which complex structures can be formed.

In human systems, there are two structural levels of articulation. The first level consists of the units themselves available for constructing larger structures. In the binary system, the units are 0 and 1. Complex units that are made up from this pair occur at the secondary level. So, when combined according to rules of positional value, these two digits can represent any numerical concept imaginable: 100 = three (3 in decimal notation), 11010 = twenty-six (26). Now, the units at the first level lack meaning in themselves (digits, phonemes, etc.), whereas those at the secondary level (such as morphemes, actual numbers) bear meaning and function. The first-level units show what Saussure (1916) called *différence*. The secondary-level units have combinatory function, since they are combinations from the set of units at the first level and thus possess meaning in themselves. Saussure referred to this as *valeur.*

Double articulation does not seem to occur in the communication systems of animals, making it, likely, a unique property of human semiosis. Nöth (1990: 155) puts it as follows:

> Among these features, *double articulation* most certainly does not occur in natural animal communication systems. Most probably, not even the "ape language" Yerkish is decoded as a system with double articulation. Some authors who ascribe the feature of double articulation to bird calls and other animal "languages" seem to take the mere segmentability of acoustic signals for a level of second articulation, However, a prerequisite of a truly phonemic patterning is that the same minimal but meaningless elements are

> combined to form new messages. When they are substituted for each other, the substitution results in a semantic difference. This type of patterning seems to be absent from animal communication systems.

The term *efficiency* needs further commentary here, since it has taken on various specialized meanings in science. In general, it is the ability of organisms or machines to do something successfully without waste (of time, energy, and other resources). It is thus related to the concept of optimization in computer science—it is the measure of the extent to which an input is used optimally for an intended output, with a minimum amount or quantity of waste, expense, or effort. Efficiency is thus a measurable phenomenon, in terms of the ratio of output to input. As applied to the E-E law, it is the underlying psycho-biological force behind the operation of extension. Extensions increase efficiency, rendering obsolete anything that goes against them. Symbols can now be defined explicitly as efficient forms, encoding all kinds of information in them without the need for further symbolism to encode them separately.

The tetrad is, in sum, a useful model of how technology, social change, and human psycho-biological propensities operate in tandem. Technologies and media (include symbols) are the vehicles through which we reify the tool-making impulse within us. In a phrase, we are the makers of our own destiny. If we bring about something negative because of our technologies, that is, if we bring about amputations of something worthwhile to human life, then we seek to find ways around them to retrieve values and take recuperative action, as discussed. As McLuhan satirically put it: "Instead of scurrying into a corner and wailing about what media are doing to us, one should charge straight ahead and kick them in the electrodes" (McLuhan 1960: 148). Extensions are neither good nor bad; they are what we make of them. When asked about this very idea, McLuhan (1987: 300) responded as follows:

> My main theme is the extension of the nervous system in the electric age, and thus, the complete break with five thousand years of mechanical technology. This I state over and over again. I do not say whether it is a good or bad thing. To do so would be meaningless and arrogant.

The E-E law may also explain convergence of media—a form of media compression into one efficient multimedia system. As mentioned already, the term convergence was introduced in the mid-1990s to describe essentially the McLuhanian law of retrieval in the Digital Age. It refers to the integration and amalgamation of media, technologies, and their content through digitization. It also refers to the merging of different modes of communication into one huge connected system that McLuhan (1964) called the global village. This village is very much like a real tribal village, where a new virtual form of orality has emerged accompanied by the retrieval of *mythos* (understanding through metaphysical narratives).

Epilogue

McLuhan's dictum that the "medium is the message" is a basic principle of semiotic theory. The form of the sign is a medium that extends some sensory function, and what it refers to is dynamically intertwined with the form, one suggesting the other. This is, of course, the basic definition of sign, enunciated by Saussure, whereby the signifier and the signified cannot be separated from the sign. This implies that the signifying resources and elements used to make representations are tools in the McLuhanian sense, namely extensions of the biology and psychology of the human organism making them. In effect, our signs are derivatives of ourselves.

A corollary to this notion is that media modify or recalibrate our senses. As this happens, shifts in human consciousness occur and these are then extrinsecated in forms of knowledge, understanding, and of culture. Because of the fact that media are tools extending bodily and cognitive processes they have brought about several major paradigm shifts over the course of human history. It is in this insight that semiotics can find something relevant to incorporate into its modus operandi. The tetrad is a perfect model of how evolutionary semiosis functions. An example is the cognitive shift that occurred as a consequence of the invention of writing and the spread of literacy. This led to a change in the brain. Pictures are sensed holistically. They cannot be broken up and "read sequentially." On the other hand, reading and writing activate linear decoding and thus thinking processes in the brain, because, as argued, printed ideas are laid out one at a time and can thus be connected to each other sequentially and analyzed logically in relation to each other. Orality, on the other hand, is not conducive to such precise thinking, because spoken ideas are transmitted through the emotional qualities of the human voice and are, thus, inextricable from orator who transmits them and the audiences that listen in. Oral culture was thus acoustic; literate culture is visual. Printed information can be easily categorized and preserved in some durable material form such as books. Simply put, without the advent and institutionalization of literacy, the spread of philosophy, science, jurisprudence, and the many other human intellectual activities that we now hold as critical to the progress of human civilization would simply not have been possible in the first place. But orality has not, of course, disappeared from human life. It was rendered obsolete at first, but is always being retrieved in various forms. The spoken word comes naturally; literacy does not. Through simple exposure to everyday dialogue, children develop the ability to speak with little or no effort and without any training or prompting whatsoever. Literacy, on the other hand, does not emerge through simple exposure to printed texts. It is learned through instruction, practice, and constant rehearsal. Schools were established, in fact, to impart literacy and print-based knowledge.

Culture is a sensory-extensional system, providing its own "sensorium," or environment to activate the senses in specific ways. Thus, the kinds of sensory forms and the type of sensory information available to children reared in a specific culture will shape how their mind develops. In a sense, the laws of natural selection have ceded to the laws of technological selection. And each aspect of the selection is guided by principles of semiosis, which is thus not only a law of life but also one of technology, embedded in semiotic laws lite the E-E one among others.

References

Agawu, K. (2008). *Music as Discourse: Semiotic Adventures in Romantic Music*. New York: Oxford University Press.

Ananthanarayanan, R., Esser, S. K., Simon, H. D., and Modha, D. S. (2009). The Cat Is Out of the Bag: Cortical Simulation with 10^9 Neurons, 10^{13} Synapses. *Proceedings of the Conference on High Performance Computing Networking, Storage and Analysis*. Article No. 63.

Andersen, H. (1989). Markedness Theory: The First 150 Years. In: O. M. Tomic (ed.), *Markedness in Synchrony and Diachrony*, 11-16. Berlin: Mouton de Gruyter.

Andersen, H. (2001). Markedness and the Theory of Linguistic Change. In: H. Andersen (ed.), *Actualization*, 19-57. Amsterdam: John Benjamins.

Andersen, H. (2008). Naturalness and Markedness. In: K. Wellems and L. De Cuypere (eds.), *Naturalness and Iconicity in Language*, 101-119. Amsterdam: John Benjamins.

Andersen, P. B. (1997). *A Theory of Computer Semiotics*. Cambridge: Cambridge University Press

Andrews, E. (1990). *Markedness Theory*. Durham: Duke University Press.

Andrews, E. (2003). *Conversations with Lotman: Cultural Semiotics in Language, Literature, and Cognition*. Toronto: University of Toronto Press.

Andrews, E. and Tobin, Y. (eds.) (1996). *Toward a Calculus of Meaning: Studies in Markedness, Distinctive Features and Deixis.* Amsterdam: John Benjamins.

Aristotle (1952). *Rhetoric*. In *The works of Aristotle*, Vol. 11, W. D. Ross (ed.). Oxford: Clarendon Press.

Arnheim, R. (1969). *Visual Thinking*. Berkeley: University of California Press.

Asch, S. (1955). On the Use of Metaphor in the Description of Persons. In: H. Werner (ed.), *On Expressive Language*, 29-38. Worcester: Clark University Press.

Ashby, W. R. (1956). *An Introduction to Cybernetics*. London: Chapman and Hall.

Aston, E. and Savona, G. (1991) *Theatre as a Sign System.* London: Psychology Press.

Augustine, St. (1887). *De doctrina christiana. Patrologia latina, migne tomus XXXIV*. Paris: Hachette.

Bain A. (1868). *The Senses and the Intellect*. London: Longmans.

Bakhtin, M. M. (1981). *The Dialogic Imagination.* Trans. C. Emerson and M. Holquist. Austin: University of Texas Press.

Bakhtin, M. M. (1984). *Rabelais and His World.* Bloomington: Indiana University Press.

Bar–Hillel, Y. (1960). The Present Status of Automatic Translation of Languages. *Advances in Computers* 1: 91-163.

Barkow, J., Cosmides, L., and Tooby, J. (1992). *The Adapted Mind: Evolutionary Psychology and the Generation of Culture*. Oxford: Oxford University Press.

Barthes, R. (1957). *Mythologies.* Paris: Seuil.

Barthes, R. (1964a) *Éléments de sémiologie*. Paris: Seuil.

Barthes, R. (1964b). Rhetoric of the Image. Reproduced in: C. Handa (ed.), *Visual Rhetoric in a Visual World: A Critical Sourcebook.* New York: Bedford/St. Martin's.

Barthes, R. (1967). *Système de la mode,* Paris: Seuil.

Barthes, R. (1977). *Image-Music-Text.* London: Fontana.

Barthes, R. (1981) Theory of the Text. In: R. Young (ed.), Untying the Text, 31-47. London: Routledge.

Bateson, G. (1972). *Steps to an Ecology of Mind.* New York: Ballantine.

Battistella, E. L. (1990). *Markedness: The Evaluative Superstructure of Language.* Albany: State University of New York Press.

Battistella, E. L. (1996). *The Logic of Markedness*. Oxford: Oxford University Press.

Baudrillard, J. (1983). *Simulations*. New York: Semiotexte.

Benvenistc, E. (1946). Structure des relations de personne dans le verbe. *Bulletin de la Société de Linguistique de Paris* 43: 225-236.

Berger, J. (1972). *Ways of Seeing.* Harmondsworth: Penguin.

Bergin, T. G. and Fisch, M. (1984). *The New Science of Giambattista Vico*. Ithaca: Cornell University Press.

Berlin, B. and Kay, P. (1969). *Basic Color Terms*. Berkeley: University of California Press.

Berlinski, D. (2000). *The Advent of the Algorithm.* New York: Harcourt.

Bickerton, D. (2009). *Adam's Tongue: How Humans Made Language, How Language Made Humans.* New York: Hill & Wang.

Birdwhistell, R. L. (1952). *Introduction to Kinesics*. Ann Arbor, MI: University of Ann Arbor.

Birdwhistell, R. L. (1970). *Kinesics and Context: Essays on Body Motion Communication.* Harmondsworth: Penguin.

Black, M. (1962). *Models and Metaphors*. Ithaca, NY: Cornell University Press.

Bloomfield, L. (1933) *Language*. New York: Holt, Rinehart, and Winston.

Bogdan, C. (2002). *The Semiotics of Visual Languages*. New York: Columbia University Press.

Bolinger, D. (1968). *Aspects of Language*. New York: Harcourt, Brace, Jovanovich.

Bor, D. (2012). *The Ravenous Brain: How the New Science of Consciousness Explains Our Insatiable Search for Meaning*. New York: Basic Books.

Brier, S. (2008). *Cybersemiotics.* Toronto: University of Toronto Press.

Broca, P. (1861). Remarques sur le siège de la faculté du langage articulé suivies d'une observation d'aphémie. *Bulletin de la Société d'Anatomie* 36: 320-357.

Brown, R. (1958). *Words and Things: An Introduction to Language.* New York: The Free Press.

Brown, R. (1970) *Psycholinguistics: Selected Papers*. New York: Free Press.

Bühler, K. (1908). On Thought Connection. In: D. Rapaport (ed.), *Organization and Pathology of Thought*, 81-92. New York: Columbia University Press.

Bühler, K. (1934). *Sprachtheorie: Die Darstellungsfunktion der Sprache*. Jena: Fischer.

Buss, D. M. (2004). *Evolutionary Psychology: The New Science of the Mind.* Boston: Pearson.

Carnap, R. (1942). *Introduction to Semantics*. Cambridge, Mass: Harvard University Press.

Cassirer, E. (1944). *An Essay on Man.* New Haven: Yale University Press.

Church, A. (1935). Abstract No. 204. *Bulletin of the American Mathematical Society* 41: 332-333

Church, A. (1936). An Unsolvable Problem of Elementary Number Theory. *American Journal of Mathematics* 58: 345-363.

Conway, J. H. (2000). *On Numbers and Games.* Natick, Mass.: A. K. Peters.

Crow, D. (2010). *Visible Signs: Introduction to Semiotics in the Visual Arts.* New York: Ava.

Damasio, A. R. (1994). *Descartes' Error: Emotion, Reason, and the Human Brain.* New York: G. P. Putnam's.

Danesi, M. (2007). *The Quest for Meaning: A Guide to Semiotic Theory and Practice.* Toronto: University of Toronto Press.

Danesi, M. (2013). *Signs of Crime: Introducing Forensic Semiotics.* Berlin: Mouton de Gruyter.

Danesi, M. (2016). *The Semiotics of Emoji*. London: Bloomsbury.

Danesi, M. (2019). *Enigmatology: The Science of Puzzles*. München: Lincom Europa.

Danesi, M. (2020). *Pythagoras' Legacy: Mathematics in Ten Great Ideas.* Oxford: Oxford University Press.

Danesi, M. and Zukowski, N. (2019). *Medical Semiotics*. München: Lincom Europa.

Davis, P. J. and Hersh, R. (1986). *Descartes' Dream: The World According to Mathematics*. Boston: Houghton Mifflin.

Dawkins, R. (1976). *The Selfish Gene*. Oxford: Oxford University Press.

Dawkins, R. (1985). *River Out of Eden: A Darwinian View of Life*. New York: Basic.

Dawkins, R. (1987). *The Blind Watchmaker*. Harlow: Longmans

Dawkins, R. (1998). *Unweaving the Rainbow: Science, Delusion and the Appetite for Wonder*. Boston: Houghton Mifflin.

Deely, J. (2001). *Four Ages of Understanding: The First Postmodern Survey of Philosophy from Ancient Times to the Turn of the Twentieth Century.* Toronto: University of Toronto Press.

Déjerine, J. (1892). Contribution à l'étude anatomo-pathologique et clinique des différents variétés de cécité verbale. *Comptes Rendus des Sciences de la Société de Biologie* 9: 61-90.

Derrida, J. (1967). *De la grammatologie.* Paris: Minuit.

Derrida, J. (1976). *Of Grammatology*, trans. by G. C. Spivak. Baltimore: Johns Hopkins Press.

Descartes, R. (1633) *De Homine.* Amsterdam: Elsevier.

Douglas, M. (1966). *Purity and Danger*. Harmondsworth: Penguin.

Eco, U. (1976). *A Theory of Semiotics*. Bloomington: Indiana University Press.

Eco, U. (1979). *The Role of the Reader: Explorations in the Semiotics of Texts.* Bloomington: Indiana University Press.

Eco, U. (1989). *The Open Work*. Cambridge, Mass.: Harvard University Press.

Eco, U. (1990). *I limiti dell'interpretazione*. Milano: Bompiani.

Ekman, P. (1982). Methods for Measuring Facial Action. In: K. R. Scherer and P. Ekman (eds.), *Handbook of Methods in Nonverbal Behavior*, 45-90. Cambridge: Cambridge University Press.

Ekman, P. (1985). *Telling Lies.* New York: Norton.

Ekman, P. (2003). *Emotions Revealed.* New York: Holt.

Eliasmith, C., Stewart, T. C., Choo, X., Bekolay, T. DeWolf, T., Tang, Y., and Rasmussen, D. (2012). A Large-Scale Model of the Functioning Brain. *Science* 338: 1202-1205.

Engelbart, D. (1962). *Augmenting Human Intellect: A Conceptual Framework.* SRI Project No. 3578, Stanford Research Institute.

Enninger, W. (1992). Clothing. In: R. Bauman (ed.), *Folklore, Cultural Performances, and Popular Entertainments*, 123-145. Oxford: Oxford University Press.

Epes Brown, J. (1992). Becoming Part of It. In: D. M. Dooling and P. Jordan-Smith (eds.), *I Become Part of It: Sacred Dimensions in Native American Life*, 1-15. New York: Harper Collins.

Fan-Pei, G. Y., Bradley, K., Huq, M., Wu, D-L, and Krawczyk, D. C. (2013). Contextual Effects on Conceptual Blending in Metaphors: An Event-Related Potential Study. *Journal of Neurolinguistics* 26: 312-326.

Fauconnier, G. and Turner, M. (2002). *The Way We Think: Conceptual Blending and the Mind's Hidden Complexities*. New York: Basic.

Fisher, H. (1992). *Anatomy of Love.* New York: Norton.

Flanagan, O. J. (1984). *The Science of the Mind.* Cambridge, Mass.: MIT Press.

Foucault, M. (1972). *The Archeology of Knowledge*, trans. by A. M. Sheridan Smith. New York: Pantheon.

Frege, G. (1879). *Begiffsschrift eine der Aritmetischen nachgebildete Formelsprache des reinen Denkens.* Halle: Nebert.

Freud, S. (1901). *The Interpretation of Dreams*. New York: Avon.

Gardner, M. (1970). The Fantastic Combinations of John Conway's New Solitaire Game "Life." *Scientific American* 223: 120-123.

Ghiselin, M. T. (1973). Darwin and Evolutionary Psychology. *Science* 179: 964-968.

Gitlin, T. (2001). *Media Unlimited: How the Torrent of Images and Sounds Overwhelms Our Lives*. New York: Picador.

Goertzel, B. (2010). *A Cosmist Manifesto: Practical Philosophy for the Posthuman Age.* Humanity+ Press.

Good, I. J. (1965). Speculations Concerning the First Ultraintelligent Machine. *Advances in Computers* 6: 31-83.

Goode, J. (1992). Food. In: R. Bauman (ed.), *Folklore, Cultural Performances, and Popular Entertainments*, 233-245. Oxford: Oxford University Press.

Greimas, A. J. (1966). *Sémantique structurale.* Paris: Larousse.

Greimas, A. J. (1970). *Du sens.* Paris: Seuil.

Hall, E. T. (1959). *The Silent Language*. New York: Anchor.

Hall, E. T. (1966). *The Hidden Dimension.* New York: Doubleday.

Halliday, M. A. K. (1985). *Introduction to Functional Grammar.* London: Arnold.

Haraway, D. (1989). *Primate Visions: Gender, Race, and Nature in the World of Modern Science*. London: Routledge

Haraway, D. (1991). *Simians, Cyborgs, and Women: The Reinvention of Nature*. London: Free Association Books.

Hawkins, J. and Blakeslee, S. (2004). *On Intelligence.* New York: Times Books.

Hegel, G. W. F. (1807). *Phaenomenologie des Geistes*. Leipzig: Teubner.

Heidegger, M. (1976). *Phaenomenologie und Theologie*. Frankfurt: Klostermann.

Hjelmslev, L. (1939). Note sur les oppositions supprimables. *Travaux de Cercle Linguistique de Prague* 8: 51-57.

Hjelmslev, L. (1959). *Essais linguistique*. Copenhagen: Munksgaard.

Hobbes, T. (1656). *Elements of Philosophy.* London: Molesworth.

Hollander, A. (1988). *Seeing Through Clothes.* Harmondsworth: Penguin.

Honeck, R. P. and Hoffman, R. R. (eds.) (1980). *Cognition and Figurative Language*. Hillsdale, NJ: Lawrence Erlbaum Associates.

Humboldt, W. von (1836). *On Language: The Diversity of Human Language-Structure and Its Influence on the Mental Development of Mankind.* Cambridge: Cambridge University Press.

Husserl, E. (1890). *Philosophie der Arithmetik*. The Hague: Nijhoff.

Huxley, J. (1957). *New Bottles for New Wine*. London: Chatto & Windus.

Jakobson, R. (1939). Observations sur le classement phonologique des consonnes. *Proceedings of the Fourth International Congress of Phonetic Sciences,* 34-41.

Jakobson, R. (1942). *Kindersprache, Aphasie und algemeine Lautgesetze*. Uppsala: Almqvist and Wiksell.

Jakobson, R. (1960). Linguistics and Poetics. In: T. A. Sebeok (ed.), *Style and Language*, 34-45. Cambridge, Mass.: MIT Press.

James, W. (1890). *The Principles of Psychology.* New York: Henry Holt.

Janet, P. (1893). *The Mental State of Hystericals: A Study of Mental Stigmata and Mental Accidents*. New York: G. P. Putnam's Sons.

Jappy, T. (2013). *Introduction to Peircean Visual Semiotics*. London: Bloomsbury.

Jenkins, H. (2006). *Convergence Culture: Where Old and New Media Collide*. New York and London: MIT.

Johnson, M. (1987). *The Body in the Mind: The Bodily Basis of Meaning, Imagination and Reason*. Chicago: University of Chicago Press.

Jung, C. G. (1983). *The Essential Jung*. Princeton: Princeton University Press.

Kant, I. (1790). *Critique of Judgment*. New York: Hafner Press.

Kay, P. (1975). Synchronic Variability and Diachronic Change in Basic Color Terms. *Language in Society* 4: 257-270.

Kendon, A. (2004). *Gesture: Visible Action as Utterance*. Cambridge: Cambridge University Press.

Köhler, W. (1925). *The Mentality of Apes*. London: Routledge and Kegan Paul.

Korzybski, A. (1933). *Science and Sanity.* Brooklyn: Institute of General Semantics.

Kristeva, J. (1980). *Desire in Language: A Semiotic Approach to Literature and Art*. New York: Columbia University Press.

Kull, K. (1999). Biosemiotics in the Twentieth Century: A View from Biology. *Semiotica* 127: 385-414.

Kurzweil, R. (1999). *The Age of Spiritual Machines*. New York: Viking Press.

Kurzweil, R. (2005). *The Singularity Is Near.* Harmondsworth: Penguin.

Kurzweil, R. (2012). *How to Create a Mind: The Secret of Human Thought Revealed.* New York: Viking.

Lakoff, G. (1987). *Women, Fire, and Dangerous Things: What Categories Reveal about the Mind*. Chicago: University of Chicago Press.

Lakoff, G. and Johnson, M. (1980). *Metaphors We Live By*. Chicago: Chicago University Press.

Lakoff, G. and Johnson, M. (1999). *Philosophy in the Flesh: The Embodied Mind and Its Challenge to Western Thought*. New York: Basic.

Langacker, R. W. (1987). *Foundations of Cognitive Grammar*. Stanford: Stanford University Press.

Langacker, R. W. (1990). *Concept, Image, and Symbol: The Cognitive Basis of Grammar*. Berlin Mouton de Gruyter.

Langacker, R. W. (1999). *Grammar and Conceptualization*. Berlin Mouton de Gruyter.

Langer, S. K. (1948). *Philosophy in a New Key.* New York: Mentor Books.

Langer, S. K. (1957). *Problems of Art: Ten Philosophical Lectures*. London: Routledge.

Lashley, K. S. (1929). *Brain Mechanisms and Intelligence*. Chicago: University of Chicago Press.

Lepik, P. (2008). *Universals in the Context of Juri Lotman's Semiotics*. Tartu: Tartu University Press.

Lévi-Strauss, C. (1958). *Anthropologie structurale.* Paris: Plon.

Lévi-Strauss, C. (1962). *La pensée sauvage.* Paris: Plon.

Lévi-Strauss, C. (1964). *The Raw and the Cooked.* London: Cape.

Lévi-Strauss, C. (1971). *L'Homme nu.* Paris: Plon.

Licklider, J. C. R. (1960). Man-Computer Symbiosis. *IRE Transactions on Human Factors in Electronics, HFE-1*: 4-11.

Lippmann, W. (1922). *Public Opinion*. New York: Macmillan.

Locke, J. (1690). *An Essay Concerning Humane Understanding*. Oxford: Clarendon Press.

Lombardo, A. (1981) *Il testo e la sua performance*. Rome: Bulzoni Editore.

Lotman, Y with Salvestroni, S. (1981). " La semiotica della scena" in «Strumenti critici : rivista quadrimestrale di cultura e critica letteraria», vol. XV, n. 44, Turin, pp. 1-29.

Lotman, Y. (1991). *Universe of the Mind: A Semiotic Theory of Culture.* Bloomington: Indiana University Press.

Ludden, D. (2015). Fifty Shades of Grue: The Intimate Relationship Between Language and Color Perception. *Psychology Today* (psychologytoday.com/us/blog/talking-apes/201502/fifty-shades-grue).

Magnus, M. (1999) *Gods of the Word: Archetypes in the Consonants.* Kirksville, Missouri: Thomas Jefferson University Press.

Magnus, M. (2013) A History of Sound Symbolism. In: K. Allan (ed.), *The Oxford Handbook of the History of Linguistics*, 191-212. Oxford: Oxford University Press.

Malinowski, B. (1923) The Problem of Meaning in Primitive Languages. In: C. K. Ogden and I. A. Richards, *The Meaning of Meaning*. London: Routledge and Kegan Paul.

Markram, H. (2008). Fixing the Location and Dimensions of Functional Neocortical Columns. *Human Frontier Science Program* 2: 132-135.

Martinet, A. (1955). *Économie des changements phonétiques*. Paris: Maisonneuve and Larose.

Maturana, H. R. and Varela, F. (1973). *Autopoiesis and Cognition: The Realization of the Living*. Dordrecht: Reidel.

McLuhan, M. (1951). *The Mechanical Bride: Folklore of Industrial Man*. New York: Vanguard.

McLuhan, M. (1960). Report to the National Educational Broadcasters Association, quoted in: *Marshall McLuhan: The Medium and the Messenger,* by Philip Marchand, Cambridge: MIT Press.

McLuhan, M. (1962). *The Gutenberg Galaxy: The Making of Typographic Man*. Toronto: University of Toronto Press.

McLuhan, M. (1964). *Understanding Media: The Extensions of Man*. Cambridge: MIT Press.

McLuhan, M. (1968). *Through the Vanishing Point.* New York: Harper & Row.

McLuhan, M. (1969). *Counterblast*. New York: Gingko Press.

McLuhan, M. (1970). *Culture is Our Business*. New York: Wipf & Stock.

McLuhan, M. (1985). *Tyuonyi*, Volumes 1-2 (entire volumes).

McLuhan, M. (1987). *Letters of Marshall McLuhan*, ed. by M. Molinaro and C. McLuhan. Oxford: Oxford University Press.

McLuhan, M. (1998). *The Agenbite of Outwit*, published posthumously in *McLuhan Studies*, Volume 1, Issue 2 (January 1998).

McLuhan, M. (2011). *The Book of Probes: Marshall McLuhan*. Designed by David Carson, edited by Marshall McLuhan Project, W. Terrance Gordon, Eric McLuhan, Philip B. Meggs. New York: Gingko Press.

McLuhan, M. and Barrington, N. (1972). *Take Today: The Executive as Dropout*. New York: Harcourt, Brace, & Jovanovich.

McLuhan, M. and McLuhan, E. (1988). *The Laws of Media.* Toronto: University of Toronto Press.

McNeill, D. (1992). *Hand and Mind: What Gestures Reveal about Thought.* Chicago: University of Chicago Press.

Metz, C. (1974). *Film Language: A Semiotics of the Cinema.* Chicago: University of Chicago Press.

Miller, G. A. (1956). The Magical Number Seven, Plus or Minus Two: Some Limits on Our Capacity for Processing Information. *Psychological Review* 63: 81-97.

Morgan, C. L. (1895). *Introduction to Comparative Psychology*. London: Scott.

Morris, C. W. (1938). *Foundations of the Theory of Signs*. Chicago: University of Chicago Press.

Morris, C. W. (1946). *Signs, Language and Behavior.* Englewood Cliffs, N.J.: Prentice-Hall.

Morris, D. (1969). *The Human Zoo*. London: Cape.

Morris, D., Collett, P., Marsh, P., and O'Shaughnessy, M. (1979). *Gestures: Their Origins and Distributions.* London: Cape.

Müller-Lyer, F. C. (1889). Optische Urteilstäuschunge. *Archiv für Physiologie Suppl.*: 263-270.

Nattiez, J.-J. (1990). *Music and Discourse: Toward a Semiology of Music*. Princeton: Princeton University Press.

Needham, R. (1973). *Right and Left.* Chicago: University of Chicago Press.

Neisser, U. (1967). *Cognitive Psychology*. Englewood Cliffs, NJ: Prentice–Hall.

Neuman, Y. (2014). *Introduction to Computational Cultural Psychology*. Cambridge: Cambridge University Press.

Neumann, J. von (1958). *The Computer and the Brain*. New Haven: Yale University Press.

Nicaso, A. and Danesi, M. (2013). *Made Men: Mafia Culture and the Power of Symbols, Rituals, and Myth.* Lanham: Rowman & Littlefield.

Nietzsche, F. (1873). *Philosophy and Truth: Selections from Nietzsche's Notebooks of the Early 1870's*. Atlantic Heights, NJ: Humanities Press.

Nöth, W. (1990). *Handbook of Semiotics.* Bloomington: Indiana University Press.

Nuessel, F. (1992). *The Study of Names: A Guide to the Principles and Topics.* Westport: Greenwood.

Ogden, C. K. (1932). *Opposition: A Linguistic and Psychological Analysis*. London: Paul, Trench, and Trubner.

Ogden, C. K. and Richards, I. A. (1923). *The Meaning of Meaning*. London: Routledge and Kegan Paul.

O'Neill, S. (2008). *Interactive Media: The Semiotics of Embodied Interaction*. New York: Springer

Ong, W. (197). *Orality and Literacy*. New York: Methuen.

Ortony, A. (ed.) (1979). *Metaphor and Thought*. Cambridge: Cambridge University Press.

Osgood, C. E., Suci, G. J., and Tannenbaum, P. H. (1957). *The Measurement of Meaning*. Urbana: University of Illinois Press.

Pavlov, I. (1902). *The Work of Digestive Glands*. London: Griffin.

Peirce, C. S. (1931-1958) *Collected Papers of Charles Sanders Peirce*, Vols. 1-8, C. Hartshorne and P. Weiss (eds.). Cambridge, Mass.: Harvard University Press.

Penrose, R. (1989). *The Emperor's New Mind*. Cambridge: Cambridge University Press.

Piaget J. (1969). *The Child's Conception of the World*. Totowa, NJ: Littlefield, Adams & Co.

Piaget, J. and Inhelder, J. (1969). *The Psychology of the Child*. New York: Basic Books.

Plato (2006). *Meno*. Cambridge: Cambridge University Press.

Pollio, H. R., Barlow, J. M., Fine, H. J., and Pollio, M. R. (1977). *The Poetics of Growth: Figurative Language in Psychology, Psychotherapy, and Education*. Hillsdale, NJ: Lawrence Erlbaum.

Propp, V. (1928). *Morphology of the Folktale*. Austin: University of Texas Press.

Quine, W. (1953). *From a Logical Point of View*. Cambridge: Harvard University Press.

Richards, I. A. (1936). *The Philosophy of Rhetoric*. Oxford: Oxford University Press.

Roberts, D. D. (2009). *The Existential Graphs of Charles S. Peirce*. The Hague: Mouton.

Rubin, E. (1921). *Visuell Wahrgenommene Figuren: Studien in psychologischer Analyse*. Kobenhaven: Gyldendalske Boghandel.

Ruesch, J. and Bateson, G. (1951). *Communication: The Social Matrix of Psychiatry*. New York: Norton.

Samuel, A. (1959). Some Studies in Machine Learning Using the Game of Checkers. *IBM Journal of Research and Development* 3: 210-229.

Sapir, E. (1921). *Language*. New York: Harcourt, Brace, and World.

Sapir, E. (1929) A Study in Phonetic Symbolism. *Journal of Experimental Psychology* : 225-239.

Saussure, F. de (1916) *Cours de linguistique générale*, ed. by C. Bally and A. Sechehaye Paris: Payot.

Schmandt-Besserat, D. (1992). *Before Writing*, 2 vols. Austin: University of Texas Press.

Sebeok, T. A. (1977). *A Perfusion of Signs*. Bloomington: Indiana University Press.

Sebeok, T. A. (1990). *Essays in Zoosemiotics*. Toronto: Toronto Semiotic Circle.

Sebeok, T. A. (2001a). *Global Semiotics*. Bloomington: Indiana University Press.

Sebeok, T. A. (2001b). *Signs: An Introduction to Semiotics*. Toronto: University of Toronto Press.

Sebeok, T. A. and Danesi, M. (2000). *The Forms of Meaning: Modeling Systems Theory and Semiotics*. Berlin: Mouton de Gruyter.

Shackell, C. (2018). Finite Cognition and Finite Semiosis: A New Perspective on Semiotics for the Information Age. *Semiotica* 222: 225-240.

Shackell, C. (2019). Finite Semiotics: Recovery Functions, Semioformation, and the Hyperreal. *Semiotica* 227: 211-226.

Shannon, C. E. (1948). Mathematical Theory of Communication. *Bell Systems Technical Journal* 27: 379-423.

Shannon, C. E. and Weaver, W. (1949). *Mathematical Theory of Communication.* Chicago: University of Illinois Press.

Silverstein, M. (1976). Shifters, Linguistic Categories and Cultural Description. In K. H. Basso and H. A. Selby (eds.), *Meaning in Anthropology*, 11-55. Albuquerque: University of New Mexico Press.

Sirius, R. U. and Cornell, J. (2015). *Transcendence: The Disinformation Encyclopedia of Transhumanism and the Singularity.* San Francisco: Disinformation Books.

Skinner, B. F. (1938). *The Behavior of Organisms*. New York: Appleton–Century–Crofts.

Stam, J. (1976). *Inquiries in the Origin of Language: The Fate of a Question.* New York: Harper and Row.

Stjernfelt, F. (2007). *Diagrammatology: An Investigation on the Borderlines of Phenomenology, Ontology, and Semiotics*. New York: Springer.

Stross, B. (1976). *The Origin and Evolution of Language.* Dubuque, Iowa: W. C. Brown.

Swadesh, M. (1951). Diffusional Cumulation and Archaic Residue as Historical Explanations. *Southwestern Journal of Anthropology*: 1-21.

Swadesh, M. (1959). Linguistics as an Instrument of Prehistory. *Southwestern Journal of Anthropology* 15: 20–35.

Swadesh, M. (1971). *The Origins and Diversification of Language.* Chicago: Aldine–Atherton.

Tanaka-Ishii, K. (2010). *Semiotics of Programming.* Cambridge: Cambridge University Press.

Tarasti, E. (1979). Myth and Music. Berlin and New York: Mouton de Gruyter.

Tarasti, E. (1994). *A Theory of Musical Semiotics*. Bloomington: Indiana University Press.

Thorndike, E. L. (1898). *Animal Intelligence*. New York: Psychological Monographs.

Thorndike, E. L. (1905). *The Elements of Psychology.* New York: A. G. Seiler.

Titchener, E. B. (1910). *A Textbook of Psychology*. Delmar: Scholars' Facsimile Reprints.

Todorov, T. (1982). *Theories of the Symbol.* Ithaca: Cornell University Press.

Tolman, E. (1932). *Purposive Behavior in Animals and Men.* New York: Appleton-Century-Crofts.

Tomaselli, K. (2009). *Appropriating Images: The Semiotics of Visual Representation.* Højbjerg, Denmark: Intervention Press.

Tomic, O. M. (1989) (ed.), *Markedness in Synchrony and Diachrony*. Berlin: Mouton de Gruyter.

Toro, F. de (1995). *Theatre Semiotics*. Toronto: University of Toronto Press.

Trubetzkoy, N. S. (1936). Essaie d'une théorie des oppositions phonologiques. *Journal de Psychologie* 33, 5-18.

Trubetzkoy, N. S. (1939). Grundzüge der Phonologie. *Travaux du Cercle Linguistique de Prague* 7 (entire issue).

Tulving, E. (1972). Episodic and Semantic Memory. In: E. Tulving and W. Donaldson (eds.), *Organization of Memory*, 23-46. New York: Academic.

Turner, M. (2013). *The Origin of Ideas.* Oxford: Oxford University Press.

Uberfeld, A. (1977). *Lire le théâtre*, Paris, Éditions sociales.

Uexküll, J. von (1909). *Umwelt und Innenwelt der Tierre*. Berlin: Springer.

Ulam, S. (1958). Tribute to John von Neumann. *Bulletin of the American Mathematical Society* 64: 5.

Vinge, V. (1981). *True Names*. New York: Tor Books.

Vinge, V. (1993). The Coming Technological Singularity: How to Survive in the Post-Human Era. In: G. A. Landis (ed.), *Vision-21: Interdisciplinary Science and*

Engineering in the Era of Cyberspace, 11-22. NASA Publication CP-10129.

Vygotsky, L. S. (1961). *Thought and Language*. Cambridge, Mass.: MIT Press.

Watson, J. B. (1913). *Psychology from the Standpoint of a Behaviorist*. Philadelphia: Lippincott.

Weizenbaum, J. (1966). ELIZA—A Computer Program for the Study of Natural Language Communication Between Man and Machine. *Communications of the ACM* 9: 36-45.

Wernicke, C. (1874). *Der aphasische Symptomenkomplex*. Breslau: Cohn and Weigart.

Wertheimer, M. (1923). Untersuchungen zur Lehre von der Gestalt, II. *Psychologische Forschungen* 4: 301-350.

Whitehead, A. N. (1929). *Process and Reality*. New York: Free Press.

Whorf, B. L. (1956). *Language, Thought, and Reality*, J. B. Carroll (ed.). Cambridge, Mass.: MIT Press.

Whorf, B. L. (1956). *Language, Thought, and Reality*, J. B. Carroll (ed.). Cambridge, Mass.: MIT Press.

Wiener, N. (1948). *Cybernetics, or Control and Communication in the Animal and the Machine*. Cambridge, Mass.: MIT Press.

Wiener, N. (1950). *The Human Use of Human Beings: Cybernetics and Society*. Boston: Houghton, Mifflin.

Wilson, E. O. (1975). *Sociobiology: The New Synthesis*. Cambridge, Mass.: Harvard University Press.

Wilson, E. O. (1979). *On Human Nature*. New York: Bantam.

Wilson, E. O. (1984). *Biophilia*. Cambridge, Mass.: Harvard University Press.

Wilson, E. O. and Harris, M. (1981). Heredity versus Culture: A Debate. In: J. Guillemin (ed.), *Anthropological Realities: Readings in the Science of Culture*, 450-465. New Brunswick, N. J.: Transaction Books.

Wolfram, S. (2002). *A New Kind of Science*. Champaign, Ill.: Wolfram Media.

Wundt, W. (1880). *Grundzüge der physiologischen Psychologie*. Leipzig: Englemann.

Wundt, W. (1901). *Sprachgeschichte und Sprachpsychologie*. Leipzig: Eugelmann.

Zantides, E. (ed.) (2014). *Semiotics and Visual Communication: Concepts and Practices*. Cambridge: Cambridge Scholars Publishing.

Basic Glossary of Semiotics

This glossary lists many of the terms that were used in this book, and others that are found scattered throughout the field of semiotics. It can thus be used as a self-contained basic reference dictionary. The entries here do not cover related areas of cognitive science, Artificial Intelligence, etc.

A

Abduction term used by Charles Peirce to designate how a concept is formed on the basis of an existing concept or model by inference; an abduction is essentially a hunch as to what something entails or presupposes

Abstract art 20th century visual art style characterized by the use of abstract, symbolic images (rather than direct, realistic ones) conveying moods, feelings, and impressions

Abstract concept concept that cannot be demonstrated or observed directly in some physical way like some object: *justice, hope, experience*, etc.

Acculturation process by which continuous contact between two or more distinct societies causes cultural change. Acculturation unfolds in one of two ways: 1. the beliefs, conventions, customs, and codes of the societies in contact may merge producing a single culture; 2. one society may completely absorb the cultural patterns of another, transforming them radically

Actant prototypical character role that manifests itself cross-culturally in all kinds of narratives: a *hero*, an *opponent*, a *helper*, etc.

Addressee receiver of a message

Addresser sender of a message

Aesthesia 1. total sensory and emotional reaction to a physical stimulus, an idea, or a work of art; 2. heightened sensitivity to beauty

Aesthetics 1. branch of semiotics that studies the meaning and interpretation of art in general; 2. study of beauty and meaning in art and of the psychological responses to it; aesthetics deals in particular with the question of whether beauty and ugliness are objectively present in art works, or whether they exist only in the mind of the individual

Algorithm systematic, step-by-step method of solving a certain kind of problem or of representing a procedure

Allegory narrative or poem in which the plot, the characters, and the settings have a purely symbolic meaning

Alliteration repetition of the initial sound (usually a consonant or consonant cluster) in two or more words of a phrase, expression, line of poetry, etc.: *no-no, ping-pong,* etc.

Allusion indirect reference to a theme, plot, character, idea, etc. in a conversation, play, narrative, discourse, etc.

Alphabet graphic code whereby individual characters stand for individual sounds (or sound combinations)

Alphabetic writing
writing system consisting of conventional symbols known as characters that can be used singly and in combination to make up the words of a language

Alterity concept or movement emphasizing ethnic, racial, and sexual diversity in philosophy, the arts, and the sciences. This movement was given impetus by Michel Foucault's argument in the 1980s that the "Other"—that is, the person of different race, sexual orientation, etc.—had been excluded for too long from the center of Western society's representational activities

Ambiguity ambivalence or multiplicity of meaning of a word, statement, work of art, etc.: *play* (as in *a Shakespearian play* versus *I play tennis all the time*)

Analogy 1. similarity in some respects between two words, statements, concepts, etc. that are otherwise unlike; 2. process by which words, constructions, etc. are formed or created on the model of already-existing patterns in a language; 3. process of making an inference from certain resemblances between two or more things to a probable further similarity between them

Anchorage term coined by Roland Barthes referring to the ways a meaning is determined, ass for example, how captions anchor the meaning of a photograph, a figure, etc.

Animism philosophical and religious view that objects possess a life force

Anthroposemiosis human semiosis (the production and comprehension of signs) as both linked to, and different from, animal semiosis (known as zoosemiosis)

Anthroposemiotics branch of semiotics dealing with human semiosis (the capacity for producing and comprehending signs) as similar to, or different from, semiosis in other species

Anticlimax sequencing of ideas in a phrase or sentence in abruptly diminishing importance, often for rhetorical or satirical effect

Antihero main character in a dramatic or narrative work who lacks the traditional heroic qualities, such as idealism or courage

Antinomy contradiction or inconsistency between two apparently reasonable principles, or between conclusions drawn from them

Antithesis rhetorical technique by which two words, phrases, clauses, or sentences are opposed in meaning in such a way as to give emphasis to contrasting ideas

Antonomasia 1. use of an epithet or title in place of a name; 2. use of a well-known personage to describe someone

Antonym word that is perceived to have an opposite meaning with respect to another word: *love*-versus-*hate*

Antonymy relation by which different words, phrases, sentences, etc. stand in a discernible oppositeness of meaning to each other

Apologue moral fable in which animals or inanimate objects are depicted as humanlike characters

Apostrophe rhetorical technique by which an actor turns from the audience, or a writer from his or her readers, to address a person who usually is absent or deceased, an inanimate object, or an abstract idea

Arbitrariness the relation between a word and its meaning that is purely arbitrary and/or conventional

Archetype 1. original pattern or model from which all other patterns of the same kind are made; 2. in psychology, any of several innate ideas or mental images which manifest themselves typically in conversations, dreams, myths, art forms, and performances across cultures

Architectural code
code that underlies the design and construction of buildings

Architecture art and science of designing and erecting buildings

Art disciplined expressive activity that provides the people who produce it and those who observe it with a range of aesthetic, emotional, and/or intellectual experiences

Artifact object produced or shaped by human craft, such as a weapon, a vase, a tool, a piece of jewelry, etc.

Artificial intelligence
branch of computer science concerned with the development of systems capable of imitating, or actually performing, human mental activities (problem-solving, inferencing, speaking, etc.)

Automata theory 1. study of computing processes; 2. study of the relationship between psychological theories of the human mind and the operation of automated devices

Axiom statement universally accepted as true, and therefore accepted without proof

B

Ballet classical dance form characterized by grace and precision of movement and elaborate formal technique

Baroque art style which started in Europe around 1550 and lasted till around 1750, emphasizing refined ornamentation, and an overall balance of disparate parts

Basic level concept
concept that has a typological (classificatory) function: *cat* (a *feline*)

Bauhaus School architectural school, also known as *International Style* or *Modernism*, founded in Weimar, in 1919, by Walter Gropius (1883-1969), promoting a simple, unadorned style of building design

Beat gesture hand gesture accompanying discourse, resembling the "beating" of musical tempo

Behaviorism school of psychology based on the view that observable and quantifiable behavior provides the only valid data for psychologists to study

Binarism view that two forms or signs are kept recognizably distinct by the presence of a minimal difference between them: *pin*-versus-*bin* (difference between *p* and *b*)

Biosemiosis term referring to semiosis (the production and comprehension of signs) in all living things

Biosemiotics branch of semiotics studying semiosis in all life forms

Biosphere environment or habitat to which a species has become adapted. Large-scale divisions of the biosphere into regions of different growth patterns are called *biomes*

Birth and rebirth myth

myth informing people about how life can be renewed or about the coming of an ideal society or savior

C

Catachresis 1. obscure use of a word or phrase for rhetorical effect; 2. improper use of a word or phrase

Catharsis purification of the emotions through the experience of a work of art or a performance of some kind (dramatic, musical, etc.)

Channel physical system carrying a transmitted signal

Character person portrayed in an artistic piece, such as a drama or novel

Chiaroscuro technique of using light and dark colors and/or shades in pictorial representation

Chiasmus structural inversion of the second of two parallel phrases or clauses

Chromaticism 1. in painting, color perceived to have a saturation greater than zero; 2. in music, type of composition or style based on the chromatic (nonharmonic) scale

Chronemics study of how cultures: 1. divide time into regular periods, 2. arrange events in the order of their occurrence, 3. assign dates to events

Cinema visual narrative art form that encompasses the utilization of verbal and nonverbal codes

Cinéma verité style of film-making that stresses stark psychological realism in the portrayal of character

Classicism term describing the art and literature created by the ancient Greeks and Romans, as well as any style or period of creative work distinguished by qualities that suggest or are derived from classical aesthetics; the term has been applied especially to the art and music of the period that starts around 1750 and ends around 1820

Climax 1. series of ideas, images, etc. arranged progressively so that the most forceful is last; 2. decisive turning point of the action in a drama, performance, or narrative

Closed work term coined by Umberto Eco in reference to a type of text with a singular or fairly limited range of meanings

Code 1. system of signs given certain meanings; 2. system of signs and structural patterns for constructing and deciphering messages

Cognitivism school of psychology originating in the 1950s based on the idea that mental functions, can be studied by seeking parallels between the brain and computer operations

Cohesive gesture gesture used during oral discourse that serves to show how the separate parts of an utterance are supposed to hold together.

Collocation meaning acquired by a word by virtue of its association with other words that tend to occur in linkage with it: *clear cut evidence*

Comics narrative text put together by means of a series of drawings arranged in horizontal lines, strips, or rectangles called panels, and read from left to right

Commedia dell'arte

type of comedy developed in Italy in the medieval and Renaissance eras, characterized by improvisation from standard plot outlines and stock characters, often in traditional masks and costumes. Although the governments of Spain and France attempted to censor and regulate *Commedia* performances, the ribald humor and realistic character types of the *Commedia* were eventually adopted by conventional theater

Communication 1. production and exchange of messages by means of signals, facial expressions, talk, gestures, or writing; 2. art of expressing ideas, especially in speech and writing

Commutation test technique for analyzing how meaningful differences in signs unfold and are maintained, consisting of commuting structurally-corresponding elements in a pair or set of forms in order to ascertain if such a commutation is meaning-bearing: *cat*-versus-*rat* (phonological commutation test), *night*-versus-*day* (semantic commutation test)

Conative function in Roman Jakobson's model of communication, the intended effect—physical, psychological, social—that a message has or is expected to have on the target or receiver of the message

Conceit 1. fanciful or witty expression; 2. elaborate, often extravagant metaphor that makes an association between things that are normally perceived to be totally dissimilar: *This water is fiery*

Concept general thought connection or pattern made by the human mind (within cultural contexts)

Conceptual metaphor

generalized metaphorical formula that defines a specific abstraction: *people are animals*

Conceptual metonym

generalized metonymical formula that defines a specific abstraction: *the face is the person*

Concrete concept concept that is demonstrable and observable in a direct way: *cat, table*, etc.

Connotation extended, secondary, or implied meaning of a sign (word, symbol, etc.) or text (conversation, story, etc.): *cat* in *cool cat*

Connotatum connotative referent of a sign

Contact in Roman Jakobson's model of communication, the physical conditions (channel, situation, etc.) in which a message is delivered and the primary social and psychological connections that exist or are established between the participants

Context 1. parts of a sentence, paragraph, or discourse that impose a constraint on the composition of a form and/or on what a form means; 2. whole situation, background, or environment (physical, social, psychological) that determines the meaning of something

Contrast minimal difference between two elements (two words, two symbols, etc.)

Conventional sign sign that is made by humans, versus natural sign that is made by Nature

Cosmogonic myth myth explaining how the world came into being

Cubism movement in 20th century visual art characterized by a separation of the subject into cubes and other geometric forms in abstract arrangements, rather than by a realistic representation of the subject

Cuisine term meant to emphasize the difference between the biological and cultural orders in human life in the area of eating; food pertains to the biological order, cuisine to the cultural order

Cultural model constant juxtaposition of conceptual metaphors that leads to a complex abstract model of a concept

Culture interconnected system of daily living that is held together by signs, codes, texts, and other sign-based phenomena

Culture hero myth myth describing beings who discover a cultural artifact or technological process that radically changes the course of history

Cuneiform writing writing code consisting of wedge-shaped symbols used in ancient Sumerian, Akkadian, Assyrian, Babylonian, and Persian writing

Cybernetics interdisciplinary science dealing with communication and control systems in living organisms, machines, and organizations

Cyberspace space created by the "computer culture" that has developed among users of these computers

D

Dadaism movement in painting, sculpture, and literature, lasting from about 1916 to 1922, characterized by highly imaginative, abstract, or incongruous creations, and especially by the rejection of all accepted conventions of western art

Dance art form based on bodily movements and gestures connected to each other in terms of musical tempo and rhythm. The functions of dance include: 1. aesthetic representation; 2. narration through bodily movement; 3. recreation; 4. Ritual

Decoding process of deciphering the message formed in terms of a specific code

Deconstruction method of literary analysis originated by Jacques Derrida in the mid-20th century, based on his view that, by the very nature of language and literary usage, no TEXT can have a fixed, central meaning

Definition statement of the meaning of a word or phrase

Deictic gesture gesture utilized during oral discourse which serves to indicate an abstract concept that had occurred earlier in the conversation

Deixis pointing out something by a gesture, word, or symbol, in order to locate it in time, space or in relation to something else

Denotation initial meaning that a sign is designed to capture

Denotatum denotative referent of a sign

Diachrony change in signs and sign systems over time

Diagram 1. geometric figure, used to illustrate a mathematical statement, proof, etc.; 2. sketch, drawing, or plan that explains a thing by outlining its parts and their relationships; 3. chart or graph explaining or illustrating ideas, statistics, etc.

Dialectic process of examining opinions or ideas logically, often by a method of question and answer, so as to determine their validity

Dicisign in Peircean theory the term *dicisign* refers to the meanings elicited by such indexical signs like *here*, *there*, etc.

Différence Ferdinand de Sausssure's notion that a sign bears meaning by virtue of its perceptible *difference* in form from other signs

Discourse 1. communication of ideas, information, etc., by talking or writing; 2. long and formal treatment of a subject, in speech or writing; 3. system or style of communication (as in the *discourse of postmodernity*)

Discreteness term referring to the fact that signs are fashioned from a small set of elements that form meaningful oppositions with each other

Discursive form notion developed by Susanne Langer, whereby the composition of an art work is governed by the linear, syntactic properties of language

Displacement feature of signs whereby whatever they stand for can be evoked even if not present for the senses to perceive

Drama verbal performing art that involving actors on a stage or platform with the background support of setting and props

Dramatic irony dramatic effect achieved by informing an audience about an incongruity between a situation and the accompanying dialogue or action, while the characters in the play remain unaware of the incongruity

Dress code system of clothing suitable for certain occasions or for a certain place or time (such as the appropriate *dress for wedding ceremonies*)

Dualism view that the mind and body function separately, and that human beings have two essential natures, the physical and the spiritual

Duality of patterning feature of language whereby vocal sounds have no intrinsic meaning in themselves but combine in different ways to form elements (e.g. words) that do convey meanings

E

Echoism linguistic imitation of sounds heard in the environment

Ego in psychoanalysis, central part of personality that allows the individual to cope with reality. The ego is said to begin forming as soon as neonates start to become aware of their encounters with the external world, learning to modify their behavior in socially-expected ways

Emblem 1. figure with a motto or verses, allegorically suggesting some moral truth; 2. visible symbol of a thing, idea, class of people, etc.; 3. object that stands symbolically for something else

Emotive function in Roman Jakobson's model of communication, the addresser's (sender's) emotions, attitudes, social status, etc. as they are worked into and shape the message-making process

Encoding process of putting together a message in terms of a specific code

Entropy term referring to anything that is unpredictable in a message or text

Eponymy name of a city, country, era, institution, or other place or thing derived from the name of a person

Eschatological myth

myth describing the end of the world or the coming of death into the world

Euphemism rhetorical technique by which a term or phrase that has coarse, sordid, or other unpleasant associations is replaced by one that is perceived to be more delicate or inoffensive

Evolutionary psychology

contemporary school of psychology that is concerned with studying human behaviors and symbolic phenomena in terms of evolutionary theories

Exclamation rhetorical technique by which a sudden outcry expressing strong emotion, such as fright, grief, or hatred, is interpolated into a text

Exegesis critical explanation or analysis of a text

Existentialism philosophy that emphasizes the uniqueness and isolation of the individual's experience in a hostile or indifferent universe, stressing freedom of choice and responsibility for the consequences of one's acts.

Eye contact length of time involved in looking, and type of looking pattern, that people in social situations exhibit, conveying what kind of relationship they have with each other

F

Fable fictitious story meant to teach a moral lesson. In a fable the characters are usually talking animals, given the attributes of human beings; the moral is typically summed up at the end of the improbable story

Facial expression facial cast or look that conveys emotion

Fairytale story about *fairies* (diminutive, supernatural, creatures, generally in human form) dwelling in an imaginary region called *fairyland* who intervene through magic in human affairs

Fashion prevailing dress style or custom of an era, group of people, or entire society

Feedback process of detecting signals or cues issuing from the receiver of a message so that the performance or control of the communication system can be maintained or improved

Fetish object that is believed to have magical or spiritual powers, or to cause sexual arousal

Fetishism extreme devotion to objects and desires

Fetishism extreme devotion to objects

Fiction literary work whose content is produced by the imagination and is not necessarily based on fact

Firstness in Peircean theory, the first level of meaning derived from bodily and sensory processes

Focal color color category that is associated with a universal sequencing of colors

Folktale generic term for the various kinds of narrative prose literature found in the oral traditions of the world. Myths, legends, and fairytales are considered to be the three main types of folktale

Food code 1. complex rules of how to prepare food and when to eat it; 2. meanings that specific dishes have vis-à-vis group membership; 3. set of rules governing eating events

Foundation myth myth recounting the founding of cities

Functionalism 1. in architecture, 20th movement stressing functional design of a building; 2. in psychology, school of thought that stresses the study of the mind as a functioning component of the entire physiological individual

G

Gaze looking at someone intently and steadily

Gender sexual identity and role established in cultural terms

Genre works of literature, art, etc. classified together according to subject, theme, or style

Gesticulant gesture unit accompanying speech

Gesticulation use of gestures to accompany speech

Gestural code system of communication based on gesture

Gesture semiosis and representation by means of the hand, arms, and, to a lesser extent, the head

Global village Marshall McLuhan's term designating a world that depends upon electronic media for information and is thus united, electronically, as if in a village

Glossematics approach in semiotics and linguistics initiated by Louis Hjelmslev (1899-1965) and Hans Jørgen Uldall (1907-1957) which formalizes the basic notions of structuralism

Glyph symbol or figure on a public sign that imparts information nonverbally

Graffiti inscription or drawing scratched, incised, or drawn on a wall or other public surface. Graffiti have been used by linguists to reconstruct an earlier form of a language, and by social scientists to penetrate the mindset of a particular social group or subculture

Grammar 1. in Latin and Greek, term referring to the whole apparatus of language and literary study; 2. in the Medieval period it referred to the study of Latin, and hence to all learning as recorded in Latin; 3. in linguistics, it refers to the study of the form and structure of words, with their customary arrangement in phrases and sentences

Grammatology study of language from the perspective developed by Jacques Derrida whereby oral speech is seen as a derivative of writing, and not the other way around, as linguists have traditionally maintained. Derrida formulated grammatological theory on the basis of archeological evidence, which suggested to him that pictographic language preceded vocalized language

Graph 1. type of diagram (curve, broken line, series of bars, etc.) representing the successive changes in a variable quantity or quantities in mathematics; 2. unit in a writing-system representing a phoneme, a syllable, etc.

Ground 1. in metaphor theory, the meaning of the metaphor; 2. In painting, the entire or connecting surface of a scene

Gutenberg Galaxy Marshall McLuhan's term describing the radical new social order that ensued from the invention of print technology

H

Haptics 1. having to do with the sense of touch; 2. branch of semiotics studying touching patterns during social interaction

Hermeneutics 1. in semiotics, the study and interpretation of texts; 2. in psychology, the study of the meanings derived from social behavior and experience

Hero 1. in mythology and legend, a personage, often of divine ancestry, who is endowed with great courage and strength, celebrated for his bold exploits, and favored by the gods; 2. principal character in a novel, poem, or dramatic representation

Hieroglyphic writing
ancient Egyptian system of writing, in which pictorial symbols were used to represent meaning or sounds or a combination of meaning and sound

Historiography systematic study and documentation of history in general, or of the history of some nation, event, movement, discipline, etc. in particular

Holophrase one-word utterance produced by infants

Homograph word that is spelled the same as another but with a different meaning: *home (my own home)* versus *home (he hit a home run*)

Homophone: words pronounced the same but with different meanings: *ant*-versus-*aunt*

Homonymy verbal coincidence by which two or more words with distinct meanings, are pronounced and/or spelled in the same way

Hyperbole rhetorical exaggeration for effect

Hypermedia computer-based information retrieval system that enables a user to gain or provide access to texts, audio and video recordings, photographs, and computer graphics related to a particular subject. A hypermedia navigation might include links to such topics as *language*, *semantics*, *communication*, *semiotics*, and *media*

Hypertext electronic text that provides links between key elements, allowing the user to move through information non-sequentially

Hypertextuality system for linking different texts and images within a computer document or over a network

Hypoicon Charles Peirce's term for an icon that is shaped by cultural convention but which can nonetheless be figured out by those who are not members of the culture (with prompting)

Hyponym concept, expressed by a word, that is inclusive of another *rose* is an example of *flower*

Hyponymy semantic relation whereby one concept embraces another

I

Icon 1. sign that is made to resemble its referent through some form of replication, resemblance, or simulation (such as onomatopoeic words: *splash, bang*, etc.); 2. a visual image of some kind; 3. picture of a sacred or sanctified Christian personage; 4. one who is the object of great attention and devotion (an idol); 5. in computer science, picture on a screen that represents a specific command

iconic gesture gesture used while speaking that bears a close resemblance to what is being talked about

Iconicity process of representing things with iconic signs (onomatopoeic words, photographs, etc.)

Id in psychoanalytic theory, the element of personality which undergirds instinctual drives

Idealism theory of reality and of knowledge that physical objects are mind-dependent and can have no existence apart from a mind that is conscious of them. This view is in opposition to materialism, which maintains that consciousness itself is purely physical, and to realism, the view that mind-independent physical objects exist and can be known through the senses

Ideogram 1. graphic sign representing an object or idea without indicating the pronunciation of the word or words that stand for the object or idea

Ideographic writing

type of writing system in which a character, known as an ideograph, may bear some resemblance to its referent, but is also in part a symbolic signifier

Idiom speech form or expression that is peculiar to itself grammatically or cannot be understood from the individual meanings of its elements: *born with a silver spoon*

Image 1. mental picture of something; 2. concept of a person, product, institution, etc. held by the general public, often one deliberately created or modified by publicity, advertising, propaganda, etc. 3. in psychoanalysis, a picture or likeness of a person, buried in the unconscious

Image schema term used by George Lakoff and Mark Johnson to refer to the recurring structures of, or in, our perceptual interactions, bodily experiences, and cognitive operations that portray locations, movements, shapes, etc. in the mind

Index sign in which the signifier has an existential connection to its signified or referent (that is, the sign indicates that something "exists" somewhere in time and/or space): *here, there, up, down, left, right*, etc.

Index sign whose function is pointing out something real or imaginary in temporal spatial or relational terms

Indexicality process of representing something with indexes. The presence of *indexicality* in representational systems across the world is evidence that human consciousness is attentive to recurrent cause and effect patterns and to the fact that referents occur in time, space, and in relation to one another: *this* or *that*, *here* or *there*, *before* or *after*, *now*, or *then*, *the one* or *the other*, etc.

Information any fact or datum that can be stored and retrieved by humans or machines

information theory

theoretical framework developed by Claude Shannon in the late 1940s for improving the efficiency of telecommunication systems. Shannon's model has come to be known as the bull's-eye model of communication, because it essentially depicts a sender aiming a message at a receiver as in a bull's-eye target:

Innenwelt specific system of understanding of a species that allows it to make sense of the input it receives from the outside world. This term is often used in biosemiotics, used first by Jakob von Uexküll in 1909, for referring to the fact that all organisms possess species-specific modeling capacities that allow them to respond in kind to their outer experiences

Interpretant Charles Peirce's term for the meaning that one gets from a SIGN, whereby the sign-user evaluates or responds to what the sign means socially, contextually, personally, etc.

Interpretation 1. process of deciphering what a sign or text means; 2. act or result of deriving the meaning of something; 3. realization of a person's conception of a work of art, subject, etc. through acting, playing, writing, criticizing, etc. (e*the pianist's interpretation of the Beethoven sonatas)*

Intertext culture-specific text alluded to within a main text. The text can be cited, rewritten, prolonged, or transformed by the main text

Intertextuality allusion within a text to some other text of which the interpreter would normally have knowledge

Irony 1. humorous or subtly sarcastic expression in which the intended meaning of the words stands in direct opposition to their usual sense; 2. cool, detached attitude of mind, characterized by recognition of the incongruities and complexities of experience

K

Kineme basic unit of bodily-based meaning: a pose, a facial expression, etc.

Kinesic code 1. science or study of human muscular movements, especially as applied in physical education; 2. a code based on some aspect of bodily semiosis

Kinesics study of bodily semiosis

Kinestheme minimal unit of significant bodily movement: a posture, a pose, a look, etc.

L

Langue term used by Ferdinand de Saussure to refer to the largely unconscious knowledge that speakers of a language share about what forms and grammatical structures are appropriate in that language

Legal semiotics branch of semiotics aiming to study the representational system underlying law-making

Legend story derived from folk history that differs from myth in that it tells about what has happened in the world since the period of its creation

Legisign in Peircean theory, a representamen (signifier) that designates something by convention: *a whistle used by a referee.* Peirce viewed all legisigns as provisional

Lexical field set of lexical items (words) related to each other thematically (weather vocabulary, geometrical terms, etc.)

Lexicon 1. compilation of special words or terms of a particular author, field of study, etc.; 2. record or inventory of all words and terms collected in a volume or a language

Libido in psychoanalysis, the psychic and emotional energy associated with instinctual sexual drives. According to the theories of Austrian psychoanalyst Sigmund Freud, the libido is the sex instinct, which can be rechanneled as artistic creation. Swiss psychiatrist Carl Jung rejected the sexual basis, believing that the general will to live is the force that drives creativity

Litotes rhetorical technique involving understatement for enhancing the effect of the ideas expressed

Logo a distinctive company or brand signature, trademark, colophon, motto, newspaper nameplate, etc.

Logocentrism notion that language shapes worldview and personal attitudes; logocentric cultures are those that depend on the written word for gaining knowledge

Logogram symbol representing an entire spoken word without expressing its pronunciation

Logograph full symbol or character representing a word

Logographic writing
highly symbolic writing system in which a character, known as a logograph, resembles its referent only in small part

M

Map 1. drawing (by hand or electronically) or other representation, usually on a flat surface, of all or part of the earth's surface, ordinarily showing countries, bodies of water, cities, mountains, etc.; 2. similar representation of part of the sky, showing the relative position of the stars and planets

Markedness view that ibn an opposition, such as *off*-versus-*on* one of the two poles is the default (expected one), called *unmarked*, and the other the derived or subsidiary one, called *marked*: in an alarm system, the *off* mode is unmarked (expected) while the *on* is marked (unexpected)

Mask 1. material covering for the face or part of the face, to conceal the identity of the wearer; 2. figure of a head worn on the stage by an ancient Greek or Roman actor to identify a character and amplify the voice

Materialism in philosophy, theory of reality and of knowledge that posits consciousness as being the result of purely physical (evolutionary) processes

Meaning what is referred to or understood by a sign, a text, etc.

Medium 1. any means, agency, or instrument of communication; 2. the physical means by which a sign or text is encoded (put together) and through which it is transmitted (delivered, actualized)

Meme term coined by sociobiologist Richard Dawkins to refer to the units of information and conceptualization (fashions, tunes, ideas, etc.) that are acquired and transmitted in cultural settings

Message 1. communication (information, feelings, ideas, etc.) passed on or transmitted by talking, writing, etc.; 2. in software, a piece of information passed from the application or operating system to the user

Metacommunication
theory or statement about communication whose purpose it is to examine the nature of communication

Metafiction fiction about fiction, whose purpose it is to examine the nature of fiction and narrative

Metalanguage theory or statement about language, whose purpose it is to examine the nature of language

Metalingual function in
Roman Jakobson's model of communication communicative function by which the code being used is identified: *This noun is a noun*

Metaphor application of a word or phrase with one meaning to another that has a different meaning, thus creating a new meaning by association: *The professor is an eagle*

Metaphoric gesture

gesture accompanying discourse that depicts the vehicle (concrete part) of a metaphor being utilized in the discourse

Metaphorology branch of semiotics studying metaphor and figurative language generally

Metaphysics branch of philosophy dealing with the nature of reality, including the relationship between mind and matter. Metaphysics is customarily divided into ontology, which examines the question of how many entities compose the universe, and metaphysics proper, which is concerned with describing the most general traits of reality

Metonymy signifying process by which an entity is used to refer to another that is related to it: *the face* for *human personality*

Mimesis 1. imitation in art, literature or representation; the imitation or representation of aspects of the sensible world, especially human actions, in literature and art; 2. in biology, physical or behavioral resemblance of one species to another that benefits the mimicking species or sometimes both species

Minimal pair two items which are the same except for one element in the same position: *cat*-versus-*rat*

Modeling system species-specific system that allows a species to make models of things in the world

Modernism technique in architecture also known as the Bauhaus school

Music art based on vocal or instrumental tones put together on the basis of a system of melody, harmony, rhythm, and timbre

Myth 1. ancient story dealing with supernatural beings, ancestors, or heroes; 2. any story or narrative that aims to explain the origin of something in metaphysical ways

Myth of the culture hero

myth describing the actions and characters of beings who are responsible for the discovery of a particular cultural artifact or technological process

Mytheme anthropologist Clause Lévi-Strauss's term referring to a basic event, role, or theme that goes into the make-up of a mythical story

Mythology 1. branch of semiotics and anthropology studying myths; 2. use and/or evocation of mythic themes in contemporary behaviors and performances

N

Name sign that identifies a person or place

Naming process by which names are assigned to persons, places, and things

Narrative something told or written, such as an account, story, tale

Narrative grammar
theory that the categories if narrative correspond to the categories of linguistic grammar

Narrative structure
universal patterns of plot, character, and setting in storytelling

Narrativity innate human capacity to produce and comprehend narratives

Narratology branch of semiotics that studies narrativity, narrative structure, and narratives

Natural sign 1. sign produced by Nature (a symptom, an unwitting signal); 2. sign that has been constructed to simulate some property of its referent

Naturalism 1. system of thought holding that all phenomena can be explained in terms of natural causes without attributing spiritual or metaphysical significance to them; 2. in art, practice of reproducing subjects as precisely as possible

Nickname descriptive name added to or replacing the actual name of a person

Nihilism term applied to various radical philosophies, usually by their opponents, implying that adherents reject all positive values and believe in nothing. The term was first used to describe Christian heretics during the Middle Ages. It was applied in Russia in the 1850s and 1860s in reference to young intellectuals who repudiated Christianity, considered Russian society backward, and advocated revolutionary change. The best-known fictional nihilist is Bazarov in the Russian novel *Fathers and Sons* (1862) by Ivan Turgenev (1818-1883)

Noise in communication theory, anything that interferes with the reception and successful decipherment of a message. In radio and telephone transmissions, *noise* is electronic static; in voice transmissions, it can vary from any interfering exterior sound (physical noise) to the speaker's lapses of memory (psychological noise)

Nominalism doctrine of the late Middle Ages that all universal or abstract terms are mere necessities of thought or conveniences of language and therefore exist as names only

Nonverbal branch of semiotics studying signs and codes based on the body: for example, gesture, facial expression, eye contact, etc.

Novel fictional prose narrative in which characters and situations are depicted within the framework of a plot

O

Object 1. in grammar, noun or other substantive that directly or indirectly receives the action of a verb, or is governed by a preposition; 2. in philosophy, anything that can be known or perceived by the mind; 3. in semiotics, a synonym for signified or referent (what a sign refers to)

Onomastics study of names

Onomatopoeia coining of a word in imitation of the natural sound associated with the object or action to which it refers: *splash*, *bang*, etc.

Ontology branch of metaphysics dealing with the nature of being, reality, or ultimate substance

Open work semiotician Umberto Eco's notion of a text with (in theory) an unlimited range of meanings

Opposition process by which signs are differentiated through a minimal change in their form or meaning: *cat*-versus-*rat* (form), *night*-versus-*day* (meaning)

Oxymoron rhetorical technique by which two seemingly contradictory or incongruous words are combined: *This is sharply dull*

P

Pantomime	1. in ancient Rome, an actor who played a part by gestures and action without words; 2. any theatrical presentation without words, involving only action and gestures
Paradigmatic	structural relation between signs that keeps them distinct and therefore recognizable
Paradox	statement that appears contradictory or inconsistent
Parallelism	repetition of linguistic patterns
Parody	work imitating the characteristic style of someone or some other work in a satirical or humorous way
Parole	term used by Ferdinand de Saussure to refer to the use of a language for various purposes, such as communication
Perception	discernment of objects, qualities, etc. by means of the senses
Performance	1. formal exhibition or presentation before an audience, of a play, a musical program, etc.; 2. representation and communication of some text, framed in a special way and put on display for an audience; 3. in linguistics, the actual use of language in concrete situations
Persona	1. voice or character representing the speaker in a literary work; 2. character in a dramatic or literary work; 3. in psychoanalysis, role that one assumes or displays in society as distinguished from the inner Self
Personification	portrayal or characterization of inanimate objects, animals, or abstract ideas as if they were living beings: *My cat speaks Italian*
Perspective	art of representing objects or a scene in such a way, so as to show them as they would appear to the eye in real three-dimensional space
Petroglyph	carving or line drawing on rocks or cave walls, especially one made by prehistoric people
Phatic function	in Roman Jakobson's model of communication, communicative function by which contact between addresser and addressee is established: *Hello*, *How's it going?*
Phenomenology	20th-century philosophical-psychological movement aiming to describe the forms and manifestations of experience as they present

themselves to consciousness, without recourse to any theoretical or explanatory framework

Phoneme minimal unit of sound in a language that allows its users to differentiate meanings

Photographic art art involving representation with photography, the process of recording images by means of a camera and reproduced on a photosensitive surface

Physicalism view that all psychic reality, including human emotions and intelligence, can be studied and understood in terms of physical processes

Phytosemiosis semiosis (sign processes) in plants

Phytosemiotics branch of semiotics studying semiosis in plants

Pictograph 1. picture or picture-like symbol representing an idea in primitive writing; 2. diagram of an object conveying an idea, information, etc.

Pictographic type of writing system in which a character, known as a pictograph, bears pictorial resemblance to its referent

Poetic function in Roman Jakobson's model of communication, type of message constructed to deliver meanings effectively

Poetic logic term used by philosopher Giambattista Vico referring to the innate capacity of all human beings to invent symbols, expressions, etc. to represent the world that are in direct connection with the properties of the sensible world

Poetics branch of semiotics and literary criticism concerned with the study of poetry and poetic communication generally

Poetry verbal art based on the acoustic, rhythmic, and imagistic properties of words

Polysemy process by which a sign bears multiple meanings: *table* as in *Let's eat on the table* versus *Learn your multiplication tables*

Pop art visual art movement that began in the 1940s-1950s, principally in the United States and Great Britain, whereby scenes and objects from mass culture were represented in painting or sculpture, sometimes with actual objects incorporated into the artwork

Pop culture form of culture, characteristic of 20th-century technological societies, that emphasizes the trivial and the routine in its artistic and various other forms of representation. Pop culture includes television programs, advertising, comic books, popular music (rock n' roll, hip hop, etc.), fashion, and the like

Pose bodily position that says something about the person's mood, attitude, social class, etc.

Postmodernism movement in philosophy and the arts that took hold in the latter part of the 20th century attacking traditions and value systems as concoctions of human fancy, rather than as systems reflecting a teleological purpose to life. The term *postmodernism* was coined by architects to designate an architectural response against the earlier BAUHAUS style (characterized by box-like skyscrapers, tall apartment buildings, etc.) that had degenerated into sterile and monotonous formulas, reintroducing traditional or classical elements of architectural design in an eclectic way. Postmodern architects called for greater individuality, complexity, and eccentricity in design, while also demanding acknowledgment of historical precedent and continuity—through the innovative reinterpretation of traditional ornamental symbols and patterns. Shortly after its adoption in architecture, the notion of *postmodernism* started to catch on more broadly, becoming a more general movement in philosophy and the arts

Poststructuralism anti-structuralist movement in semiotics based on a denial of the fundamental structuralist tenet that human signifying systems, including culture, manifest regularity, systematicity, patterning, predictability, and above all else, a central system of meanings

Pragmatics branch of semiotics and linguistics concerned with how language or some other code is used in social situations. The pragmatic study of language deals with *who* says *what* to *whom* in specific situations

Pragmatism philosophical movement developed by Charles S. Peirce and William James distinguished by the tenet that the validity of an idea or a proposition lies in its observable practical consequences

Presentational term used by philosopher Susanne Langer referring to the form of an art work that conveys meaning through feeling

Proxemic code social code regulating how people maintain spaces between each other when interacting, and how they orient their bodies in social situations

Proxemics branch of semiotics and anthropology that studies the symbolic structure of the physical space maintained between people in social contexts

Psychoanalysis 1. field studying so-called unconscious mental processes; 2. method, developed by Sigmund Freud, of treating neuroses, based on the assumption that mental disorders are the result of the rejection by the conscious mind of factors that persist in the unconscious

Q

Qualisign in Charles Peirce's theory, type of sign that refers to a quality: i.e. it is a sign that draws attention to, or singles out, some quality of its referent

R

Reader person decoding or interpreting a text, especially a literary text such as a novel, a play, or a poem

Realism 1. Scholastic doctrine, opposed to nominalism, positing that universals exist independently of the particular systems of thought that have generated them; 2. in modern philosophy, term applied to the view that ordinary objects of sense perception have an existence independent of their being perceived

Receiver 1. person or mechanism capable of receiving and decoding a signal; 2. entity or system, organic or mechanical, to which/whom a message is directed

Receiver person to whom a message or text is directed

Redundancy in communication systems, feature that counteracts NOISE. In many systems, such as language, redundancy can be seen in the predictability built into certain structures (forms, sentences, etc.)

Reference process of directing attention to something or someone in the world

Referent what a sign (a word, a symbol, a drawing, etc.) stands for (a thing, an idea, an event, etc.)

Referential	in Roman Jakobson's model of communication, function whereby a message is constructed to convey information, referring to something other than itself
Relativism	1. view in anthropology and semiotics that an individual's actions and behaviors are shaped primarily in relation to the culture in which s/he has been reared; 2. philosophical view that there is no absolute, universal moral or ethical code
Representamen	Charles Peirce's term referring to the physical strategy of representation itself (the use of sounds, hand movements, etc. for some representational purpose)
Representation	activity of using signs to capture, portray, simulate, or relay impressions, sensations, perceptions, or ideas that are felt or deemed to be identifiable, knowable, and/or memorable
Rheme	Charles Peirce's term designating the meaning that is derivable from a sign that captures some quality (known technically as a qualisign)
Rhetoric	1. art of using words effectively in speaking or writing 2. branch of philosophy and semiotics studying the various verbal techniques used in all kinds of discourses, from common conversation to poetry
Rococo	style of art (especially architecture and painting), characterized by elaborate ornamentation, that originated in France in the early 18th century, especially by arabesques, shells, elaborate curves, and iridescent pastel colors
Russian Form	school of semiotic analysis prominent from 1916 to about 1930 which emphasized the power of poetic thinking in shaping all of discourse and literature

S

Scholasticism	system of logic, philosophy, and theology of certain university scholars from the 10th to the 15th century, based upon Aristotelian logic, the writings of the early Christian fathers, and the authority of tradition and dogma
Secondness	Charles Peirce's term referring to a second level of meaning derived from verbal processes. Secondness shows an ability to separate sensory knowledge of an object from recognition of the object. It is the awareness of cause and effect

Semantic Differential
experimental technique developed by three psychologists, C. E. Osgood, G. J. Suci, and P. H. Tannenbaum in their 1957 book, *The Measurement of Meaning*, to assess the emotional connotations evoked by words or concepts. This technique consists in posing a series of questions to subjects about a specific concept—*Is it good or bad? weak or strong?* etc.—as seven-point scales, with the opposing adjectives at each end. The answers are then analyzed statistically in order to sift out any general pattern from them

Semantics in linguistics and semiotics study of meaning in language

Semaphore apparatus for signaling, such as traffic lights, flags, and mechanical arms on railroads

Semasiology study of relationships between signs and symbols and what they represent

Semeiotics older spelling of semiotics

Sememe minimal unit of meaning that goes into the composition of the overall meaning of a word

Semiology Ferdinand de Saussure's term for the science of signs

Semiosis innate capacity that underlies the comprehension and production of signs. Semiosis is an activity of the brain that underlies the production and comprehension of signs, from simple physiological signals to highly complex symbols

Semiosphere the world of signs and codes to be differentiated from the biosphere (the physical life-supporting environment)

Semiotic square semiotician A. J. Greimas's theory of signification whereby, given a unit of sense (*rich*), its meaning is gleaned only in terms of its relation with its contradictory (*not rich)*, its contrary (*poor*), and its contradictory (*not poor*). Greimas claimed that the course of a narrative corresponds to a movement along this square: the narrative unfolds in terms of operations leading from a given unit to its contrary (or contradictory)

Semiotics 1. discipline considered to be both a science, with its own corpus of findings and its theories, and a technique for studying meaning in human systems of representation; 2. generally defined as the science of signs

Sender	entity or system, organic or mechanical, who/which originates and transmits a message
Sense	1. ability of the nerves and the brain to receive and react to stimuli through specific bodily organs and the nerves associated with them (sight, touch, taste, smell, and hearing); 2. feeling, impression, or perception through the senses; 3. original sense-based meaning of something
Sense ratio	term coined by Canadian communication theorist Marshall McLuhan designating the degree to which a physical sense is used in processing information
Sign	something that stands for something else in some capacity
Sign language	language code based on gestures and grammatical rules that share some common points with the spoken language, used in place of vocal speech among people lacking a common spoken language, or by people physically incapable of speech or hearing
Signal	an emission or movement that naturally or conventionally triggers some reaction on the part of a receiver
Signification	1. meaning of a sign(s) in specific context(s); 2. process of generating meaning through the use of signs
Significs	Lady Victoria Welby's term for the 'study of the nature of significance in all its forms and relations
Signified	that part of a sign that is referred to
Signified	what a sign refers or calls attention to
Signifier	1. that part of a sign that does the referring; 2. the physical part of a sign
Simile	rhetorical technique by which two ideas are compared explicitly with the word *like* or *as*
Sinsign	in Peircean theory, a representamen (signifier) that draws attention to, or singles out, a particular object in time-space
Sociobiology	science studying the codependency of biological factors with social ones in the evolution of all species. The main claim of sociobiology is that there is a high degree of innate control in all social behaviors
Socratic irony	feigning of ignorance in argument, in order to make a point more forcefully

Sound symbolism process by which referents (objects, ideas, events, actions, etc.) are represented through some form of vocal simulation

Source domain class of vehicles that deliver a conceptual metaphor

Spatial code set of meanings and rules of conduct ascribed systematically to spaces in buildings and in other physical spaces of a society

Speech vocalized or articulated language

Stream of consciousness

literary technique by which a novel, film, or play is structured to unfold through the thoughts and feelings of a character as they develop

Structuralism mode of inquiry in semiotics, linguistics, anthropology, and other human sciences aiming to understand the sensory, emotional, and intellectual structures that undergird both the production and interpretation of signs. The basic tenet of structuralism is that signs and concepts beget their meanings and functions through binary oppositions

Structure any repeatable, systematic, patterned, or predictable aspect of signs, codes, texts

Style 1. manner or mode of expression in language, as distinct from the ideas expressed; 2. way of using words to express thoughts; 3. in any art, period, or work, the way in which anything is made or done; 4. in clothing, a synonym for *fashion*

Stylistics 1. branch of linguistics studying style in language; 2. study of style as a means of analyzing works of literature and their effects

Subordinate level level on which a concept has a detailing function: *Siamese* for *cat*

Subtext text (message) hidden within a text, alluding to mythical themes (good vs. evil), narratives, etc.: for example, an allusion to eating a forbidden fruit or to the figure of a snake constitutes a Biblical subtext

Superego in psychoanalytic theory, the element of personality that automatically modifies and inhibits instinctual impulses that tend to produce antisocial actions and thoughts

Superordinate level

level on which a concept has a highly general classificatory function: *feline* for *cat, lion, tiger,* etc.

Surrealism 20th-century literary and artistic movement founded by French poet and critic André Breton (1896-1966) in Paris in 1924; the movement wanted artists to express the imagery of their unconscious mind through fantastic and incongruous juxtaposition of subject matter in their works

Syllabary writing system based on characters representing syllables

Syllable word or part of a word pronounced with a single, uninterrupted sounding of the voice (usually a vowel) and generally one or more sounds of lesser sonority (usually consonants)

Symbol 1. sign that represents or refers to something in an arbitrary, conventional way; 2. any sign referring to an abstract notion

Symbolicity production, comprehension, and utilization of symbols

Symbolism property of something that has highly symbolic features (symbolist poetry, painting, etc.)

Symptom bodily sign that stands for some ailment, physical condition, disease

Synchrony signs, codes, texts as they exist at a specific point in time

Synecdoche signifying process by which a part stands for the whole, the whole for a part, the species for the genus, etc.

Synesthesia 1. sensation felt in one part of the body when another part is stimulated; 2. fusion of two sensory forms of representation (sight and hearing, touch and sight, etc.)

Synonym word having the same or nearly the same meaning as another in the same language: *close* for *near*

Synonymy relation by which the meanings of different signs overlap

Syntagmatic structural relation that combines signs in code-specific ways

Syntax 1. arrangement of words, phrases, and clauses in language-specific ways to form sentences; 2. study of how words are combined in a language to make sentences

T

Tactile code social code that regulates the patterns of touch in social interpersonal situations

Target domain part of a conceptual metaphor constituting the abstract topic (the 'target' of the conceptual metaphor): *people* in *people are animals*

Technology system of objects made by humans

Tenor subject of a metaphor (topic)

Territoriality mechanism by which animals seek out territories or stake boundary zones around themselves for survival

Text anything put together with SIGNS to represent or communicate something—conversations, letters, speeches, poems, myths, novels, television programs, paintings, scientific theories, musical compositions, etc.

Theater reenactment of some event in nature, in life, in society in some carefully scripted way, involving actors and a spatial location, such as a raised stage, around which an audience can view and/or hear the performance

Thirdness in Peircean theory, the third level of meaning derived from symbolic processes

Topic subject of a metaphor (tenor)

Topic what a metaphor is about: the *A* in the formula *A is B*, which shows the general (explicit or implicit) form of metaphor

Transmission 1. physical process of sending messages to a receiver; 2. the physical conveyance of broadcast signals

Trope 1. word used in a figurative sense; 2. figure of speech (metaphor, metonym, etc.); 3. figurative language in general

U

Umwelt the world of experience that is processed by a specific species: term used in biosemiotics and traced to Jakob von Uexküll (1909)

V

Valeur Ferdinand de Saussure's term designating the relation that holds between signs

Vehicle part of a metaphor to which a tenor is connected: *snake* in *He is a snake*

Visual semiotics study of visual signs, visual codes, and visual representation generally

Z

Zoosemiosis term coined by Thomas A. Sebeok to refer to semiosis in and across animal species

Zoosemiotics term coined by Thomas A. Sebeok referring to the branch of semiotics studying semiosis in and across animal species

Index

LINCOM Studies in Semiotics

In this series

01 Marcel Danesi & Nicolette Zukowski	**Medical Semiotics** Medicine and Cultural Meaning
02 Marcel Danesi & Donato Santeramo	**Semiotics** The Science of Signs